AF899683

Dimensions of Constitutional Democracy

Anupama Roy · Michael Becker
Editors

Dimensions of Constitutional Democracy

India and Germany

Springer

Editors
Anupama Roy
Centre for Political Studies,
School of Social Sciences
Jawaharlal Nehru University
New Delhi, India

Michael Becker
Institute of Political Science
and Sociology
University of Würzburg
Würzburg, Germany

ISBN 978-981-15-3898-8   ISBN 978-981-15-3899-5 (eBook)
https://doi.org/10.1007/978-981-15-3899-5

© Springer Nature Singapore Pte Ltd. 2020
This work is subject to copyright. All rights are reserved by the Publisher, whether the whole or part of the material is concerned, specifically the rights of translation, reprinting, reuse of illustrations, recitation, broadcasting, reproduction on microfilms or in any other physical way, and transmission or information storage and retrieval, electronic adaptation, computer software, or by similar or dissimilar methodology now known or hereafter developed.
The use of general descriptive names, registered names, trademarks, service marks, etc. in this publication does not imply, even in the absence of a specific statement, that such names are exempt from the relevant protective laws and regulations and therefore free for general use.
The publisher, the authors and the editors are safe to assume that the advice and information in this book are believed to be true and accurate at the date of publication. Neither the publisher nor the authors or the editors give a warranty, express or implied, with respect to the material contained herein or for any errors or omissions that may have been made. The publisher remains neutral with regard to jurisdictional claims in published maps and institutional affiliations.

This Springer imprint is published by the registered company Springer Nature Singapore Pte Ltd.
The registered company address is: 152 Beach Road, #21-01/04 Gateway East, Singapore 189721, Singapore

Preface and Acknowledgement

This volume is an outcome of two conferences organised in the Julius-Maximilians-University of Würzburg on 7th and 8th December 2017 and in Jawaharlal Nehru University on 15th and 16th March 2018. The conference in Würzburg focused on key conceptual categories that provide the analytical frameworks for making comparisons among contemporary democracies. The papers presented in the conference focused on constitutionalism, nationalism, democracy, development, political culture and secularism. The conference in Jawaharlal Nehru University brought together presentations on specific dimensions of constitutional democracy around which contemporary debates on constitutional frameworks and democratic practices have accumulated. The papers presented in the conference engaged with questions pertaining to the idea of transformative constitutionalism in countries making the transition to constitutional democracies concerning themselves with the Indian and German experiences. Thus, questions pertaining to constitutional morality and constitutional patriotism, rule of law, law and sovereignty, privacy, and the rights to speech and to resources became the focus of discussions. Both the conferences, the inaugural one in JMU, Würzburg and the follow up conference in JNU, Delhi, foregrounded salient normative frameworks for studying the past and present of constitutional democracies and some significant concepts around which debates on constitutionalism and democracy have endured. Starting from the premise that constitutional democracies may be understood as having distinct antecedents and contemporary forms, the papers attempted to place these experiences along universal norms, so that Germany and India could be seen as presenting specific trajectories of post-World War II transitions to democracy and not unbridgeable parallel incidences located in the binaries of East and West.

It is in this context that the volume affirms the idea of transformative as a methodological manoeuvre to explore how temporally coincident constitutions imagined their democratic futures. While the idea of the transformative has been associated specifically with the constitution giving experiences of South Africa, in this volume we look at the transformative in terms of 'a historic bridge' that rearticulates the relationship between the past and the future. The notion of change is intrinsic to this relationship and the contradictions that emerge in the process of charting a way to the democratic future are seen as providing the space for the continual recreation of the political. The papers from the two conferences that eventually made their way into this volume engage with the way and the forms in which constitutional democracies have endured. The ideas of nationalism, sovereignty, secularism and rights are given salience to understand how contesting ideas of the 'people' compete and cohabit in democracy and the constitutional order. It is these contestations that help us understand the complexities of democracy, the anchor constitutionalism provides for evaluating actually existing democracies, and the different sources from which ideas of solidarity are drawn to install a democratic state amidst social, economic, political and ideological contradictions. These ideas are elaborated in a comprehensive introduction which attempts to give a cohesive analytical frame to the different concerns raised in each chapter.

We would like to thank all the paper presenters for enriching the deliberations in the two conferences including Valerian Rodrigues, Ujjwal Kumar Singh, Shubhra Nagalia, Janaki Srinivas, Ashish Abrol, Gautam Bhatia, Anuj Bhuwania, Christoph Mohamad-Klotzbach, Heba Ahmed and Ikshula Arora, whose papers are not part of this volume. We thank the contributors to this volume whose papers have made it possible to address complex and often fraught questions pertaining to contemporary democracies. We are grateful to the University Grants Commission of India (UGC) and the Deutscher Akademischer Austauschdienst (DAAD) for providing the funds to support the project on 'Foundations of the India-Europe Strategic Partnership: Comparative Perspectives on Indian and European Political Ideas, Policy and International Cooperation' as part of the Indo German Partnership in Higher Education programme. We thank Salma Ummu Bava and Gisela Müller-Brandeck-Bocquet in JNU and JMU, respectively, for steering the project. Two doctoral students, Heba Ahmed and Aditya Pandey, visited JMU under the project to conduct research. Aditya Pandey's chapter in this volume is an outcome of his research stay in JMU. We thank Matthias Gsänger and Timo Lowinger for their support and students at both JMU and JNU who helped in organising the conferences.

New Delhi, India Anupama Roy
Würzburg, Germany Michael Becker

Contents

Editors and Contributors

Editors

Anupama Roy is a Professor at the Centre for Political Studies in Jawaharlal Nehru University, Delhi. Her research interests straddle legal studies, political anthropology of political institutions, political ideas, and gender studies. She obtained her MPhil degree from University of Delhi, and her PhD degree from the State University of New York at Binghamton, USA. She is the co-author of the book *Election Commission of India: Institutionalising Democratic Uncertainties* (OUP, 2019) and author of the books *Citizenship in India* (Oxford India Short Introduction Series, OUP, 2016), *Mapping Citizenship in India* (OUP, 2010, reprinted 2015), and *Gendered Citizenship: Historical and Conceptual Explorations* (Orient Longman, 2005, paperback, 2013). She has co-edited *Poverty, Gender and Migration in South Asia* (Sage, 2008). Her research articles have appeared in various national and international journals including Asian Studies Review, Australian Feminist Studies, Critical Asian Studies, Contributions to Indian Sociology, Economic and Political Weekly and Election Law Journal.

Anupama Roy was a senior fellow in the Centre for Women's Development Studies, before she joined the Centre for Political Studies in JNU. She has been a visiting scholar in Sydney University, University of Warwick and University of Würzburg, Germany. She was Sir Ratan Tata post-doctoral Fellow at the Institute of Economic Growth in Delhi and KTP Fellow at University of Technology, Sydney, Australia.

Michael Becker is a Professor at the Institute of Political Science and Sociology, Julius-Maximilians-University, Würzburg. He received his PhD 1991 at Johannes-Gutenberg University at Mainz and did his Habilitation at Otto-Friedrich-University at Bamberg in 2002. Between 2003-2005 he was Substitute Professor at the Universities of Bamberg, Landau and Konstanz. Since

2007 he is Professor for Political Science at the Institute for Political Science and Sociology at Würzburg University. His Fields of Research are Modern and Contemporary Western Political Philosophy, Constitutional Democracy; Modern Indian Political Thought. Since 2013 he has been Guest Professor at Indian Universities (Delhi, Chandigarh, Mangalore). He participates in the DAAD sponsored "Indo-German-Partnership" (IGP) and is a Member of the BMBF sponsored "International Centre for Advanced Studies – Metamorphoses of the Political" (ICAS-MP) (https://micasmp.hypotheses.org/).

Major Publications: Rechtsstaat und Demokratie (co-editor), Wiesbaden 2001; Verständigungsorientierte Kommunikation und rechtsstaatliche Ordnung (Habilitation), Baden-Baden 2003; Politik und Recht (special issue of Politische Vierteljahresschrift) (co-editor), Wiesbaden 2006; Politische Philosophie (co-author), Paderborn 2006 (4th ed. 2017); Grundstrukturen der Politik in der Bundesrepublik Deutschland, Opladen 2011, Politischer Liberalismus und wohlgeordnete Gesellschaften (ed.), Baden-Baden 2013.

Contributors

Amir Ali Centre for Political Studies, Jawaharlal Nehru University, New Delhi, India

Michael Becker Institute of Political Science and Sociology, Julius-Maximilians-University, Würzburg, Germany

Radhika Chitkara Jindal Global Law School, Delhi, India

Krishna Swamy Dara Department of Political Science at Jamia Millia Islamia, New Delhi, India

Garima Dhabhai Presidency University, Kolkata, India

Oliver Hidalgo Department of Politics, University of Münster, Münster, Germany; University of Regensburg, Regensburg, Germany

Mirjam Künkler The Netherlands Institute for Advanced Study, Amsterdam, The Netherlands

Aditya Pandey Centre for Political Studies, Jawaharlal Nehru University, New Delhi, India

Shaunna Rodrigues Department of Middle Eastern, South Asian and African Studies (MESAAS), Columbia University, New York, USA

Anupama Roy Centre for Political Studies, Jawaharlal Nehru University, New Delhi, India

Anushka Singh School of Law, Governance and Citizenship, Ambedkar University Delhi, Delhi, India

Tine Stein University of Göttingen, Göttingen, Germany

Chapter 1
Dimensions of Constitutional Democracy

Anupama Roy and Michael Becker

Abstract Constitutional democracies have distinctive antecedents and contemporary forms. The history of constitutional democracies is informed by past and continuing histories of the struggle over democratisation of power. These struggles have shaped constitutional moments and have produced constitutional orders of juridical norms and democratic practices. The durability of constitutional democracy depends on the spread of constitutional morality as a precondition for a democratic society and polity. It requires that both the government and citizens agree to live by constitutional values which embody norms of pluralism and freedom, basic rights, and respect for difference. Yet the relationship between the constitutional order and democracy is a fraught one. It is important to study constituent moments as holding out the promise of transformation against the legacies of past wrongs. The conflict between the promise of democracy and the actual unfolding of 'normal' politics produces constituent power, restoring faith in constitutionalism as an affirmation of sovereign power of the people.

1.1 Introduction

As a political and legal regime, constitutional democracy has a pedigree that can be traced to the end of the eighteenth century in the 'new world'. Over the past 200 years and more, constitutional democracy has expanded its scope to encompass most of the world. It is commonly agreed that constitutional democracy is one in which a higher order legal framework guarantees fundamental and inalienable rights to citizens and provides the moral norms for the organisation of the government of a polity. This higher order law, which can be entrenched to variable degrees, is the result of a democratic process. A democracy constituted in this manner postulates a combination or fusion of two strands of thought which accumulated around the concepts of 'rights of

A. Roy (✉)
Centre for Political Studies, Jawaharlal Nehru University, New Delhi, India
e-mail: anupamaroy@mail.jnu.ac.in; royanupama07@gmail.com

M. Becker
Institute of Political Science and Sociology, Julius-Maximilians-University, Würzburg, Germany

© Springer Nature Singapore Pte Ltd. 2020

A. Roy and M. Becker (eds.), *Dimensions of Constitutional Democracy*,
https://doi.org/10.1007/978-981-15-3899-5_1

man' and 'popular sovereignty' (Hamilton et al. [1987/88] 1961; Rousseau [1762] 2000) and became significant with the beginning of modernity. Over the years these two strands have generated contest over the form and substance of democracy, in particular the relationship between constitutionalism embodying the sovereign people and democracy as people possessing rights that predate the constitutional order (Tushnet 2003).

Studies of comparative constitutionalism propose that constitution making has taken place in successive waves (Elster 1995; Tushnet 2014; Lerner 2016). Constitution-making processes in the twentieth century have shown that almost all constitutions emerged in postcolonial (e.g., India, Pakistan, and South Africa), post-war (e.g., Germany and Japan), and post-conflict (e.g., Nepal) contexts as well as in the process of transition from authoritarian regimes (e.g., Brazil). These constitutions passed through distinct practices of framing, assumed different forms, and emphasised specific and often dissimilar core components; but the promise of democratic transition and consolidation marked the birth of all of them. Writing in the 1950s, W. B. Gallie had persuaded us to recognise the 'essentially' contested character of democracy, which he argued, was a manifestation of its 'vagueness' and the 'inchoate' conditions of its growth. The contested nature of democracy was, however, as Gallie contended, not simply about the *usage* of the term, but fundamentally about the meaning one ascribed to it, and a manifestation of ongoing and unresolved dispute over what one *means* when one uses the word democracy. The philosophical enquiry, which is the result of such disputes, has made democracy an internally complex concept amenable to a variety of descriptions in which its components are graded in different orders of importance. More importantly, however, they have made democracy an appraisive concept—indeed, *the* appraisive political concept *par excellence* (Gallie 1955–1956: 184). *Constitutional* democracy may be seen as giving a distinctive anchoring to the appraisive content of democracy *and* the internal ordering of its content, by making constitutionalism the normative and substantive framework within which commitment to democracy may be both evaluated and ensured.

Debates on constitutionalism and studies of actually existing constitutional democracies have arrayed around positions which refer to limited government and effective restraints on governmental power through the rule of law (Friedrich 1950) to those that see constitutionalism as a manifestation of a collective identity of the people (Wolin 1989), and others who see it as providing the ideological contexts within which constitutions emerge and function (Baxi 2000). Upendra Baxi sees constitutionalism as 'providing for structures, forms and *apparatuses of governance* and modes of *legitimation of power*' (Ibid.: 540). He also argues, however, that constitutionalism is not only about governance; it 'provides contested sites' where 'narratives of rule' contend with 'ideas and practices concerning justice, rights, development and individual/associational autonomy' (Ibid.). As higher order legal rules and principles that provide a legitimate framework for bringing about political and social change, constitutionalism has animated narratives of resistance in societies making the transition to democracy. The idea of change, indeed transformative change, is a historic constituent moment in the life of constitutional democracies involving a conscious and meticulous sequestering from the past (Mehta 2010a, b: 16). The promise of constitutionalism in such societies was one of self-rule, and the installation of democratic government which derived its powers from the people and was constrained by rule of law. The constituent moment was often also, as in the case of India, tied to the nation-building project, and in the case of both India and Germany, to the institution of republican citizenship and constitutional patriotism.

Holding that constitutional democracies may be understood as having distinctive antecedents and contemporary forms, this volume locates the Indian and German experiences as distinctive products of post-war/postcolonial tendencies towards democratisation. The chapters remind us of visions of a future society they promised, the modalities through which the new future could be realised, and how they emerged in practice. The history of constitutional democracy in this sense may be seen as the culmination of past and continuing histories of the struggle over democratisation of power, which shaped the specific project of writing a constitution, and also the production of the legal ensemble, which generated specific modes of governance and juridical norms (Baxi 2002, 2008). The durability of constitutional democracy depended on the spread of constitutional morality (Mehta 2010a, b; Singh and Roy 2017), which was a precondition for setting up a democratic society and polity in which both the government and the citizens agreed to live by constitutional values which embodied norms of pluralism and freedom, basic rights, and respect for difference.

In this volume, therefore, the chapters ask questions and elicit discussions on how to understand constitutionalism and the idea of the transformative in specific contexts. Is there a perceptible notion of modernity and corresponding political cultures and traditions, which mark out a distinctive trajectory for democratic futures? How do we understand the contestations and promises which surround constitutional democracy? How did the dominant idioms of democracy emerge and what were the strands which were lost in the process? What are the lifeworlds that the constitution has inhabited over a period of time, to come to us as a living document? How have specific constitutional principles evolved so as to achieve commensurability with democracy? The questions they ask pertain to the ongoing state formative practices and the forms they assume within contending notions of constitutionalism, democracy, nationalism, religion, and the struggle over resources. They also concern themselves ultimately with the relationship between the constitutional architecture and institutional edifice of democracy. Within such a framework the chapters in this book explore the themes—constitutionalism, nationalism, secularism, sovereignty, the rule of law, freedoms, and rights—to study how contestations over democratic transitions and democratic futures have unfolded in India and Germany. The purpose is to give the readers an insight into how the normative frameworks of constitutional democracy take concrete forms along specific sites of democratic and constitutional imagination, and the relationship between state and religion in the writings of public intellectuals and political and legal philosophers. The book also focuses on specific sites of contestation in democracies including the relationship between sovereignty and citizenship, free speech and sedition in liberal democracies, the questions of land rights in the context of economic and political changes in contemporary contexts, and the rights of communities in international conventions and domestic law.

1.2 The Constitutional Moment and Democracy

Despite its acceptance as a legitimate legal order, the concept of constitutional democracy has faced at least two lines of critique: firstly, is it possible to speak of a *constituted* democracy or is such a combination contradictory, and secondly, if not contradictory, is it reasonable and prudent to commit to such combination?[1] At the crux of this debate is the dispute over the idea of the sovereign and constitutional self-binding that constitutional democracy is premised upon. This contradiction was presented by Thomas Hobbes in terms of the impossibility of a self-binding sovereign since the sovereign who bound himself was also the one who could dissolve the bond. Jean-Jacques Rousseau took this argument further to say that it would be 'against the nature' of the political body to pass a basic law or constitution which he is not allowed to violate. Rousseau later argued that a 'people' is always and at every point 'sovereign' over its own laws.[2] The general anti-constitutional direction of that argument should demonstrate that the sovereign people is an absolute sovereign free to 'violate' himself by disregarding even 'good laws'. In these statements Rousseau negates the binding force of positive laws. This theoretical radicalism is a consequence of his *voluntarism* appreciating only the actual will of the people and not a prior one laid down in a constitution. If Rousseau would allow for a constitutional framework, it would only be valid as long as the sovereign would like to support it. However, one should take into account that this radicalism was probably meant to defend the revolutionary conceptual innovation because later on he wrote a draft for the constitution of Corse.

A pragmatic position would make one ask if it is at all a good idea for a people to bind themselves to the wisdom of a people who made a decision in the past to bind themselves to a constitution. There is some evidence that every age and therefore the enlightenment era too, understood itself as the 'end of history' in which no further improvements are conceivable. In the field of politics and political institutions, such a self-understanding is for different reasons considered less dangerous, than in the context of say, natural sciences. Indeed, the two 'binding' components of modern constitutions are on the one hand a list of (core) human rights, which have persisted for more than two centuries, and have been adopted in the lists of fundamental and constitutional rights in most constitutions, and on the other hand a set of institutions for representative government. According to Immanuel Kant the only necessary institutional elements of a civic constitution (besides the inborn right to freedom) are the rule of law and separation of powers. A milder version of the anti-democratic argument stems from the context of the founding phase of the US

[1]For an elaboration of these debates see Holmes (1988: 195–240).

[2]See Rousseau 2000: Book I, Chap. 7 and Book II, Chap. 12.

constitution and has been brought up by Thomas Jefferson.[3] Jefferson held that a permanent (and democracy enabling) constitution would be undemocratic in the end because it would be handed over from one generation to another, and only the first, that is founding generation was able to act democratically in the literal sense. In other words, Jeffersonians would not necessarily demand other principles than what the old constitution entails, but instead a new possibility for 'new' generations to adopt democratically old legal provisions.[4]

The relationship between constitutionalism and democracy has spawned debates in which constitutionalism has been considered as both restraining and facilitating democracy. The root of this contradictory relationship is seen as lying in the 'juridical' understanding of constitutions as merely providing a framework of government and an 'institutional' understanding of democracy as an ensemble of instruments and mechanisms for peaceful transitions of political regimes. Writing in the 1960s, Giovanni Sartori argued that a juridical understanding was prompted by the quest for a 'universal' definition of the constitution, leading to a *sequestering* of the universal trait of 'plan of government' as a 'primary component of constitution from its *garantiste* component, such as the Bill of Rights in the American Constitution'. It also became customary to make a distinction between constitution as merely a 'frame of government' referring to 'state order', and constitutionalism as its specific 'content' of guarantees (Sartori 1962: 856). Sartori, however, finds this distinction of only subsidiary importance. What mattered, he said, was the *telos*—which made it possible to find a *commonality of purpose* among different kinds of constitutionalism—'a fundamental law, or a fundamental set of principles, and a correlative institutional arrangement, which would restrict arbitrary power and ensure a limited government' (Ibid.: 855). This made constitutionalism, quite like freedom, justice, and democracy, a 'good word', having 'favourable emotive properties' (Ibid.: 859):

> And 'constitution' was in no way born as a Janus-faced concept. The term was re-conceived, adopted and cherished not because it merely meant 'political order' but because it meant much more, because it meant 'political freedom'. We may put it thus: because it denoted *the* distinctive political order which would protect their liberties; or to paraphrase Friedrich's felicitous wording – because it not only 'gave form' but also because it 'limited' governmental action. …for to us constitution means – a frame of political society, *organised through and by the law,* for the purpose of restraining power. (Sartori 1962: 860)

The unambiguous meaning of the word constitution for Sartori, does not, however, preclude the possibility of evaluating and making a distinction between what is constitutional and what is not. Lamenting that many 'authoritarian systems', particularly in the post-World War II contexts, have appropriated the term constitution, Sartori distinguishes between three categories of actually existing constitutions, which he classifies as grantiste, nominal and façade constitutions. Arguing against assuming a position of neutrality towards the definition of constitutionalism, Sartori makes a

[3]See Holmes (1988): 202 f.

[4]To identify a 'new' generation empirically is much more complicated than it seems at first glance. Interestingly, the Swiss constitution in article 193 provides the possibility of a 'total revision'. The second and until now last revision took place in 1999.

cautionary concluding note: '…[W]hen the time of trial comes, one discovers that what the "pure" jurists have really been doing—under the shield of their juridical indifference to meta-juridical matters—was to pave the way for allowing unscrupulous politicians to make a discretionary use of power under the camouflage of a good word. Politics cannot be taken out of politics, so to speak' (Ibid.: 864).

Speaking on the idea of a constitution at the annual meeting of the Association of American Law Schools in 1987, celebrating the bicentennial of the American Constitution, Hanna Pitkin similarly pointed at the way in which we 'ordinarily' and 'spontaneously' use the *word* constitution and the 'deep inconsistencies' in 'the patterns of use of such important, abstract, and politically contested words' (1987: 167). For Pitkin, 'to understand what a constitution is, one must look not for some crystalline core or essence of unambiguous meaning but precisely *at* the ambiguities, the specific oppositions that this specific concept helps us to hold in tension' (Ibid.). In this context Pitkin refers to two meanings of the constitution: one, that refers to its 'composition, constituent parts and the physical make-up', which determine its 'delicate' or 'robust' temperament, and how it has been put together; and suggesting an ethos or a way of life, of what 'we are'—the national character of a people, which is the product of their particular history and social conditions (Ibid.: 168). The other way of looking at the constitution, however, is to look at it as a dimension of our action—of not what we are, but what we 'can do'—especially to 'break the causal chain of process and launch something unprecedented':

> In this vein one might even want to argue that our constitution is more something we do than something we make: we (re)shape it all the time through our collective activity. Our constitution is (what is relatively stable in) our activity; a stranger learns its principles by watching our conduct. (Pitkin 1987: 168)

Writing, like Pitkin, in the context of the bicentennial of the American constitution, Bruce Ackerman proposed the theory of *constitutional moments*—a constitutional theory which draws upon history—to understand and explain constitutional practice (Ackerman 1991). A constitutional order can best be understood, the theory argues, 'by reflecting on the course of its historical development'. This would make the 'real' constitution, not simply the text of the constitution or its interpretation by judges, but 're-discovering' the set of principles that came to be adopted by 'We, the people' and 'extraordinary' moments of intense constitutional participation and deliberation, with or without changes in the constitutional text (Ibid.: p. 5).

These extraordinary moments are those of creation and communication of constitutional symbols and communication, which propose to establish not just a constitutional order but a democratic order as well. Yet the relationship between a constitutional order and democracy is a fraught one. The constitutional order claims to be a culmination and often the terminal point of revolutionary struggles and popular ferment of earlier generations. It sets the limits of political action, and substitutes 'the people' with forms and politics of representation affirming the claims of a political regime to speak for them (Ackerman 1988; Holmes 1988). The constitutional foundation for a different kind of politics is, however, based on the invocation of legitimacy drawn from a revolutionary legacy. Paradoxically, this foundation is also premised on the deferral of revolutionary change and conformity to politics of order. Yet, the 'pre-commitment' (Holmes, ibid.) to the constitutional order by a historically constituted majority is construed as a fetter to democratic transformations that may be envisaged by future generations. This 'counter-majoritarian dilemma' (Holmes 1988) informs the 'democratic paradox' (Mouffe 2000) and is at the heart of the conflict between constitutionalism and democracy. This conflict is articulated in different ways. Bruce Ackerman, for example, sees it in terms of the distinction between two forms of politics—*constitutional politics*, characterised as politics of the highest order, which appeals to the common good, and makes itself manifest 'during rare periods of heightened political consciousness' (Ackerman 1988: 162–63) and *normal politics*, an inferior form of politics marked by narrow individual interests (ibid.). The purpose of constitutional politics is to ameliorate the effects of normal politics to make it consistent with the higher order politics of constitutionalism. At the crux of this conflict is also the irreconcilability that is seen to exist between the institutional forms of democracy, in particular its representative institutions which claim to emulate the 'People', and its sovereign form as 'We the People' embodied in the constitution.

This contest over the representative form of the people and the sovereign people gets manifest in the debate over institutional arrangements that would make them approximate each other as closely as possible, and on the other hand the modalities through which the constitution giving process would remain as close to the original imagination as possible, sustaining the foundational majority that constituted the people in the originary constitutional moment. In the former case, contestations over parliamentary sovereignty, judicial review and separation of powers, the enhancement of judicial power and constitutional sovereignty, have taken place in the institutional domain of the state, with implications for what can be construed as a democratic constitution and constitutional government. The idea of the originary constitutional moment is often invoked to act as a constraint on temporary majorities representing myopic politics and generating constitutionally unlimited democracy (Hayek 1960). A contrary position would, however, view questions of constitutionalism not in institutional arrangements but in the way in which constitutions fetter or enable the right of the people to *alter* or *abolish* any *form of government* which becomes 'destructive' of their life and liberty (Holmes 1988: 199). It would also offer arguments which buttress 'the prohibition against binding the future' (Holmes Ibid., Hume 1963) and the affirmation of the 'consent of the living' (Holmes 1988: 200; Paine 1991).

This brings us to another element of the contemporary debate where it is not the *substance* but the *procedure* of adopting a normative framework which becomes central to constitutionalism. Accordingly, there is a split between so-called substantialists and proceduralists, whereupon the former tend more to the camp of liberals and the latter to the group of pure democrats or republicans: (Republican) proceduralists, in certain respects the inheritors of Rousseau's radical democracy, recognise for example that there are some very important rights, but the rights they have in mind are the ones which are 'integral to the democratic process', that is freedom of expression and freedom of assembly. Other rights, like that of economic equality, are necessary, but not 'integral' to the democratic process.[5] (Liberal) substantialists hold that there is an inalienable (inborn or 'natural' or evolutionary) individual right—the right to individual freedom—which exists prior to the democratic process and cannot be understood as 'given' by a human sovereign. It is rather the other way around and the sovereign *has to respect* this normative claim and transform it into positive law. Liberals would not deny the importance of the majority rule and democratic process on both levels of norm production: normal and constitutional, but insist that some substantive principles necessarily need to be part of a constitution: in the first place a much broader understanding of the liberty principle which should enable not only to participate politically but also to practice a religion and to unfold life plans independent of politics.[6]

1.3 The 'Transformative' and Democratic Moments

How was 'the new political world of reflection and choice' as Bruce Ackerman (1988) would say, being imagined and created? The idea of 'transformative' in the literature on comparative constitutionalism locates constituent moments in the histories of transition to the 'magnificent goal' of democracy (Baxi 2013). The central motif of transformative constitutionalism is a conscious and meticulous sequestering from the past (Mehta 2010a, b: 16). Etched on the 'temporal register' of the future, constitutions embody the momentous present, from where a vision of the future aimed specifically to repudiate and transform 'legacies of injustice' (Bhatia 2019) may be mapped.

While transformative constitutionalism has come to be associated specifically with post-apartheid constitution-making processes of South Africa, the 'transformative' may well be invoked as an analytical framework which bridges the binaries of East and West and helps us explore how temporally coincident constitutions imagined their democratic futures. Tracing the transformative in constitutional moments in India (1949/50), Brazil (1988) and South Africa (1996), Baxi (2013) sees them as historically specific moments emerging out of postcolonial, post-authoritarian, and postcolonial/apartheid conditions. The constitution in South Africa served as 'a historic bridge' paving the passage from a deeply divided and wounded society to a future in which past injustices were to be erased through therapeutic healing. The transformative moment in the history of constitutionalism in Brazil lay in the transition to a fraternal, pluralist and unprejudiced society founded on social harmony,

[5] See for these distinctions Dahl (1989), Chap. 12 (Process and Substance).

[6] See Hayek (1960), Chap. 9 (majority rule). Proceduralists would reply to the argument that a sovereign who 'has to do' something, is not really sovereign. A 'synthesis' of these two opposing positions has been offered by Jürgen Habermas: '(P)opular sovereignty and human rights go hand in hand, and hence grasp the co-originality of civic and private autonomy … (A)s soon as the legal medium is used to institutionalize the exercise of political autonomy, these rights become necessary enabling conditions; as such they cannot *restrict* the legislator's sovereignty; even though they are not to her disposition.' (1996: 127f).

elimination of poverty, political pluralism, and a pan Latin American solidarity. The constituent moment in India was a moment of interlocution between the past and future, which generated overlapping visions of future society. Jawaharlal Nehru described Indian independence as a 'tryst with destiny'—the fulfilment of a pledge made by the Indian people—to take their rightful place in the community of free nations. B. R. Ambedkar saw the constituent moment as one of contradictions—between formal equality in the political domain and a deeply unequal economic structure. The persistence of this contradiction, Ambedkar argued, could imperil Indian democracy (Constituent Assembly Debates, 25 November 1949). Yet, it also provided space for the articulation of 'constitutional insurgency', making possible the continual recreation of the political and the 'creation of a new world of life' (Baxi ibid.).

While the constitution making and giving processes in India and Germany were specific to their historical and political contexts, the constitutional promise of an enduring democratic future converged, in what may be seen as simultaneous transformative moments. The trajectories of constitution making in the twentieth century can be traced to the aftermath of the Second World War, decolonisation, and the third wave of democratisation (Tushnet 2014; Lerner 2016). The 'wave of constitutional transitions' (Lerner 2016: 56) in the 1990s was steered by the perception of 'constitutions as an instrument for democratisation' (Ibid.: p. 57.).[7] The constitution drafting process and experience for these countries was participatory to different degrees and all of them involved deliberations over the norms and principles that would constitute the foundational principles of democracy in the new state.

The Indian constitution was among the first constitutions in 'the postcolonial wave of constitution drafting' (Lerner 2016: 57) characterised by 'dramatic examples of constitution making' (Tushnet 2014: 1). These constitutions had certain common characteristics which made them different from the revolutionary constitutions of France and the United States of America. Most of these constitutions were the result of a negotiated process or the former rulers continued to exercise influence over the constitution-making process. Constitutions that emerged as a culmination of anti-colonial national movements, for example, were in most cases not autochthonous since the process was authorised by the former colonisers, which also retained the legal power to validate the final constitution. According to the theory of constitutional autochthony, as argued by the legal philosopher Hans Kelsen, an existing legal system could not become independent solely through a legal process, since such a process was premised on a transfer of power through a process recognised as 'legal' by the imperial predecessor. By this reasoning, only an 'unlawful' or 'revolutionary' act could ensure an autochthonous constitution by rending asunder all continuity with the imperial predecessor, as was the case with the United States of America. In India, Pakistan, Ireland, Sri Lanka, and Ghana, independence was the result of the

[7] The transitions in the 1990s were witnessed in the wake of the fall of communism in Eastern and Central Europe, the end of Apartheid in South Africa, and later in the post-conflict reconstruction in early-twenty-first-century Africa (e.g., Kenya and South Sudan), Asia (e.g., East Timor, Thailand, and Nepal), and the Middle East (e.g., Iraq, Afghanistan, Egypt, and Tunisia) (Lerner 2016).

British Crown-in-Parliament's enactment of statutes of independence (Swaminathan 2013). In Indonesia, Japanese rulers appointed the members of the Drafting Committee in 1945, and in 1947 in Sri Lanka and in 1957 in Malaysia, a British colonial constitutional committee reviewed and revised the draft constitutions, which also explains why postcolonial governments often sustained the old forms of colonial governmental structures (Lerner 2016; Khilnani et al. 2013).

Yet, the constitutional moments were not continuous with the colonial past and presented an 'inaugural postcolonial form' (Baxi 2000). In the case of India, even when it sustained the governance framework of the Government of India Act of 1935, the constitution broke free from the old forms of the colonial state to address the complex social and economic conditions that obtained in India, marking a rupture from colonial practices of rule. Moreover, the constitution of the sovereign people as citizens was achieved through the insertion of an 'illegality' in the procedure laid down in the Indian Independence Act 1947—an imperial Act laying down the procedures for transfer of power. This illegality was achieved consciously through what Swaminathan (2013) has called a 'deliberately designed procedural error in the adoption of the new constitution', with a view to 'severing the seamless transition of legal authority' from its imperial predecessor. The error in procedure involved a deliberate non-adherence to the procedure prescribed by the Indian Independence Act of 1947, whereby the constituent Assembly of India did not present the draft of the constitution for the approval of the British Parliament and through Article 395 of the Constitution of India, it repealed the Indian independence Act itself. In doing so, 'the framers not only repudiated the source which authorised them to enact the Constitution but it was also a denial, albeit symbolic, of Indian independence being a grant of the imperial Crown-in-Parliament. This ensured that the chain of constitutional validity did not extend all the way to the Crown-in-Parliament, thus delivering a completely autochthonous Constitution' (Swaminathan 2013).

It has become a convention among constitutional historians to trace the 'antecedents' of the Indian constitution to a series of Government of India Acts legislated by the colonial government in India. Such a history sees the reforms in representation and governmental structures in successive colonial Acts leading up to independence and republican government, affirming thereby, the 'liberal justifications of imperialism as training Indians for self-rule' (De 2016; Chatterjee 1993). A different narrative of the emergence of the constitution traces it to the republican-democratic project of the national-liberation movement (Kaviraj 2003). In this narrative, it is the Nehru Report of 1928—an outcome of the Committee set up by the Madras Congress Resolution of 1927 under the chairmanship of Motilal Nehru—which is considered as the precursor of the Constitution of India (Austin 1966; De 2016). The Nehru Report, which came with the subtitle 'an anti-separatist manifesto' laid down the template of the draft *Swaraj* (self-determination) constitution—which declared that the foremost concern of Indians was to secure the Fundamental Rights which were denied to them. It also proposed special safeguards for the rights of the minority communities (Nehru Report, 1928). The special rights to freedom of conscience and the free profession and practice of religion were considered important for the protection of the rights of minority communities. In 1931, the Resolution on

Fundamental Rights and Economic and Social Change passed by the Indian National Congress in Karachi added a new dimension of social and economic conditions for the realisation of fundamental rights. As a declaration of rights and a humanitarian and socialist manifesto with a distinct Gandhian ambience, some of these provisions anticipated the Directive Principles of State Policy in the Indian constitution (Austin 1966).

An indirectly elected body set up under the Cabinet Mission Plan, the Constituent Assembly (CA) of India, articulated the principle of popular sovereignty in the Objective Resolution moved by Nehru on 13 December 1946 in the claim that it 'derived from the people… all power and authority'.[8] In addition, the CA affirmed its own sovereignty by framing the rules by which it would conduct its proceedings. The CA was according to one view, a deliberative body, which discussed the various aspects of the constitution in contexts where reasoned arguments were made to provide a normative framework to the proceedings under conditions of trust (Bhatia 2018). Others would, however, see the CA as primarily a political body, which adopted strategies which corresponded with the politics of the late colonial period in India (Bhatia ibid., Elangovan 2018). The debates in CA, according to the second view, show a preference for centralisation of power amidst the turmoil of Partition and economic crisis. It also became acceptable, therefore, to set limits to fundamental rights and suspend them under conditions of 'extreme necessity'. Granville Austin refers to the Indian constitution as a 'seamless web', consisting of three strands—democracy, social revolution, and unity and integrity—to which he later added a fourth—culture. The working of the constitution of India reflected the interaction between these strands, which were assumed to be harmonious, but often existed in conflict with each other (Austin 1966, 1999, 2002).

Under conditions of deep 'ideational disagreement' (Lerner 2016), the Indian constitution sought to address questions of national unity and identity, while recognising and protecting cultural and social diversity, and devise ways of correcting past wrongs. It did so in ways which have been described variously—as 'innovations' (Lerner 2016), 'original contribution' (Austin 1966: p. 311), and triumphal moments of achievement (Bhargava 2008), among others. The innovations have been found in the manner in which the CA adopted the strategy of 'constitutional incrementalism', which included the *deferral* of 'controversial decisions' on matters such as India's national language, *ambiguity* on matters of religion, and *non-justiciability* as far as socio-economic rights as inscribed in the Directive Principles of State Policy were concerned (Lerner 2016). Writing in 1966 Austin had pointed out the following as the original contribution of the Indian CA: *decision-making by consensus*, which made the means by which a decision was reached more important than the decision itself, *the principle of accommodation*, reflecting the ability to harmonise without changing

[8]The CA was not constituted on the principle of universal adult franchise. The provincial legislatures, elected on the basis of limited franchise, elected the Assembly—in ratio to their population, and separate representations were accorded to minority communities according to their percentage of the province's population. The Princely states had 93 members selected in consultation with the CA (Austin 1966). The process of drafting the constitution began in December 1946, 7 months before Indian Independence, and culminated with the enactment of the constitution in January 1950.

the content of categories, which may appear incompatible to the European or American observer (Austin 1966: 311–318). The constitutional text adopted by the CA was not derivative or imitative but cosmopolitan (Choudhry et al. 2016) and transformative (Baxi 2013) based on the 'categorical principle of inclusion' (Bhargava 2008, 2006) as reflected in the ideas of inclusive citizenship and universal adult franchise. A republican citizenship affirmed the secular foundation of the Indian constitution and Indian nation and also congealed the relationship between democracy and the political imagination of 'the people' in India. Ornit Shani, for example, argues that the implementation of universal franchise elicited 'both a sense of Indianness and commitment to democratic nationhood…', indeed, in the process of preparation of the electoral roll, that political imagination itself was democratised (Shani 2018: 18–19).

Scholars who have studied the working of the Indian constitution and examined the 'conflict' in the seamless web of the constitutional edifice, have cited instances where 'democracy' strand of the constitution has collided with the 'social revolution' and 'national unity and integrity' strands (Austin 2002). These conflicts have prompted scholars to reconsider the idea that the constitution was the result of a consensus pushed by nationalism (Elangovan 2018), to see it as a 'series of conflicts', of which several remained unresolved (De 2016). Indeed, the status of secularism as a basic feature of the Indian constitution was affirmed in the course of the 'inner conflict' (Mehta 2002) in the constitution between parliamentary sovereignty and judicial power. In a decisive extension of its power of judicial review to exercise scrutiny over the legislative *and* constituent powers of the Parliament, in the case *Kesavananda Bharati versus State of Kerala* (1973), the Supreme Court decided that certain features of the Indian constitution were part of its basic structure, and could not be amended by the Parliament. In articulating the basic structure doctrine, the Supreme Court may be seen as invoking the idea of an overlapping deliberative consensus that was present at the constituent moment.

The German Basic Law (*Grundgesetz*) may similarly be seen as an articulation of transformative constitutionalism in the aftermath of the Second World War. The German Basic Law succeeded two constitutions, and all three came with distinct visions of 'free democratic basic order' (Freiheitlich-demokratische Grundordnung). Yet, the prehistory of constitutional democracy in Germany is somewhat confusing. Seen from the perspective of political philosophy things looked optimistic at the beginning of the modern era, if one recalls the American and French Revolution at the end of the eighteenth century. On the one side Immanuel Kant welcomed the revolutionary events in France and in his piece on 'Perpetual Peace' he postulated in the first 'definitive article', adopting the concept of a republic from his predecessor Jean-Jacques Rousseau, that the civic constitution of a state should be republican. His young contemporary Wilhelm von Humboldt developed a strong 'Idea' of a liberal state (which would influence John Stuart Mill half a century later), and finally Georg Wilhelm Friedrich Hegel, in the early years of the nineteenth century, postulated that the 'reasonable' in terms of the legal principle of the rule of law (*Rechtsstaat*) was nearly realised in Prussia. But on the other side and nearly at the same time, the German Empire, more precisely, the Holy Roman Empire of German Nationality, which consisted in the aftermath of the Westphalian Peace order of 1648 of several hundred more or less small principalities, was defeated by Napoleonic troops in 1806. The German state ceased to exist at the same time when German Political Philosophy had reached its peak.

Although numerous European rulers tried to turn back the clock and strived for the re-establishment of conservative monarchies during this post-revolutionary period of *Restauration*, only shortly later first signs of early constitutionalism appeared on the territory of the former German Empire.[9] Simultaneously, an all-German national movement was reanimated, and in both cases small groups of German liberals were responsible. This development showed that constitutionalism and nationalism in those early days had been tied closely together. In December 1848 the National Assembly in *Paulskirche* in Frankfurt passed the *Reichsverfassung*, whose catalogue of rights can be considered as a blueprint for the German *Grundgesetz* after World War II. The National Assembly itself had been created in an exemplary way when a committee of liberals invited the so-called 'pre-parliament' (*Vorparlament*) to stipulate voting principles. The Federal Assembly—the already existing quasi-constitutional organ of the German Federal Convention (*Deutscher Bund*) consisting of 38 'states'—accepted these principles and in May 1848 the constituent *German National Assembly* convened. The *Reichsverfassung*, the first modern German constitution, declared Germany to be a constitutional monarchy, but in the end, it was not adopted due to disagreements between the Emperor and the states. Liberalism in Germany in the middle of the nineteenth century, despite its famous intellectual pedigree, was too weak to be successful in the political realm.[10]

During the turmoil after World War I, a new attempt to frame a liberal constitution was undertaken. A social democratic initiative under Friedrich Ebert decided to invite the heads of important federal institutions and state governments, and they agreed to convene a constituent National Assembly. Members of that assembly came in the first place from the Social Democratic Party, the Centre Party (Zentrum), and the German Democratic Party. They discussed and later on accepted a draft from legal theorist Hugo Preuß. The so-called *Weimarer Verfassung* provided, by taking the ideas from 1848 seriously, a comprehensive rights catalogue and at the same time emphasised legal duties (e.g., 'property obliges'). The failure of that liberal constitution was because of numerous internal as well as external reasons: among others, the reparation costs Germany had to pay following the war had been overwhelming, and the world economic crisis intensified this situation; the highly problematic 'emergency ordinances' allowed for government legislation without parliamentary procedure being followed; and the increasing radicalisation of the population prevented the new constitution from acquiring a binding force. The strong left-wing and right-wing camps, the Communist Party on the one side, and different nationalist parties on the other, understood the constitution only as an interlude which they

---

[9]For the following see Zippelius (1994), Chaps. 3 and 4.

[10]The second German Empire was founded in 1870/71. It had a constitution, the Bismarck Reichsverfassung, which was not democratically legitimised and lasted until the end of World War I.

thought could be overcome more or less soon and taken into one or the other political direction.

After the 13 years of the totalitarian 3rd Reich, in 1948/9 a third and until now the last initiative to install a constitutional democracy was undertaken in Germany. When the split of the country into a Western and an Eastern part became unavoidable, the Western allies requested the German politicians in the West to start the constitution giving process. But those politicians were not willing to act accordingly because they thought that such a process should be a matter of the whole, that is united German people. They offered to develop something which they called an 'administrative statute' which should be able to fulfil exclusively executive functions (the administration) for West Germany. The allies were, however, not satisfied by this offer and insisted that the Germans develop a solution which would come closer to a full-fledged constitution. The result was the *Grundgesetz* (Basic Law) which differed not only in its name from a 'normal' constitution: in May 1949 it was not accepted by the (West) German people but only by the majority of the *Länderparlamente* (state legislatures) which were already in place. Apart from these two 'anomalies' and the fact that the first impulse came from the allies, the constitution-giving process took a more or less normal course: at first the Prime Ministers of the *Länder* convened an expert committee which gathered in August 1948 at the small island of *Herrenchiemsee* in Southern Bavaria to discuss normative and technical questions of the planned legal order. The proper constituent assembly, the Parliamentary Council (*Parlamentarischer Rat*) (which again did avoid all connotations of being *constitution giving*), consisted of 65 persons who had been elected by state legislatures according to proportional representation and who gathered together in September 1948. After 9 months of deliberations this committee accepted the draft of the *Grundgesetz*. The 'Frankfurt Documents' of the Western occupying powers originally stipulated that the people in two-thirds of the Länder should accept the draft, but the German side achieved that not through the acceptance by the people but two-thirds of the state legislatures. So it came about that the *Grundgesetz* has been adopted by all German *Landtage*, except the Bavarian, who nevertheless determined that if the *Grundgesetz* would be ratified by all others, it would be valid in Bavaria too.

While studying the constitutional status of the Preamble of the German Grundgesetz, Silagi (2011) points at what may be considered 'the transformative' in the Preamble's vision of the future of Germany. The special circumstances of occupation by allied powers, in which the Basic Law was framed, had initially compelled the Parliamentary Council to refer to 'severe limitations' to its sovereignty. Eventually, however, the Preamble avoided any mention of curtailment of sovereignty, to foreground the 'constituent power' of the 'German People', and their 'resolve' to preserve the 'national and political unity' of Germany: 'The entire German people is called upon to accomplish, by free self-determination, the unity and freedom of Germany' (Preamble 1949/50). This call for achieving the goal of a free and united Germany was made on behalf of an 'entire' people—even those 'Germans to whom participation was denied' (Quint 1991: p. 12). According to Silagi, in invoking the German people with reference to national and political unity, the Preamble was effectively alluding to the context of a 'divided post-war Germany', which made 'the enforced territorial partition' and 'the invitation of other, still excluded, parts of Germany to accede to the newly formed State', relevant to the future of 'German unity'. It is in this context that the declaration was made that the German people in enacting the Basic Law had also acted on behalf of those who were excluded and to whom participation was denied. The declaration is followed by an emphatic exhortation to achieve 'in free self-determination the unity and freedom of Germany'. Self-determination was an essential condition for Germany to become an 'equal partner in a united Europe' (2011: 56), and for human dignity (Article 1) which was fundamental to a just and peaceful world.

Theoretically, the breakdown of the Berlin wall in 1989 and the subsequent German reunification in 1990 was an ideal 'constitutional moment', to use the conception coined by Bruce Ackerman.[11] The East Germans had overturned the authoritarian and corrupt socialist government and strived for constitutionalised liberties and broader participation. Besides these substantial arguments, a larger number of democrats in both parts of Germany argued for a new CA, because they thought that after 40 years the time had come to give the *Grundgesetz* a real democratic legitimation (Guggenberger et al. 1991). But the sceptics and conservative politicians of the West in the end had the last word: they argued that the already existing constitution has proved itself to be effective and that one should not take imprudent steps which could endanger this solid legal fundament. This reluctance was underpinned by some overdrawn postulates and expectations from the East German side and the general confusing situation of that time. Of course, one could say that a chance and a symbolic moment for a real constitution giving process has been missed, but in the end, the substance of a normative order has been preserved for all Germans. In a way, substance prevailed over the process in those days.

1.4 Locating the Chapters: Constitutionalism and Democratic Practice

In their book *Endurance of National Constitutions*, Elkins, Ginsburg and Melton (2009) suggest that modes of looking at survival of national constitutions are based on both the way they are designed and the environment in which they unfold. While most constitutions that have emerged in the wake of democratisation after the Second World War and the processes of decolonisation, especially in South Asia, have experienced interruptions and continual deferrals, the Indian constitution has survived though not in the form in which it was inaugurated. In the 1990s, the German Basic Law came to encompass a united Germany. Through integration into a European Union, it also offered space for change in notions of sovereignty and citizenship. The

[11] With reference to Ackerman (1989: 546) who defined constitutional moments 'as moments when political movements succeed in hammering out new principles of constitutional identity that gain the considered support of a majority'. See also Ackerman (1998).

chapters in this book have addressed questions pertaining to constitutional design and change, the contexts in which changes occur, and what is considered unchangeable even when flexibility and dynamism are regarded as appropriate for constitutional durability. The promise of democracy in the transformative moment, the emphatic power of the constituent moment, the struggles around constitution-giving processes that represent 'constitutional politics' and its relationship with 'normal politics' of political majorities, provide an anchor for the chapters in this book. This anchor has persuaded the authors to weave arguments around themes which emerge out of a 'moral' reading of constitutions and the 'constitutional essentials' that suggest a deliberative consensus over the normative frameworks of democracy. At the same time, the authors examine how the consensus was fraught with contestations over their substance and form, and the relationship between constitutional order, institutional arrangements, and democratic practice. The contributions in this volume are organised broadly around two themes: 'Transition' and 'Transformative'. The theme 'Transition' focuses on secularism and nationalism as frameworks for the evaluation of processes of democratisation and the relationship between democracy and constitutional identity. The second theme—'Transformative'—brings together contributions which focus on constitutional democracy as an aspect of transformative constitutionalism, focusing on sovereignty and citizenship as constituting the conditions that provide the bridge between the past, present, and the future. This theme sees the transformative in tandem with constitutional morality as a condition for the sustenance of constitutional democracy. In this context the historical trajectory of 'offences against the state', especially sedition as a speech-crime in new contexts of popular sovereignty and rights to resources such as forests and land, that have become increasingly disputed, have been addressed. All the chapters, however, straddle the two themes and are not confined to one or the other.

1.4.1 Transition and Constitutional Identity

An intrinsic aspect of transition to constitutional democracy was the affirmation of 'a people' who had agreed to be governed by a constitution that they had given themselves. Declaratory statements in constitutions, such as the one made by the Preamble of the Irish constitution, among others, ascribe identities to the people. The 1937 constitution of the Republic of Ireland, for example, invoked the Holy Trinity as the source of 'all authority' and acknowledged 'obligation' to Jesus Christ. It simultaneously remembered with gratitude—the 'heroic' and 'unremitting' struggles of their ancestors in achieving independence—and affirmed their commitment to work for 'the common good, with due observance of Prudence, Justice, and Charity'. The preamble identifies the Irish people as Roman Catholic (Tushnet 2010: 671) imparting a 'coherent narrative of sameness and selfhood'—an identity in other words of the constitutional subject, (Rosenfeld 2009 cited in Tushnet, Ibid.: 673). It also presents a constitutional worldview, offering a different possibility of pinning an identity. Jocobsohn (2010) speaks of constitutions themselves assuming an identity, which distinguishes one constitution from another. The idea that constitutions can be identified on the ground of having salient features that make them distinguishable, assumes the existence of a 'discernable identity' (Ibid.: 3). Most constitutions, however, possess 'conflicting, even radically inconsistent, ideas at one and the same time' (Tribe 1987: 173 cited in Jacobsohn ibid.). Yet, in moments of constitutional rupture, e.g., the transition from Ottoman rule to secular republicanism in Turkey, an identity may emphatically be claimed. Unlike those who argue that a central unifying idea confers an unambiguous and lasting meaning to constitutionalism, Jacobsohn argues that 'constitutional disharmony' is 'critical' for the development of constitutional identity, throwing up challenges periodically for elaborating the substance of that identity (2010: 4). The uneasy relationship of constitutionalism and constitutional democracy with religion and nationalism provides the critical points of dissonance, where the conflict over constitutional identity assumes significance.

The Western literature on constitutionalism does not explicitly mention religion as a worldview which in one way or the other relates to a constitution as a normative order. While positive or negative religious freedoms a constituted legal order should guarantee, are mentioned nearly everywhere, only rarely is its compatibility with a different normative order scrutinised. From a liberal perspective, which is dominant in the field of constitutionalism, citizens of a constitutional democracy are conceived in the first place as individuals who try to realise their life plans within a given legal frame. The communitarian critique of (Rawlsian) liberalism criticised among other things an 'unencumbered self', meaning that liberal theory would not be able to do justice to the social and cultural embeddedness of individuals. If one takes this argument seriously one has to respect that the majority of citizens will normally adhere to one or another worldview, and an important question is how these different conceptions can coexist under the rule of law or, at least, how 'reasonable pluralism' is envisioned or accommodated in constitutional worldviews.

To indicate the direction in which an answer could lie, it is not necessary to refer to an accurate reconstruction of the history of constitutionalism here, it suffices to point out that a legal constitution in the modern sense is 'the work of centuries' as German philosopher Hegel (1991: §274, supplement) once said. This means that constitutive ideas—like human rights, rule of law, sovereignty and autonomy—have to develop over a longer period and a 'constitutional moment' at a certain point of time (e.g., 1787 or 1789) is to be understood as an endpoint of this development. In Europe, one could say, it started with the religious wars in the sixteenth and seventeenth century when ideas of political sovereignty and tolerance had been developed. Rawls considered both as important elements of the Westphalian peace order (1648). In other words, something like a common ground which guaranteed at least a temporary coexistence of inimical religious groups or nations emerged out of a standstill and not according to a master plan. Rawls called this historical situation a 'modus vivendi', which has been 'accepted' by the different parties only for strategic reasons. But sovereignty, tolerance, and human rights are by nature normative concepts and the rival religions had to find out if and how they could support and meet the normative requirements of these principles because in turn they would protect the integrity of religious values.

If the opponents would reach a positive answer for this question, meaning that the basic elements of their respective worldviews are respected or included, then this fundament would not only be of strategic, but also of intrinsic value—a 'constitutional consensus' would be reached.[12]

The message from this brief sketch of Western constitutionalism is twofold: the first is sobering because it became clear that the first modern constitutions had not been developed and implemented overnight, as for example the quick sequence of constitutions in revolutionary France demonstrated. Also, there is no guarantee that a modus vivendi automatically transfers into a constitutional consensus—the Weimar constitution is a telling example for such a failure. The second lesson is more optimistic: once a more or less liberal version of a constitution has been realised and has proved its worth for different worldviews, religious and secular, one could expect learning effects even across cultural boundaries so that a successful legal paradigm can be imported. The Germans, for example, shaped their *Grundgesetz* according to the US model; and the former became itself a blueprint for East European constitutional assemblies after the political turmoil from 1989.

Significantly, the post-apartheid South African Constitution of 1996 veered away from the invocation of God, that occurred in the Preamble of the 1961 Constitution: 'In HUMBLE SUBMISSION to Almighty God, Who controls the destinies of nations and the history of peoples…'. (Preamble 1961). The 'people of South Africa' in the 1996 Republican constitution recognised the injustices of the past, pledged to honour those who suffered for justice and freedom, and committed themselves to the future of a united and democratic South Africa. The Indian constitution of 1950 sought an inclusive and non-sectarian national identity by invoking democratic ideas of liberty, equality and fraternity, religious pluralism, non-discrimination, and civic allegiance. Gandhi saw the relation between religion or truth as one of harmony. Indeed, self-rule was ultimately about moral transformation which encompassed the realm of politics (Kapila 2007) and formed the basis of his vision of Hindu–Muslim cooperation in India and Indian secularism (Lal 2013). In this volume, Shaunna Rodrigues makes a case for looking at the role religious justification played in shaping a plural political conception. Examining in particular the elaboration of an Islamic justification by Maulana Abul Kalam Azad, Rodrigues argues that the ideas of *tawahid* (unity of God), *jihad* (struggle), and self-rule were deployed by Azad to build a political field in which pluralism could be aligned with Islamic ideals. The domain of moral politics erected through these ideals, paved the way for notions of democratic equality as the basis of an inclusive people as constitutive of constitutional identity.

The idea of strict separation of religion/church and politics defined the *laicite*—an organising principle of a French national identity—which enabled it to accommodate religious minorities. Several states that made the transition to democracy in the twentieth century, including Turkey, through an amendment in 1928 in its 1924

[12]The third stage, following the modus vivendi and the constitutional consensus, is 'overlapping consensus' in which the different worldviews not only recognise the normative substance of a constitution but also the existence of the other worldviews as related to groups supporting the legal order. See Rawls (1993).

Constitution, included the principle of separation of religion and state. The German Basic Law and the Indian constitution have both guaranteed freedom of religion, without specifically inscribing a strict wall of separation. The word 'secularism' did not form part of the 1950 Indian constitution. It was inserted in the Preamble through an amendment in 1976 and was declared part of the basic structure of the constitution, in a judgement of the Supreme Court of India in 1994 (*S. R. Bommai versus Union of India* 1994). Scholars have pointed out that secularism in India is distinctive and does not conform to the 'western model' of strict separation of religion from politics. Politics in India maintains a 'principled distance' (Bhargava 2006, 2010, 2013) from religion, which allows the state to take decisions to preserve religious pluralism, and equality among religions (Bhargava ibid., Parekh 2008). Two chapters in this volume—by Oliver Hidalgo on constitutional democracy and secularism, and by Mirjam Künkler and Tine Stein on Ernst-Wolfgang Böckenförde's notion of the state's open neutrality—focus on the idea and practice of secularism from a comparative perspective, engaging in particular with Bhargava's framework of 'principled distance'. Hidalgo considers democracy a complex structure of *antinomies* which makes it a domain of sustained struggle between conflicting principles such as plurality versus social harmony, liberty versus equality, and individual rights versus collective claims.The idea of *antinomies* enables Hidalgo to see these principles, all of which lay claims to reasonableness, spawn an evaluative framework to distinguish legitimate political struggles from extreme political demands. In this context, Hidalgo finds Bhargava's framework an effective paradigm for understanding how religious diversity can be accommodated in the public domain without exceeding the limits of constitutional democracy. Künkler and Stein, however, find Bhargava's use of 'wall of separation', to describe the relationship between state and religion in the West, inadequate and misleading. Questioning its appropriateness in the German context, they explain the distinctiveness of the German idea of secularism. Presenting Ernst-Wolfgang Böckenförde's model of 'encompassing open neutrality' as a response to Bhargava's framework, they show another modality for designing a democratic relationship between religion and politics. A judge, jurist, and public intellectual, Böckenforde's writings were influential in shaping German jurisprudence. His idea of encompassing open neutrality accords room to religion in the public sphere—in 'school, educational institutions, and in what is summarily referred to as the public order'—without 'any form of identification' to 'create a balance', so that 'affirming and leading a life in accordance with religion, to the extent that it is compatible with the secular goals of the state, is permitted also within the public sphere by the legal system and is incorporated into the latter' (Böckenförde 1991).

The idea of belonging formed the ideological foundation of anti-colonial nationalisms, which proclaimed its sovereignty in the domain of culture, and inserted itself into a new public sphere constituted by the processes and forms of the modern state. The colonial state justified its existence on the ground that it would bring modernity to the colonies. The colonial state's power was premised on the 'rule of colonial difference' or the preservation of the alienness of the ruling race/group. Apart from rolling back the rule of colonial difference, anti-colonial movements were an expression of solidarity among people claiming a shared and distinctive past to define themselves as a nation. This self-definition as a nation inspired the 'ideal of independence' (Smith 1983: 171) and sovereignty—implying the freedom from external interference to frame its own rules and set up its own institutions, in accordance with its needs and 'character' (Ibid.).

While national liberation movements led to the installation of constitutional democracies, nationalism has not been seen as integral to constitutionalism. Nationalism, Michael Becker argues in this volume, performs the task of achieving the pre-political integration of the demos, which is an essential precondition for constituting the state. Becker engages with some of the alternatives to nationalism which have been suggested by philosophers for offering more appropriate forms of solidarity, e.g., social capital and constitutional patriotism, among others. He concludes that the old forms of closed national communities are no longer possible, but the realities of living as single collectives under a constitutional order precludes the possibility of unlimited expansion.

In a sense, Michael Becker's chapter draws attention to another question—what is it that holds together a constitutional order and makes it democratic? While Becker searched for answers in the old and new forms of nationalism and their alternatives, Amir Ali's chapter brings to scrutiny the relationship between Islam and constitutional democracy through an exploration of specific sites of conflict from the contemporary Islamic world. Drawing upon the ideas of fragile constitutionalism and unstable constitutionalism, Ali brings this relationship to reflexive scrutiny and raises possibilities of rethinking 'unstable constitutionalism' in Islamic countries by looking for the commitment to constitutionalism in Islam and the Islamic rejection of nationalism. Krishna Swamy Dara in this volume takes the discussion on nationalism forward by understanding the different 'minor' strands of nationalism in India that emerged in opposition to the colonial state and also to the hegemonic nationalism of both the Congress and the Hindu Right. Dara's chapter is an exploration of the discursive field of nationalist thought in India in the late colonial period, focusing in particular on the Dalit-Bahujan critique as an ideological engagement with dominant forms of nationalism. It provides a reading of Ambedkar's 'argumentative' stance on nationalism which offered the possibility of opposing oppression, and simultaneously making space for inclusive forms of membership.

1.4.2 The Transformative and Constitutional Morality

As discussed earlier, transformative constitutionalism is a term largely associated with the South African constitution making experience. It has, however, come to be used with reference to constitutions in the Global South, as a model different from the constitutions of the North and distinct from Western liberal constitutional models

(Hailbronner 2017). Hailbronner has, however, argued that the quick dismissal of Northern examples as irrelevant to transformative constitutionalism does not take into account the manner in which some Northern countries such as Germany have adopted important features of a transformative understanding of law, especially the broader emancipatory project, and the key role of the state in pursuing change (Ibid., p. 2). The chapters in this book may be located in a specific framework of transformative constitutionalism which goes beyond the economic and social revolution components to focus on the meaning and modality of change. The 'traditional metaphor of a bridge' (Langa 2006: 353) in the Preamble of the interim constitution of South Africa, according to Pius Langa, did not suggest a terminal point in the process of passage or crossing over to the desired destination. The bridge is 'a space between an unstable past and an uncertain future'… 'the value of the bridge lies in remaining on it, crossing it over and over to remember, change and imagine new and better ways of being'. In this perspective, transformation 'is a permanent ideal':

> …. a way of looking at the world that creates a space in which dialogue and contestation are truly possible, in which new ways of being are constantly explored and created, accepted and rejected and in which change is unpredictable but the idea of change is constant. (Langa 2006: 354)

Seen in this way, the idea of transformative constitutionalism becomes encompassing and foregrounds the intrinsic value of *dialogue* and *contestation* in propelling change. Emphasising the importance of constitutional morality when the Constituent Assembly of India was adopting the Constitution of India, B. R. Ambedkar invoked George Grote to argue that the diffusion of constitutional morality was essential for the peaceful working and sustenance of a democratic constitution. Intrinsic to such working was a commitment to the 'spirit of the constitution', which could be achieved only when 'people are saturated with constitutional morality'. Till the time constitutional morality had spread wide and deep among the Indian people and they were saturated with it, the legislatures could not be trusted with prescribing the form of administration (Singh and Roy 2017). Interestingly, Vilhena et al. use the expression 'aspirational' to refer to the attempts by India, South Africa, and Brazil, to transform their past and present (of colonialism, apartheid, and military regime) through a constitutional process to establish a durable moral order of rights and the rule of law. The constitutional texts which emerged out of these efforts at transformation can be seen primarily as normative texts, which lay down a framework for ensuring the 'ambitious constitutional promises' (Vilhena et al. 2013: 3–4). The framers of both the Indian constitution and the German Basic Law had to inscribe into their respective constitutions the tenets of a constitutional democracy with the memory of an undemocratic past. The inscription of human dignity and fundamental rights in both the Indian constitution and the Basic Law marked moments of aspirational universalism. At the same time, the commitment to universal principles were anchored in convictions that could be provided by the constitutional dictum.

The colonial state in India exercised sovereignty over Indians as a form of power in which the native became a protégée to be improved through domestication (Mbembe 2001). Independence from colonial rule carried a powerful affective appeal of transition to sovereign, self-determining camaraderie of equal citizenship—an appeal which was integral to the constitutive moment of transformative constitutionalism. In her chapter Garima Dhabhai offers a legal-anthropological insight into a postcolonial context where traditional forms of sovereignty existed through deference legitimation and the modalities through which they were transformed for accommodation in the constitutional order. Dhabhai demonstrates this by tracing the trajectory of the transition of sovereignty from 'princely' to a 'popular' form in the erstwhile princely domains of India after independence, and a corresponding transition of princes into citizens, especially after the abolition of privy purses by the Indian government through the 26th Constitution Amendment Act of 1971. The process of this transformation, Dhabhai argues, involved the affirmation of constitutional power and the sovereign power of the postcolonial state which supplanted but also coexisted, in an uneasy relationship with the residual but influential symbols and practices of its 'predecessor's' domain of sovereignty.

Any discussion of sovereignty must necessarily grapple with its relationship with rule of law and state authority. Law and politics are deeply intertwined. This relationship has several aspects. While constitutionalism and the rule of law are sometimes seen as performing a function of legitimation for the government, they provide limits to governmental action. The question of pedigree of law is important in thinking about law, as are the questions which pertain to the use of law. The latter has to do with the way in which law gets transformed and also transforms lives, conveying thereby both the normative concerns of law as well as the kinds of political subjectivities it generates. While law is central to the exercise of state power and sovereignty (Thompson 1975), the principle of 'rule of law'—deeply associated with liberal constitutionalism—both defines and limits state authority, and marks it out from the realm of everyday power (Ocko and Gilmartin 2009). It also brings into play the question of legitimate authority and additional concerns which surround it—who gives the law (a question of pedigree or source of law), why should people obey laws (a question of both source and content of law), and what are the means through which conformity to law may legitimately be achieved. Anushka Singh's chapter on the interpretative practices associated with the 'sedition law' in India may be located in the debates on the right to speech as a constitutional right in liberal democracies and the reasons of state invoked by a political regime to preserve itself against what it construes to be seditious speech. In this context, Singh examines the iterative practices of law to show how legal regimes which violate democratic rights are often preserved through both executive action and judicial interpretations that validate regime persecution.

The domain of law and politics is a field which opens up multiple possibilities of exploration. Normative questions address law's origins and intentions, the constitutive site of law, and the proliferation of law through processes that are inflected by struggles over just law as distinct from efficient law. Indeed, the three chapters by Anushka Singh, Radhika Chitkara, and Aditya Pandey, interrogate in different ways, the sites of production of law. While institutional contexts (courts, trials, and judgments) are ordinarily seen as constituting the legitimate sites of production of law, the chapters bring our attention to social and cultural contexts, the lifeworlds or habitus of law, and the manner in which they generate legal subjects and political subjectivities.

Radhika Chitkara's chapter in this volume explores the right to natural resources and international regimes of human rights, constitutional practice and democratic politics, and importantly, how people engage with law in specific contexts. A constitutional democracy allows for different ways of life (cultures) under the condition that the core values of cultural groups are compatible with the constitution and the constitution is recognised by those groups. In this context, exploring the complex question of indigenous women's human rights to resources, Chitkara has looked at specific cases pertaining to rights of indigenous women over forest resources within various international and regional human rights conventions, to explore how effective these frameworks have been in prescribing the normative 'minimums' as compared to domestic legal and constitutional protections. She examines this question in the context of collective right to self-determination over resources amidst the historical conflicts between states and indigenous peoples over land and resource sovereignty, along with contest over constitutional guarantees of non-discrimination in collective and individual rights of use, access, and governance. Aditya Pandey's chapter on the 'land question' in Germany and India brings the two countries together for a comparative study. Pandey's study finds that despite the distinct histories of land relations, land system, and agrarian structures in the two countries, there are points of convergence in the manner in which the land question is framed. Shifts in policy occur in both countries in response to state formative practices and market imperatives. The redistribution of land and reforming land relations was a primary concern during the formative moment of constitutional democracy in India as well as in the political considerations of state formation in divided Germany. The chapter focuses in particular on the dramatic revival of interest in land from the last decade of the twentieth century, beginning with the unification of Germany and liberalisation of the Indian economy, respectively. Despite differences in characteristics like percentage of population dependent upon land in agriculture, landholdings size, and share of agriculture in economy, both the countries show a qualitative similarity in the way the land question gets shaped by structural path of commodification of land and its continuous transformation as a site of improvement.

References

Ambedkar, B. R. (1949, November 25). Speech in constituent assembly. *Constituent assembly debates* (Vol. X–XII, Book no. 5). New Delhi: Lok Sabha Secretariat.

Austin, G. (1966). *The Indian constitution: Cornerstone of a nation*. Oxford: Clarendon Press.

Austin, G. (1999). *India's living constitution*. Delhi: OUP.

Austin, G. (2002). The expected and the unintended in working a democratic constitution. In Z. Hasan, E. Sridhran, & R. Sudarshan (Eds.), *India's living constitution: Ideas, practices, controversies* (pp. 319–343). Permanent Black: Delhi.

Ackerman, B. (1988). Neo-federalism. In J. Elster & R. Slagstad (Eds.), *Constitutionalism and democracy: Studies in rationality and social change* (pp. 153–193). Cambridge: Cambridge University Press.
Ackerman, B. (1989). Constitutional politics/constitutional law. *Yale Law Journal, 99*(3), 453–547.
Ackerman, B. (1991). *We the people: Foundations*. Cambridge, MA: The Belknap Press of Harvard University Press.
Ackerman, B. (1998). *We the people: Transformations*. Cambridge, MA: The Belknap Press of Harvard University Press.
Baxi, U. (2000). Postcolonial legality. In H. Schwarz & S. Ray (Eds.), *A companion to postcolonial studies* (pp. 540–555). Malden: Blackwell.
Baxi, U. (2002). The (im)possibility of constitutional justice. In Z. Hasan, E. Sridharan, & R. Sudarshan (Eds.), *India's Living Constitution: Ideas, practices, controversies* (pp. 31–63). Delhi: Permanent Black.
Baxi, U. (2008). Outline of a 'theory of practice' of Indian constitutionalism. In R. Bhargava (Ed.), *Politics and ethics of the Indian constitution* (pp. 92–118). Delhi: Oxford University Press.
Baxi, U. (2013). Preliminary notes on transformative constitutionalism. In O. Vilhena, U. Baxi, & F. Viljoen (Eds.), *Transformative constitutionalism: Comparing the apex courts of Brazil, India and South Africa* (pp. 19–47). Johannesburg: Pretoria University Law Press.
Bhargava, R. (2006). The distinctiveness of Indian secularism. In T. N. Srinivasan (Ed.), *The future of secularism* (pp. 20–53). New Delhi: Oxford University Press.
Bhargava, R. (Ed.). (2008). *Politics and ethics of the Indian constitution*. Delhi: Oxford University Press.
Bhargava, R. (2010). Indian secularism. An alternative, trans-cultural ideal. In R. Barghava (Ed.), *The promise of India's secular democracy* (pp. 63–105). New Delhi: Oxford University Press.
Bhargava, R. (Ed.). (2013). *Secular states and religious diversity*. Vancouver: UBC Press.
Bhatia, U. (Ed.). (2018). *The Indian constituent assembly: Deliberations on democracy*. London and New York: Routledge.
Bhatia, G. (2019). *The transformative constitution: A radical biography in nine acts*. Noida: Harper Collins.
Böckenförde, E.-W. (1991). Die Entstehung des Staates als Vorgang der Säkularisation. In E.-W. Böckenförde (Ed.), *Recht, Staat, Freiheit* (pp. 92–114). Frankfurt: Suhrkamp.
Chatterjee, P. (1993). *The nation and its fragments: Colonial and postcolonial histories*. Princeton: Princeton University Press.
Choudhry, S., Khosla, M., & Mehta, P. B. (2016). Locating Indian constitutionalism. In S. Choudhry, M. Khosla, & P. B. Mehta (Eds.), *The Oxford handbook of the Indian constitution* (pp. 1–13). Oxford: Oxford University Press.
Dahl, R. (1989). *Democracy and its critics*. New Haven and London: Yale University Press.
De, R. (2016). Constitutional antecedents. In S. Choudhry, M. Khosla, & P. B. Mehta (Eds.), *The Oxford handbook of the Indian constitution* (pp. 17–37). Oxford: Oxford University Press.
Elangovan, A. (2018). "We the People?": Politics and the conundrum of framing a constitution on the eve of decolonisation. In U. Bhatia (Ed.), *The Indian constituent assembly: Deliberations on democracy* (pp. 10–37). London and New York: Routledge.
Elkins, Z., Ginsburg, T., & Melton, J. (Eds.). (2009). *The endurance of national constitutions*. Cambridge: Cambridge University Press.
Elster, J. (1995). Forces and mechanisms in the constitution making process. *Duke Law Journal, 45*(2), 364–396.
Friedrich, C. J. (1950). *Constitutional government and democracy* (rev ed.). Boston: Ginn and Company.
Guggenberger, B., Preuß, U. K., & Ullmann, W. (Eds.). (1991). *Eine Verfassung in Deutschland. Manifest, Text, Plädoyers*. München: Hanser.
Habermas, J. (1996). *Between facts and norms. Contributions to a discourse theory of law and democracy*. Cambridge: MIT Press.

Hailbronner, M. (2017). Transformative constitutionalism: Not only in the global south. *American Journal of Comparative Law, 65*(3), 527–565.
Hamilton, A., Madison, J., & Jay, J. (1961). *The federalist papers [1787/88]*. New York: Mentor Books.
Hayek, F. A. (1960). *The constitution of liberty*. Chicago: University of Chicago Press.
Hegel, G. W. F. (1991). *Elements of the philosophy of right* (A. W. Wood, & H.-B. Nisbet (Eds.)). Cambridge: Cambridge UP.
Gallie, W. B. (1955–1956). Essentially contested concepts. *Proceedings of the Aristotelian Society, 56*, 167–198. New Series.
Holmes, S. (1988). Precommitment and the paradox of democracy. In J. Elster & R. Slagstad (Eds.), *Constitutionalism and democracy* (pp. 195–240). New York: Cambridge University Press.
Hume, D. (1963). Of the original contract. In D. Hume (Ed.), *Essays: Moral, political, and literary* (pp. 209–219). London: Oxford University Press.
Jacobsohn, G. J. (2010). *Constitutional identity*. Cambridge: Harvard University Press.
Kapila, S. (2007). Self, spencer and swaraj: Nationalist thought and critiques of liberalism, 1890–1920. *Modern Intellectual History, 4*(1), 124–127.
Kaviraj, S. (2003). A state of contradictions: The post-colonial state in India. In Q. Skinner & B. Strath (Eds.), *State and citizens: History, theory, prospects* (pp. 145–166). Cambridge: Cambridge University Press.
Khilnani, S., Raghavan, V., & Thiruvengadam, K. (Eds.). (2013). *Comparative constitutionalism in South Asia*. New Delhi: Oxford University Press.
Langa, P. (2006). Transformative constitutionalism. *Stellenbosch L R, 17*(3), 351–360.
Lal, V. (2013). Gandhi's religion: Politics, faith, and hermeneutics. *Journal of sociology and social anthropology, 4*(1–2), 31–40.
Lerner, H. (2016). The Indian founding: A comparative perspective. In S. Choudhry, M. Khosla, & P. B. Mehta (Eds.), *The Oxford handbook of the Indian constitution* (pp. 55–70). Oxford: Oxford University Press.
Mbembe, A. (2001). *On the postcolony*. Berkeley: University of California Press.
Mehta, P. B. (2002). The inner conflict of constitutionalism: Judicial review and the basic structure. In Z. Hasan, E. Sridharan, & R. Sudarshan (Eds.), *India's living constitution: Ideas, practices, controversies* (pp. 179–206). Delhi: Permanent Black.
Mehta, P. B. (2010a). What is constitutional morality? *Seminar, 615*, 17–22.
Mehta, U. S. (2010b). Constitutionalism. In N. G. Jayal & P. B. Mehta (Eds.), *The companion volume to politics in India* (pp. 15–27). Delhi: OUP.
Mouffe, C. (2000). *The democratic paradox*. London: Verso.
Ocko, J., & Gilmartin, D. (2009). State, sovereignty, and the people: A comparison of the "Rule of Law" in China and India. *The Journal of Asian Studies, 68*(1), 55–133.
Paine, T. (1991). *The rights of man: Being an answer to Mr. Burke's attack on the French revolution*. London: J.S. Jordon.
Parekh, B. (2008). The constitution as a statement of Indian identity. In R. Bhargava (Ed.), *Politics and ethics of the Indian constitution* (pp. 43–58). New Delhi: Oxford University Press.
Pitkin, H. F. (1987). The idea of a constitution. *Journal of Legal Education, 37*(2), 167–169.
Quint, P. E. (1991). *The imperfect union: Constitutional structures for German unification*. Princeton: Princeton University Press.
Rawls, J. (1993). *Political liberalism*. New York: Columbia University Press.
Rousseau, J. J. (2000) [1762]. *The social contract and other later political writings* (V. Gourevitch (Ed.)). Cambridge: Cambridge UP.
Rosenfeld, M. (2009). *The identity of the constitutional subject: Selfhood, citizenship, culture, and community*. London: Routledge.
Sartori, G. (1962). Constitutionalism: A preliminary discussion. *American Political Science Review, 56*(4), 853–864.
Shani, O. (2018). *How India became democratic: Citizenship and the making of universal franchise*. Gurgaon: Penguin/Viking.

Singh, U. K., & Roy, A. (2017). Ambedkar and the ideas of constitutionalism and constitutional democracy. *Summerhill IIAS Review, 23*(2), 3–11.
Smith, A. D. (1983). *Theories of nationalism*. London: Duckworth.
Wolin, S. (1989). *The Presence of the past: Essays on the state and the constitution*. Baltimore: Johns Hopkins University Press.
Silagi, M. (2011). The preamble of the German grundgesetz: Constitutional status and importance of preambles in German law. *Acta Juridica Hungarica, 52*(1), 54–63.
Swaminathan, S. (2013, January 26). India's benign constitutional revolution. *The Hindu*. Retrieved January 27, 2013, from http://www.thehindu.com/opinion/lead/indias-benign-constitutional-revolution/article4345212.ece.
Tribe, L. H. (1987). The idea of the constitution: A metaphor-morphis. *Journal of Legal Education, 37*(2), 170–173.
Thompson, E. P. (1975). *Whigs and hunters: The origins of the black act*. New York: Pantheon.
Tushnet, M. (2003). *The new constitutional order*. Princeton: Princeton University Press.
Tushnet, M. (2010). How do constitutions constitute constitutional identity? *International Journal of Constitutional Law, 8*(3), 671–676.
Tushnet, M. (2014). *Comparative constitutional law*. Cheltenham: Edward Elgar Publishing.
Vilhena, O., Baxi, U., & Viljoen, F. (Eds.). (2013). *Transformative constitutionalism: Comparing the apex courts of Brazil, India and South Africa*. Johannesburg: Pretoria University Law Press.
Zippelius, R. (1994). *Kleine deutsche Verfassungsgeschichte. Vom frühen Mittelalter bis zur Gegenwart*. München: Beck.

Anupama Roy is a Professor at the Centre for Political Studies in Jawaharlal Nehru University, Delhi. Her research interests straddle legal studies, political anthropology of political institutions, political ideas, and gender studies. She obtained her MPhil degree from University of Delhi, and her PhD degree from the State University of New York at Binghamton, USA. She is the co-author of the book *Election Commission of India: Institutionalising Democratic Uncertainties* (OUP, 2019) and author of the books *Citizenship in India* (Oxford India Short Introduction Series, OUP, 2016), *Mapping Citizenship in India* (OUP, 2010, reprinted 2015), and *Gendered Citizenship: Historical and Conceptual Explorations* (Orient Longman, 2005, paperback, 2013). She has co-edited *Poverty, Gender and Migration in South Asia* (Sage, 2008). Her research articles have appeared in various national and international journals including Asian Studies Review, Australian Feminist Studies, Critical Asian Studies, Contributions to Indian Sociology, Economic and Political Weekly and Election Law Journal.

Anupama Roy was a senior fellow in the Centre for Women's Development Studies, before she joined the Centre for Political Studies in JNU. She has been a visiting scholar in Sydney University, University of Warwick and University of Würzburg, Germany. She was Sir Ratan Tata post-doctoral Fellow at the Institute of Economic Growth in Delhi and KTP Fellow at University of Technology, Sydney, Australia.

Michael Becker is a Professor at the Institute of Political Science and Sociology, Julius-Maximilians-University, Würzburg. He received his PhD 1991 at Johannes-Gutenberg University at Mainz and did his Habilitation at Otto-Friedrich-University at Bamberg in 2002. Between 2003-2005 he was Substitute Professor at the Universities of Bamberg, Landau and Konstanz. Since 2007 he is Professor for Political Science at the Institute for Political Science and Sociology at Würzburg University. His Fields of Research are Modern and Contemporary Western Political Philosophy, Constitutional Democracy; Modern Indian Political Thought. Since 2013 he has been Guest Professor at Indian Universities (Delhi, Chandigarh, Mangalore). He participates in the DAAD sponsored "Indo-German-Partnership" (IGP) and is a Member of the BMBF sponsored "International Centre for Advanced Studies—Metamorphoses of the Political" (ICAS-MP) (https://micasmp.hypotheses.org/).

Major Publications: Rechtsstaat und Demokratie (co-editor), Wiesbaden 2001; Verständigungs-orientierte Kommunikation und rechtsstaatliche Ordnung (Habilitation), Baden-Baden 2003; Politik und Recht (special issue of Politische Vierteljahresschrift) (co-editor), Wiesbaden 2006; Politische Philosophie (co-author), Paderborn 2006 (4th ed. 2017); Grundstrukturen der Politik in der Bundesrepublik Deutschland, Opladen 2011, Politischer Liberalismus und wohlgeordnete Gesellschaften (ed.), Baden-Baden 2013.

Part I
Transitions and Constitutional Identity

Chapter 2
Constitutionalism and Nationalism—Revisited

Michael Becker

Abstract Western Nationalism has come under serious attack primarily in Germany and France. Leading politicians consider it as a dangerous ideology represented exclusively by right-wing parties. Although there is truth in the assertion that extremists have recently captured the national question, the "nationalist turn" to some extent has been a reaction to ineffective refugee politics of the European Union. This chapter explores the crucial role nationalism played in the early days of constitutional democracy. In the first part of the paper, nationalism will be taken seriously as a non-extremist theory which is able to integrate both: firstly, a horizontal or *other-directed dimension* in which individuals are seen as fellow citizens under the rule of law, and secondly, a *state-directed dimension* in which citizens support and maintain their constitutionally framed democracy. The second part of the paper will scrutinise contemporary alternatives to nationalism. One of these is "social capital" which consists, according to Paul Collier and Robert Putnam, of strong feelings of reciprocity and intersubjective trust. Social capital presupposes, and here lies a parallel to nationalism, that limited collectives are able to preserve this resource and do control the inflow of outsiders. The second alternative is called "Associative ownership". This approach stems from Ryan Pevnick and develops further the Lockean property right argument. It shows that citizens of a (nation-) state can be understood as the owners of their political institutions and therefore are allowed to exercise exclusive control over those. David Miller with his conception of "Compatriot Partiality" shows that citizens of a nation state develop certain duties to each other which have an intrinsic value. His reference to "fellow nationals" is close to a reformulation of classical nationalism. Finally, "Constitutional Patriotism" plays a role in reconsidering or replacing national ideology. Jürgen Habermas developed this conception of loyalty to the constitutional order before the background of Germany's disastrous experiences with nationalism which would not allow relying on national ideology anymore. The result of this search for substitutes for old nationalism is twofold: firstly, it is difficult to reformulate a contemporary theory of nationalism or to reanimate an old one. Above this, conceptions of a more or less closed national community cannot convince anymore under circumstances of globalisation. But, secondly and at the

M. Becker (✉)
Institute of Political Science and Sociology, Julius-Maximilians-University, Würzburg, Germany
e-mail: Michael.Becker@uni-wuerzburg.de

© Springer Nature Singapore Pte Ltd. 2020
A. Roy and M. Becker (eds.), *Dimensions of Constitutional Democracy*,
https://doi.org/10.1007/978-981-15-3899-5_2

same time, it becomes clear, that in the context of global migration single collectives which live under a constitutional order cannot or should not expand unlimitedly. Justifications for a qualified limitation are still necessary.

2.1 Introduction

Nationalism has become discredited in many countries at present for at least three reasons: firstly, in the West there is an influential strand of anti-nationalist argument in the public discourse insofar as adherents to a European integration think nationalism and the nation state are outdated models of political order. Secondly, cosmopolitans, another camp of nationalism critics, sometimes argue in the same direction, holding that national and therefore controlled or even closed borders are a violation of the human right to free movement. And thirdly, another strand of arguments holds that nowadays nationalism has a strong affinity to populism and right-wing extremism, and both are under attack by the political mainstream because of their nationalistic agenda. Anti-nationalists and nationalists clashed during the refugee crisis of 2015: the former welcomed the huge masses of refugees from the Middle East and therefore applauded the politics of the German Chancellor, saying that closed borders were obstacles for a true Human Rights policy, whereas the right-wing parties and groups, but also a lot of conservatives, argued that such a "policy" would endanger the functioning of the (German) nation state which is embedded in a malfunctioning European Union. Ironically, in this case the anti-nationalism of the advocates of European integration and cosmopolitans provoked or caused at least in part a revival of old-fashioned nationalism.

In this paper it will be argued that both camps either overestimate nationalism or underestimate it: Europhiles and cosmopolitans don't think it plays or should play an important role anymore whereas right-wing opponents tend to think it to be the only relevant frame of politics. The intention of these remarks is not to turn back time or naively rehabilitate a political conception which has recently been devalued so strongly in many speeches of prominent politicians.[1] Instead it will be explored if substitutes for nationalism do exist, conceptions to fill the gap which arose from a, sometimes unqualified, nationalism bashing.

But is nationalism or are alternatives to it necessary at all for a discussion of "constitutional democracy"? The answer must be affirmative if one considers the "subject" of a constitution: on the one side there is of course the process of democracy

[1]During the 100th anniversary of the ceasefire at the end of World War I, French President Macron called nationalism "the opposite of patriotism" (a surprising comparison from the leader of the "Grande Nation"); German Federal President Steinmeier, speaking in 2018 at the occasion of the commemoration of the "Night of Broken Glass" in 1938, spoke of an "aggressive new nationalism" of the right-wing parties and postulated "a democratic patriotism". At least German politicians who are in charge within the Grand Coalition to easily forget that the criticised increase of nationalism (which they sometimes seem to equate with National Socialism) is to a certain degree a direct result of their failures in connection with the refugee politics of 2015 and the years before.

or self-government that has to be constituted in one or the other way and which is sometimes called the "organisational part" of a constitution. On the other side constitutional democracy refers to a group of people who have the goal to govern themselves democratically, and the question of the "nature" of this group or collective arises automatically. Constitutional theories normally do not discuss this, probably because most of them adhere to the liberal paradigm in which individualism prevails all forms of communitarianism.[2] This political collective had different names over time: "demos", "people" or "nation", and the main difference between the demos of a classical, let's say Athenian city state, and a territorially extended modern state is not only that in the latter the demos can't assemble at one place and a certain point of time. Rather this group has to be constituted at all as a group of people who want to act together politically in the future. In other words, before the process of constituting in the political sense can occur some pre-political form of integration must already be established, and nationalism, at least in part, achieves this task.

The overall argument which will be developed in the following tries to demonstrate this, and offers something of a way in between the two camps mentioned a moment ago, and roughly consists of two parts: firstly, the constructive and probably indispensable role Western nationalism played for the rise of the modern state will be remembered (1) and a brief sketch of central Western ideologies will be given if connections or overlaps with nationalism do exist (2).

Secondly, some contemporary alternatives to the seemingly old-fashioned conceptions of nationalism will be scrutinised. In this context, references to social capital, associative ownership, compatriot partiality and finally to the constitutional patriotism will be made (3).

2.2 Nationalism and the Nation State

Nationalism can be considered to be a specific ideology with origins in Central Europe in the second half of the eighteenth century. It came later than liberalism but earlier than conservatism and socialism and one reason for this is that, like most other ideologies, it developed within a specific context. Nationalism of the late eighteenth and nineteenth century was a phenomenon of Western modernity in social, cultural and political respects. Beside this it is often argued that nationalism is not a freestanding conception in the same sense as the three ideologies of liberalism, socialism and conservatism. And indeed, in the nineteenth and twentieth century, at least in Germany, it often appeared in compositions such as "national-liberalism", "national-bolshevism" and "national-socialism", and, as the latest development, even "national-conservatism" seems to make sense as a right-wing ideology. Although it is true that the first three composite conceptions have the prefix "national" in common, which sets so to say geographic or group-related limits to basically universal ideologies, one can also argue the other way around: namely that from the beginning

[2] There are of course exceptions; see Tamir (1995).

nationalism must be understood as a conception of a limited political community which can appear in combination with one of the three other ideologies.

Nationalism has many faces and it is impossible to identify the one and only valid version. It is helpful to distinguish theories of "manifestations" of nationalism from explanations of its "origin". Concerning *manifestation* there is a difference between "old" and "new" conceptions (Wehler 2001: Chaps. ii–iv). *Old* conceptions reach back to the romantic strands of the enlightenment period and are best represented by German philosopher Johann Gottfried Herder, who holds that nations (as large homogenous groups of people) do exist from the beginning, that at one point in time those "natural" collectivities then strive to reach a political organisation called "state" respectively "nation state" and that finally an ideology called "nationalism" arises to legitimise the origin and continuous existence of that particular political being.[3] In the late twentieth century, this conception has been criticised by "*new*" conceptions, e.g. of Anderson (Anderson 1983), Gellner (1983) and Hobsbawm (1990) which identified a reverse order holding that in the beginning of political modernity nationalism as an intellectual concept was developed which rapidly succeeded in creating the modern form of political organisation: the nation state. Although there is much evidence that the second, new approach fits the historic processes of the late eighteenth and nineteenth century better than the first, in the end no one explanation is convincing on its own. But this question needs not to be decided here, because there is another important differentiation which deserves attention: that between the political-voluntaristic understanding of a nation and the ethnic-cultural one (Böckenförde 1999: 34f.).

The *political-voluntaristic* version occurs if a state as an organisation of the rule of law over a large territory already exits and if its legitimation must change from the monarchical-autocratic to the democratic mode. Consequently, if the king and aristocracy are not the only representatives of the state anymore and if larger parts of the population of a territory are supposed to participate in political power, this larger political body somehow has to be constituted. If the "whole" nation or at least larger parts of the population are going to enter the stage, then the main membership condition is the will(ingness) to participate in political affairs and to share the national burdens—most importantly paying taxes and carrying out military service. In contrast, the *ethnic-cultural* version of nationalism is understood as a pre-political conception. The nation is not generated by deliberate will of individuals but by descent or ethnos and culture, that is language, literature and fine arts in general. In a way this conception is communitarian, meaning that a collective with its specifics is prior to its members. In the beginning is the unintentional belonging of an individual to its group, which can and must be transformed into a deliberate consent later on.

One can easily see that the *old* nationalism is embedded in the *ethnic-cultural* conception with its emphasis not on descent (or even race), but on culture as an achievement of a linguistically integrated group, whereas the *new* nationalism mirrors the *political-voluntaristic* conception due to the accent on creation and "imagination" in

[3]See Forster (2002). It is worth mentioning that without difficulty Herder combines his early conception of nationalism with the perspective of humankind, that is cosmopolitanism.

the process of nation building. The telling example for the first version of nationalism is France and Germany for the second one. France can be considered a nation of citizens ("Staatsbürgernation") and Germany a nation of culture ("Kulturnation").

Finally, a third version of nationalism besides the political-voluntaristic and the ethnic-cultural one has been created by the United States: at the end of the eighteenth century, the people in the North-American colonies strived to become politically and legally independent. Although the Puritans would also have fulfilled the main criterion of an ethnic-cultural group, they founded "the first new nation" on the universal culture-independent grounds of individual liberty and equality—values which already figured in the Declaration of Independence from 1776. Especially the US-example clearly shows that from the early days of the modern rule of law, nationalism and constitutionalism belonged together and overlapped: the New England-settlers created a nation by democratically deciding on a federal constitution understood as a document which provided for government institutions and later on entailed a Bill of Rights.

Despite this variety of conceptions, respectively histories, of nationalism, the three illustrated types have something important in common: nationalism or national ideologies have been successful in constituting a large group of people on a clear-cut territory—either integrated by tradition, fate and descant or by common will—and helped this group to develop a special relationship to the organisation called "the state" as well as to the fellow nationals. Therefore, one can say that nationalism includes, firstly, a *state-directed dimension*, meaning that this constitutionally integrated group supports and maintains the institutional apparatus called the state, and secondly an*other-directed dimension* focusing on the very existence of those intersubjective "sympathies" which are constitutive to an in-group.

Concerning the *origin* of nationalism (in contrast to manifestation), three approaches can be distinguished:

1. From a *social* point of view, firstly, early capitalistic societies suffered a dramatic change in the nature of their social ties. To use a distinction of German Sociologist Ferdinand Tönnies (2010): former value-based "communities" characterised by a feudal order, their estates and a strict control of its members changed into "societies",[4] in which individuals enjoyed a much higher degree of personal liberty but experienced a formerly unknown degree of social isolation at the same time. Societies required standardised communication (a national language) and education, which replaced more traditional local standards (Gellner 1983: Chap. 3).
2. Secondly, roughly at the same time, enlightenment and French Revolution relativised the importance of religion and pushed societies into a more secular direction so that politics and religion became two more or less separate spheres. Against this background of a *cultural* approach, nationalism can be understood as a substitute religion in which the nation(-state) held a quasi-sacred status (Elias 1997: Chap. 2).

[4]The translation of the German "Gesellschaft" into "Civil Society" is misleading, because the former has none of the political implications the latter often has.

3. Thirdly, there is a *political* dimension to nationalism often ignored by modern social and cultural approaches, which do not take into account that the new mode of political legitimacy, people's sovereignty, needed an answer to the question of who would belong to this people or who should constitute it at all? It is this third question which will be of interest in the remainder of part one of this article. In the second part of the paper too, references to the explanations from a social point will be made.

Several political theorists of the eighteenth and nineteenth century concentrated on the political dimension of nationalism. Jean-Jacques Rousseau, the theorist of political autonomy, belongs to this group of thinkers. In his "Social contract" (1997: II, 7), he postulates the following: the process of founding a Republic, the only political system in which autonomy can be exercised, needs input from outside, that is an ingenious individual called "Législateur" has to more or less "persuade" a group of people to create this republican "body politick" and thereby transform egoistic men into moral beings. On the one side this shows that founding a Republic depends heavily on a process of *constructing a people* from "above" or top down by a single person (although this person should not be a member of the respective people), and on the other side it is clear that some social collectivity must already exist before the founding process can succeed. Rousseau holds that such a people must already be unified to a certain degree by "origin, interest and tradition" and that a Législateur must be able to start his unifying project at the right moment, not too early and not too late (1997: II, 10). It is clear that according to Rousseau, state building and nation building do overlap.

Emmanuel Joseph Sieyes, a follower of Rousseau, is more explicit on nation building in his 1789 article "What is the Third Estate?" (Sieyes 2003). He argues that although the third estate ("les communes") fulfils nearly all necessary social functions within the former France, in political matters its importance is "quelque facon nulle", nearly nothing. Therefore, it tries to become "something", that is to become politically relevant. In every detail he analysed how so far the third estate has been represented by wrong representatives and he proposed a set of fair procedures to find true delegates. The result would be a true nation understood as a "totality of united individuals who live under a common law and who are represented by the same lawgiving assembly". Although first and foremost this goal fits the existing interest of the middle class or bourgeoisie, by and large these advices can be seen as proposals for the process of nation building within an already existing monarchical state.[5]

Whereas the French authors of the two works considered so far put their focus on constructive or more *organisational* (technical) issues, it is interesting to see that in his book on "Representative Government" John Stuart Mill not only already accepted nationalism as a given and uncontested phenomenon but also referred to its *emotional* component: "A portion of mankind (!) may be said to constitute a nationality if they

[5]History of ideas includes even a try to create a nation nearly so to say "ex nihilo", when the old state doesn't exist anymore because it has been defeated. This famous try in 1808 stemmed from German philosopher Fichte (2009) after the state of the Holy Roman Empire of German Nation broke down in the course of Napoleonic Wars.

are united among themselves by common sympathies which do not exist between them and any others—which make them co-operate with each other more willingly than with other people, desire to be under the same government, and desire that it should be government by themselves, or a portion of themselves, exclusively" (Mill 1991: 308). Concerning the causes of such "common sympathies" Mill numerates race, language, religion, geographical limits and above all a national history. This list convincingly shows that nation building needs hard facts like geography, ethnicity (race) and language as well as soft facts like a common history, insofar every constructive process needs a reliable hold, a focal point in the real world. And finally, Mill's definition also contains the two dimensions of nationalism—"state directed" and "other directed"—which were already mentioned above.

Interestingly, even those who think (or thought) that the period of nationalism would be over, nowadays acknowledge its necessity in former times and agree with the aforementioned authors: in 1998 a politically closer European Union, at least a European constitution seemed possible, and Jürgen Habermas (2001) observed a weakening of the nation state. Nevertheless, he conceded that the political integration of members of a large society had been the "uncontested achievement" of the nation state.[6] During the last 20 years the situation has changed significantly. Therefore, recently Francis Fukuyama has been even more explicit on nationalism. He argued "for an international order built around national states, or for the necessity of the right sort of national identity within those states. The idea that states are obsolete and should be superseded by international bodies is flawed … Thus political order both at home and internationally will depend on the continuing existence of liberal democracies with the right kind of inclusive national identities" (Fukuyama 2018: 138f.).

This small but telling selection should demonstrate that nationalism has been one of the central topics of modern political philosophies and has been and still is estimated as a condition of the modern state.

2.3 Nationalism and "Old" Ideologies

Given the necessity of nationalism at a certain point in the transformation of political orders, the question of its relation to other ideologies arises: are they able to integrate the national perspective or do they refuse it? In the following, three ideologies, liberalism, socialism and conservatism, will be illustrated very briefly. Only central arguments of paradigmatic thinkers, classical and contemporary, in relation to the two-dimensional nationalism concept will be discussed. It will be shown that liberalism or socialism on the one side and nationalism on the other do not have much commonalities, if there are some at all, while conservatism and nationalism show

[6]Taking notice of this statement one could say that a more appropriate title of the collection would have been "postnationalistic" instead of "postnational constellation".

a strong affinity. This will be of some importance for the consideration of modern alternatives to nationalism in part two.

To begin with *liberalism:* Liberal thinking in general can be seen as an answer to the economic requirements of early capitalistic societies but also as a postulate of a steadily growing layer of citizens who argued from a right-based morality for more individual liberty in all aspects of social life. First and foremost, this morality holds that the state should guarantee individual natural rights including, according to Locke (1989), "life, liberty and property". Liberalism tries to maximise the sphere of individual liberty and therefore urges the state to guarantee such a sphere by legal means and to refrain from interference in that sphere. The leading liberal thinker of the nineteenth century John Stuart Mill argued that in a modern society, individuals are not only threatened by state power: inspired by French political theorist Alexis de Tocqueville, in *On Liberty* (Mill 1995), Mill explicated that individual thinking and acting could be restricted by the majority of society as well. To avoid such restrictions, individuals should be allowed to raise liberty claims against their fellow citizens too. Therefore contemporary communitarians criticised liberalism not only for its understanding of "rights as guns" (Frank Michelman) but also for operating with an "unencumbered self" (Michael Sandel). According to those critics, citizens in a liberal society have nothing more in common than respecting the legal order under which they live and which safeguards their private interests. Of course, the liberal focus clearly lies on a right-based moral, but this is not the whole story most liberals have to tell. At least some theories of liberalism emphasise the importance of political and social institutions and even that of intersubjective relations. For example, in his *Political Liberalism* the late John Rawls (1993: 158ff. and 212ff.) offered the conception of "public reason" to underline the importance of citizen's dialogue over a "constitutional consensus".[7] And in his book on international law he refers explicitly, while discussing the topic of "common sympathies", to Mill's understanding of a nation mentioned above (Rawls 1999: 23).

In contrast to liberalism, *socialism*, at least in Karl Marx' version, did not take individual or human rights seriously. It can be understood as a reaction to the liberal revolution in the economic field: Although the implementation of a market system with property rights and free exchange of commodities caused an enormous wealth of nations, it soon became clear that the night-watchman state inevitably would go along with a complete unequal distribution of the socially produced wealth and the complete destruction of traditional social bonds. Many Socialists held that social inequality is not a fate but a consequence of the unjust socio-economic institutions and exchange processes, and these can and must be changed. But at the same time Socialists hesitate to address their claims for a more just distribution and equality of material goods to the existing state: in "The Communist Manifesto" Karl Marx and Friedrich Engels (2012) understood the liberal state as a "committee" of the Bourgeois class, which is not at all interested in abolishing class structures and the private property of production means. At most, this bourgeois state could be used as strategic means that is for the installation of the dictatorship of the Proletariat. After

[7] See also Hayek (1978: Chap. 7).

that interim the state will wither away, political autonomy or democratic institutions are not necessary anymore.[8] Until that (distant) goal would be reached, the social value of solidarity had to come to the foreground: working men should behave and act solidary, they should be responsible for, support and help their fellows who belong to the same class and are situated in the same social position within capitalist society. The main problem of the Socialists would be to create a class for and in itself out of a working class without class consciousness. The task is, in other words, to construct a collective identity of exploited workers who know that their standing together is a precondition to reach the goal of a socialistic society. This conception of identity does entail social but not political connotations; it remains without any reference to the already existing (nation-)state.

In the late nineteenth and early twentieth century the socialist movements in many European countries had been represented in national Parliaments, but this only led to the split of the movement into a more leftist (communist) and a moderate (social democratic) wing. Where the latter took this representation seriously and tried to change society according to socialist principles by a "March through the political institutions", the former remained highly sceptical towards the resulting social state: in the 1960s German political scientist Johannes Agnoli (2004) wrote for example that political welfare programmes in liberal democracies are nothing but corruption of the workers and in the 1970s even Habermas (1975) still tried to identify serious "legitimation problems" in late liberal-capitalistic societies.[9] Contemporary theories of socialism finally involuntarily demonstrate how difficult it is to develop a convincing understanding of "solidarity" as a form of horizontal integration of individuals: in his *Idea of Socialism* Axel Honneth tried to reformulate what Marx and other socialists could have meant by solidaric intersubjective relations. In this context the meaning of "solidarity" can oscillate between "fraternity" and even "love", it is said that within a solidaric society people would not only (!) share common values, but would also realise their individual purposes only in cooperation with others, they would act "for each other" (Honneth 2016: 20–25). This is a highly ambitious revision of solidarity and in the end it remains pretty unclear what that would mean for the relationship between citizens and state. In another instance he holds that for the time being the idea of constitutional patriotism does not seem strong enough to substitute civic solidarity ("staatsbürgerliche Solidarität") (Honneth 2014: 329).

Although sometimes it is doubted if there is a coherent conservative ideology at all, one can consider *Conservatism* as a third ideological camp and as a reaction to the progressive ideas of liberalism as well as of socialism. Conservatism criticises both of them because the latter wants to transform the whole society according to a master plan whereas the former undermines traditional morals with its rights-based arguments, enhances the individualisation process and the wilful transformation of

[8]This disregard of democracy has been a serious error of Marx. In the 1970s Jürgen Habermas developed this argument in his article "Zur Rekonstruktion des Historischen Materialismus" (1976: 144–199).

[9]Habermas' change of position between this book from 1975 (the German original has been published in 1973) and his above-mentioned article from 1976 are remarkable. It has never been explained by himself.

a community into a society. A blueprint of a conservative attitude can be found in Edmund Burke's critique of the French Revolution in which he rejected the conception of an almighty people's sovereignty as well as the universalism of human rights (because the rights of the English men were already secured in England) (Burke 1999). Conservatives argue that those institutions and practices among fellow citizens, which proved worthy, should be preserved against fundamental changes and progress with uncertain consequences. As Michael Oakeshott, one of the most prominent conservative thinkers in the twentieth century puts it: Conservatives "prefer the familiar to the unknown ... the tried to the untried ... the actual to the possible" (1991: 408).

Oakeshott's political philosophy is suitable to counter the argument that conservatives do not at all have a coherent theory of a political or social collectivity and its relation to the institutional frame of politics. He developed an interesting conception of "civil association" which has to be distinguished from "enterprise association", another ideal type of social entities. The main difference is the following: members of an enterprise association try to satisfy their individual or private desires (alone or together with others). These members, the "bargainers", follow certain rules not for themselves but as useful means to realise their specific interest. Because of this contingent character of the rules and the strategic attitude of the bargainers, the enterprise association cannot be characterised by this set of rules. In contrast, members of a civil association are understood not as bargainers but as citizens or "cives". They have traditions, habits and a common language and all this together constitutes a "practice" which materialises in a set of legal rules. Within this frame, actors as citizens do not try to satisfy a private purpose by following contingent rules. Rather, they interpret those legal rules or, to use a well-known phrase from Oakeshott, they engage in the "pursuit of intimations". According to him these citizens "are related solely in terms of their common recognition of the rules which constitute a practice of civility" (1996: 128). In contrast to enterprise association, civil association can be characterised by the set of legal rules, and the self-understanding of citizens in the case of an interpersonal conflict can be seen as that of "suitors to a judicial court" (1996: 131).

According to this very brief sketch, each of the three ideologies at least indirectly comments on the two dimensions called "other-directed dimension" and "state-directed dimension". In Fig. 2.1 the main results of this discussion are assembled: for example, it can be suggested that *socialism* hasn't been (and is not?) interested in supporting the political institutions of an existing national state due to its partiality with the Bourgeois class but makes strong claims of solidarity for fellow citizens or members of the same social class. *Liberalism* postulates a "medium" state support through civil obedience and political participation and makes strong demands for the political system as a guarantor of individual rights. By common sympathies it can be acknowledged that individuals share a sociopolitical lifeworld. By and large *conservativism* is the ideology closest to nationalism. That is not surprising because both

Orientations: / 'Old' Ideologies:	Social (other directed)	Political *demands* (state directed)	Political *support* (state directed)
Liberalism	**weak** common sympathies	**strong** Guarantee of rights	**medium** participation& obey the law
Socialism	**Strong** solidarity (fraternity)	**none**	**none**
Conservatism	**strong** common practice	**strong** preservation of social structures and culture	**strong** obey the law
Nationalism	**strong** common sympathies	**strong** national identity	**strong** sovereignty

Fig. 2.1 Social and political orientations in "old" ideologies

argue in favour of a strong and sovereign state to preserve common practices, sympathies and traditions. Conservatism and nationalism both make strong arguments in favour of other- and state-directed orientations among citizens.[10]

On the one side, this means that nationalism nowadays, although it has been a progressive mode of legitimation during the formation period of the modern nation state, seems to be too conservative and therefore unable to cope with the challenges of a globalised, at least trans- or post-national world. On the other side it is not clear that in the present constellation, the world of states (or the united nations) cannot survive an enhanced globalisation. But then, if nationalism, the traditional ideology of a bounded political community under a constitution, is discredited (and misunderstood) from so many sides, it becomes inevitable to explore if there are candidates for a new nationalism or substitutes for the old one sketched in the previous section. This will be undertaken in the following second part of this article.

[10]Interestingly, Oakeshott, as one of the two reference authors of Conservatism, on the one side is not really interested in or convinced by theories of nationalism. On the other side he acknowledges (although with an ironic undertone) as a positive result of nationalism that through it the "neglected" members of society "were being able to identify themselves as valued and no longer uncared-for members of a *solidarité commune* now called 'the nation'" (1996: 304).

2.4 Modern Alternatives to Nationalism?

The two dimensions of other-directed and state-directed orientations of citizens will give structure to the analysis in this second section. The four alternatives to nationalism which shall be consulted in the following belong to contemporary Western political theory: social capital, associative ownership, compatriot partiality and constitutional patriotism. Not surprisingly three of these conceptions were developed in or can at least be applied to the context of the European refugee crisis in recent times.

2.4.1 Social Capital

After the triumph of individualistic social theory in the 1950s and 60s of the last century and especially that of social theory developed by economists in the US, the forceful critique of the "undersocialised" or "unembedded" model of human activity emerged. The theorem of social capital can be seen as an answer of the economic and individualistic social theory to this serious critique (e.g. Coleman 1990). One of its main features holds that actors generate or produce social relations by themselves through a cooperative attitude. As game theorists have shown, social capital can be generated even in extremely unfavourable conditions (Axelrod 1984: Chap. 4). The main condition is that an offer of cooperation from individual A will be answered by a complementary, positive attitude by individual B. If B's reaction to A's offer is positive, the mechanism of reciprocity can be established which is conducive to further cooperation and *trust*, which seems to be the most valuable (and maybe single) embodiment of social capital. There is some risk for actor A who tries to initiate this tit-for-tat-mechanism because the answer to his offer can be "no", which means "defection", but in general both sides of an intersubjective "cooperation" are able to achieve benefits which would not be possible if they acted alone.

The generation and maintenance of trust among actors who do not know each other is an important feature of modern societies. It explains why stable (economic) interactions among strangers are possible. Paul Collier (2013: II, 3) uses the theory of social capital to analyse the consequences of a larger inflow of migrants in domestic societies. The initial point is a Western domestic society which is characterised by an attitude he calls "mutual regard". Mutual regard allows for cooperative games, which means it enables the realisation of two important social goals: the production of public goods (characterised by non-rivalry of consumption and non-excludability) and financial transfers to citizens in need. This kind of game or the cooperative attitude can be exploited by defection and therefore it is important that free riders or rogues are punished by the majority of cooperative actors (the "principal"), respectively, the police (its "agents").

Empirical studies have now shown, Collier holds, that the frequency of non-cooperation or defection is dependent on the level of social capital, which in turn depends on the power of the constitutional state or "rule of law" to prevent defection.

In countries with a weak state, people are often opportunistic, distrustful, and not ready to cooperate: either they do not offer cooperation themselves or they answer such an offer with "defection". This unwillingness to cooperate is not irrational but the result of a rational calculation of an individual. Larger groups of these "defectors" will have alarming consequences if they occur within a cooperative domestic society. Therefore the latter will try to control and even restrict immigration to prevent the damaging or even breakdown of the valuable resource of mutual regard.[11] But this is not the point I'm interested in here in the first place. The interesting question rather is: if a constitutional state helps to maintain (and probably) create social capital due to its coercive power, is there also a connection the other way around, that the existence of that capital enables or enforces the rule of law? If so, then both, mutual regard and trust, would be good candidates to substitute old-fashioned nationalism at least in part.

This question was asked by American political scientist Robert Putnam in his book "Making Democracy Work" (1993; Becker 1999: 98f.). The objective of this study on Italian Democracy (to be more precise: on the Performance of Regional Governments in Italy) was to prove that the administration in regions with a high level of social capital that performs much better than in regions with a low level. By and large Putnam has modelling social capital in the same way as shown above: it consists of relations of reciprocity among actors and the main indicator is interpersonal trust. He then developed a so-called "civic-community" index which included referendum turnout, newspaper reading, preference vote and frequency of sports clubs and cultural associations. Putnam's intention was of course not to reformulate "Nationalism", but through his index he at least tried to grasp the core of "Republicanism": "Collective life in the civic regions is eased by the expectation that others will probably follow the rules. Knowing that others will, *you* are more likely to go along, too, thus fulfilling *their* expectations. In less civil regions nearly everyone expects everyone else to violate the rules" (Putnam 1993: 111). This quote shows that Putnam is able to demonstrate the importance of trust and rule obedience in the "horizontal", or as it was called above: "other-directed" dimension of civil society or republic. But he has not shown that it plays a role in the vertical dimension or "state-directed" dimension, that between civil society and state. For that purpose, the individual elements of his index are not significant enough.

[11] Social capital theories give important insights to migration politics and the necessity to avoid the origin and existence of so-called "parallel societies", which can be found in Germany for example in Berlin and the Ruhrgebiet: if citizens feel that the constitutional state is not able anymore to guarantee the rule of law in certain areas, because members of those special societies not only behave as "normal" defectors but also threaten the police and thereby behave as "super-rogues" (punishing those whose job it is, to punish normal defectors or rogues), then social capital in form of trust in state authorities and fellow citizens will shrink.

2.4.2 Associative Ownership and Compatriot Partiality

A second alternative to nationalism relies on specific features legally and politically integrated larger groups of people possess. It comes in two versions, both of them have been developed in the context of immigration. Version number one stems from Ryan Pevnick. He tries to find a middle ground between the postulate of completely open borders, demanded by cosmopolitans, and the thesis of hermetically closed borders, postulated by hard-nosed nationalists. One of his main arguments is that although the interests of migrants or "outsiders" cannot simply be ignored altogether, the domestic citizens or "insiders" must generally be allowed to determine their political life and future by themselves. According to Pevnick a well-known way to justify this claim is to rely on the conceptions of sovereignty and self-autonomy. Neo-realists, for example, argue that states must try to survive in a hostile international world and are therefore entitled to any decision they think would contribute to this goal. Pevnick is not convinced by this "language of power", instead he wants to explain restrictions with reference to the characteristics of domestic political institutions.

The core of this argument holds that democratic institutions "respect citizens as part owners of the relevant institutions" (Pevnick 2014: 31). One can assume that among the important institutional arrangements for self-government and autonomy, there are institutions "with persons", that is parliament and government, and those "without persons", that is first and foremost the legal constitution. The "ownership"-component of the argument goes back to John Locke's justification of property which says that an individual who applies labour force to an unpossessed object is (under certain conditions) the owner of this treated object. The reason is that an individual is the owner of its force and if this is mixed with another object the individual is the owner of this mixed good too. Pevnick wants to transfer this argumentative structure to the object "state" to explain the "associative"-component.

A state is said, firstly, to be a non-voluntary association because its members normally were not asked if they wanted to join this community or not (although liberal and even non-liberal states concede the right to leave the state). Nevertheless, efforts to maintain and develop political institutions can be made by domestic people or citizens even if they did not join the state voluntarily, and due to their *collective* maintenance of labour those people are allowed to raise *associative* ownership claims. Secondly, the associative-component is still valid even if one says that "maintenance" is an *intergenerational* project, because political institutions, like other material and intellectual goods, can be and are passed from one person to another and from one generation on to the other. This legally framed process of inheritance creates the difference between insiders and outsiders: the successive generations of insiders can continue their labour on the institutions of autonomy and outsiders are excluded from this inherited collective "property", they are not allowed to participate in the use of it and cannot complain on grounds of justice.

On the one side one must concede that Pevnick's approach is innovative in relying on the property and ownership frame which allows drawing a comparatively clear line between owner and non-owner, insiders and outsiders. But on the other side this reference to labour leads to a misunderstanding of the activity a political association is really engaged with. This is not labour in the literal sense, because labour (and work) are essentially unpolitical, they take place not between persons but during an occupation with nature and inanimate objects and materials. In contrast to that, "acting" and speaking are political activities par excellence.[12] Pevnick (2014: 35) seems to see that the category of "labour" is not quite appropriate for his purposes, in one instance he speaks of the "creative and directive qualities" of the kind of labour he has in mind. Creative "work" of maintenance and development of institutions first and foremost is communication, reaching understandings or bargaining, which happens within parliamentary debates and in the course of application of legal norms. Therefore, associative ownership relies much more, one could say, on the membership of an interpretive community which lives under a constitutional order. This perspective will be discussed in a moment.

The second version of associationalism comes from David Miller. The basic question in his latest book "Strangers in our Midst" is "whether states are obliged to weigh the interests of all human beings equally when deciding upon their policies [of immigration; M.B]"(Miller 2016: 11). Miller tries to show that the strong version of moral cosmopolitanism, according to which the duties citizens of a respective state owe to other human beings are always the same, irrespective of the relationship in which these citizens are involved, is not convincing. The argument does not deny that there are some duties domestic citizens do have (for example, because of their burning fossil fuels and other costs of their living standard) towards people who are outside of the state borders, that is foreigners, but it asserts that the ties among the fellow citizens are special ones which allow making a difference. And these special ties, so the argument goes, would result in "associative obligations". Miller starts with an analysis of *personal relationships* between friends, which according to him have two characteristics: firstly, they result in *special duties*, friends owe each other more than they are obliged to do for other persons, otherwise the relationship cannot be called friendship. And secondly, Miller says, this type of relationship has an *intrinsic value* which makes our lives "simply better"—which is not quite a happy expression, because it sounds too utilitarian. Perhaps he should have said that sometimes friendship affords certain actions that may only have positive consequences for the friend and not for the actor himself.

But the more important question is if this special kind of relationship can be transferred to the nation state and its citizens. According to Miller, members of such a state generally are involved in three different kinds of relationships:

- as *economising individuals* they are involved in an economic system or in a scheme of cooperation which allows for individual benefits;
- as *citizens* they *participate* in the elaboration of the legal scheme under which they live;
- as *fellow nationals* they share a "set of cultural values and a sense of belonging to a particular place" (Miller 2016: 26).

Out of the first two relationships, within the frame of *economy and democracy*, "associative obligations" arise: to respect the existing laws and other rules of

[12]For this basic differentiation between kinds of activities, see Arendt (1958).

cooperation. Miller also calls them "obligations of reciprocity", which brings the findings of Collier's and Putnam's theory of social capital to mind. But what about the third involvement, that of the fellow nationals? Miller argues: "With national identity comes a kind of solidarity that is lacking if one looks just at economic and political relationships. People feel emotionally attached to one another because they share this identity. They feel that they belong together and have responsibilities to each other that are not simply the result of existing institutions and practices … National identity attaches the community to a particular homeland whose special features often contribute in an important way to the identity itself" (2016: 27f.). This statement about national identity strongly reminds one of the classical nationalism illustrated above, and in the end Miller is not interested in developing an alternative to "old" nationalism but seems to evoke the spirit of this older ideology directly.

2.4.3 Constitutional Patriotism

The fourth and final possibility for an alternative to nationalism is "Constitutional Patriotism". This approach has so to say German origins and exists in two slightly different versions. The first and original conception was proposed by German Political Scientist Dolf Sternberger. On the occasion of the 30th anniversary of the German Grundgesetz in 1979 he said, while the German national feeling that all Germans should belong to one nation state has been and keeps on being wounded, it should not be forgotten that "we live under a complete constitution, in a complete constitutional state, and this is by itself a kind of fatherland" (Sternberger 1990: 13). He concedes that in the nineteenth century in Germany as well as in other countries "patriotism" was connected to the "nation" whereas a constitution, for example that of Weimar, was considered a mere juridical document. Constitution as an object of a patriotic attitude is more than a collection of basic rights. These rights are of course an important element but must be supplemented with representative institutions, a controlled government and independent judiciary. In short, a constitution must embody a liberal-democratic basic order. In sum Sternberger holds that constitutional patriotism is the core meaning of the classical understanding of patriotism and not just a substitute for a national patriotism in countries such as Germany in which a recourse to a glorious past isn't possible anymore.

The second version of Constitutional Patriotism was developed by Jürgen Habermas. At first he used the term in the so-called "Historikerstreit", a debate among historians in 1986 concerning the Nazi period in Germany and its significance for the German self-understanding and history. He criticised the historians who tried to relativize German guilt and obligation with recourse to totalitarianism in the former Soviet Union and said because of the contamination of their past the Germans would have no other option to prevent an alienation from the West than to develop a constitutional patriotism understood as a tie to universal constitutional principles anchored in individual beliefs (Habermas 1987: 135). Now, this early version has been criticised heavily, for example by Ernst-Wolfgang Böckenförde who considered it to be nothing more than a seminar's idea, and by others who viewed it as nothing more than an anaemic conception which would be unable to enter the lifeworld of average citizens.

Later on, with his project of a post-metaphysical justification of the liberal constitutional state, Habermas (2007) concretised his conception by pointing not only to the negative rights a constitution entails but also to the positive or participation rights: The unifying element the critiques are missing in the secular state consists of the principles of the democratic process itself and at the very least, active citizens try to find the right understanding and meaning of their constitutional order. With all this the republican attitude has emancipated itself from nationalism. At first glance, it seems doubtful that this second approach can really escape the former critique because interpretation of the constitution is a matter for legal experts. But if one recalls the piece on "public reason" from Rawls' Political Liberalism, on the one side it becomes clear that even ordinary people who try to justify their position in basic political questions rely on constitutional principles in one or the other way. On the other side Jan-Werner Müller rightly observed that Habermas' understanding tends towards a "Schuld-Patriotismus" ("patriotism of guilt") (Müller 2007: 16ff.) from the beginning: The reason why Germans do and should live according to the Grundgesetz is the recognition of the fact that Germans committed the crime of the century, the absolute evil. The Holocaust, and not some version of political freedom or liberation, becomes the focal point of the German community of fate. Seen from this perspective, constitutional patriotism is the result of a "negative nationalism" which makes it impossible to rely on any positive feature of German history and culture (Fig. 2.2).

Orientations / **Modern alternatives**	**Social** (other directed)	**Polical*demands*** (state oriented)	**Political*support*** (state directed)
Social Capital	**strong** trust	**strong** economic liberties, no state interference	**weak** obey the rules
Associative ownership	**strong** common ‚labour'	**weak**	**strong** political participation
Compatriot partiality	**strong** solidarity	**strong** make a difference	**strong** political participation
Constitutional patriotism	**strong** interpretive community / public reason	**Weak**	**strong** constitutional sovereignty

Fig. 2.2 Social and political orientations in modern alternatives to nationalism

2.5 Summary: A New Nationalism?

In the first part of the paper important political ideologies of the eighteenth and nineteenth century, including nationalism, were illustrated. It has been demonstrated that nationalism played an important role in the origin and stabilisation of the regime of a nation state. At least in those early days, nationalism helped to create a large nation as an "imagined community". At the same time nationalism was one of the necessary conditions to realise and institutionalise the new political principle of people's sovereignty. In its second part, the paper scrutinised the thesis if certain approaches to social and political integration could be considered as modern alternatives to old nationalism. Two results crystallised.

Firstly, all four alternative conceptions showed that domestic societies are economically, politically, or culturally integrated collectivities and that these forms of integration should be understood as a public good that has to be preserved and protected—for example against negative consequences of an unlimited and unprincipled immigration policy.

Secondly, it became clear that two out of four contemporary approaches cannot be considered as full-fledged substitutes for nationalism. They are too one-sided in the sense that social capital approaches emphasise the other-directed dimension (Collier), whereas constitutional patriotism approaches concentrate on the state-directed dimension (Sternberger, Habermas). Only the "compatriot partiality" approach (Miller) can count as a clear-cut version not of a new but more of an "old" version of nationalism. The "associative ownership" approach (Pevnick) made the interesting point that citizens as supporters of their (inherited) political institutions are their owners united in an ownership association at the same time. This could count as a moderate version of a new nationalism.

Compared to these demanding two models of a national community, one can say that constitutional patriotism is a shrunken version of it because the only reference points are the catalogue of universal rights and the blueprint for democratic government. One can not only consider these principles as the minimum content or the backbone of a liberal constitution but of a liberal nationalism as well. The question is if this is enough for a reliable identity of a political collectivity. Walzer (1987) once compared the scarce content of (moral) universalism with the rooms of an international hotel chain: they are purposeful, everybody can live there for a certain time, but nearly all would prefer rooms created or chosen by themselves. One can transfer this argument to the question of nationalism and conclude that in contemporary Germany a tiny but influential minority of cosmopolitans postulates that Germans should permanently live in constitutional "hotel rooms" because this is the lesson they have to learn from history. It is to hope that this instruction by well-meaning people will not prevail and the way to a liberal nationalism compatible with the Grundgesetz will be cleared.

References

Agnoli, J. (2004) [1968]. *Transformation der Demokratie*. Hamburg: Konkret Literatur Verlag.

Anderson, B. (1983). *Imagined communities: Reflections on the origin and spread of nationalism*. London: Verso.

Arendt, H. (1958). *The human condition*. Chicago: Chicago UP.

Axelrod, R. (1984). *The evolution of cooperation*. New York: Basic Books.

Becker, M. (1999). Zivilgesellschaft. *Kommunikation und institutionelle Performanz. Associations, 3*(1), 91–119.

Böckenförde, E.-W. (1999). Die Nation – Identität in Differenz. In: E.-W. Böckenförde: *Staat, Nation, Europa. Studien zur Staatslehre, Verfassungstheorie und Rechtsphilosophie* (pp. 34–58). Frankfurt: Suhrkamp.

Burke, E. (1999) [1790]. *Reflections on the revolution in France*. Indianapolis: Liberty Fund.

Coleman, J. S. (1990). *Foundations of social theory* (Vol. 1). Cambridge: Harvard UP.

Collier, P. (2013). *Exodus: Immigration and multiculturalism in the 21st century*. London: Allen Lane.

Elias, N. (1997). *The Germans: Power struggles and the development of habitus in the nineteenth and twentieth centuries*. London: Blackwell.

Fichte, J. G. (2009). *Addresses to the German Nation*. Ed. by Gregory Moore. Cambridge: Cambridge UP.

Forster, M. N. (2002). Introduction. In: M. N. Forster (Ed.), *Johann Gottfried Herder. Philosophical Writings* (pp. xxx-xxxii). Cambridge: Cambridge UP.

Fukuyama, F. (2018). *Identity. Contemporary Identity Politics and the Struggle for Recognition*. London: Profile Books.

Gellner, E. (1983). *Nations and Nationalism*. Oxford: Oxford UP.

Habermas, J. (1975). *Legitimation Crisis*. Boston: Beacon Press.

Habermas, J. (1976). Zur Rekonstruktion des Historischen Materialismus. In J. Habermas (Ed.), *Zur Rekonstruktion des Historischen Materialismus* (pp. 144–199). Frankfurt: Suhrkamp.

Habermas, J. (1987). Apologetische Tendenzen. In J. Habermas (Ed.), *Eine Art Schadensabwicklung* (pp. 120-136). Frankfurt: Suhrkamp.

Habermas, J. (2001). The Postnational Constellation. In J. Habermas, *The Postnational Constellation. Political Essays* (pp. 58–111). Cambridge: Cambridge UP.

Habermas, J. (2007). Prepolitical Foundations of the Constitutional State? In J. Habermas (Ed.), *Between Naturalism and Religion: Philosophical Essays* (pp. 101–113). London: Polity Press.

Hayek, F. A. (1978). *The Constitution of Liberty*. Chicago: Chicago UP.

Hobsbawm, E. (1990). *Nations and Nationalism since 1780. Programme, Myth, Reality*. Cambridge: CambridgeUP.

Honneth, A. (2014). *Freedom's Right: The Social Foundations of Democratic Life*. Cambridge: Polity Press.

Honneth, A. (2016). *The Idea of Socialism*. London: Polity Press.

Locke, J. (1989) [1690]. 2nd Treatise. In: P. Laslett (Ed.) *Two Treatises of Government* (pp. 265–428). Cambridge: Cambridge UP.

Marx, K. and Engels, F. (2012) [1848]. *The Communist Manifesto*. A Modern Edition, ed. by E. Hobsbawm. London: Verso.

Mill, J. St. (1991) [1861]. *Considerations on Representative Government*. Amherst: Prometheus Books.

Mill, J. St. (1995) [1859] On Liberty. In: St. Collini (Ed.), *On Liberty and Other Writings* (pp. 1–115). Cambridge: Cambridge UP.

Miller, D. (2016). *Strangers in our Midst*. Cambridge/Mass. and London: Harvard UP.

Müller, J.-W. (2007).*Constitutional patriotism*. Princeton: Princeton UP.

Oakeshott, M. (1991). On being conservative. In M. Oakeshott, *Rationalism in Politics and other Essays* (pp. 407–437). Indianapolis: Liberty Fund.

Oakeshott, M. (1996). [1975]: On Human Conduct. Oxford: Oxford UP.

Pevnick, R. (2014). *Immigration and the constraints of Justice. Between open borders and absolute sovereignty*. Cambridge: Cambridge UP.
Putnam, R. D. (1993). *Making Democracy Work. Civic Traditions in Modern Italy*. Princeton: Princeton UP.
Rawls, J. (1993). *Political Liberalism*. New York: Columbia UP.
Rawls, J. (1999). *The Law of Peoples*. Cambridge/Mass. and London: Harvard UP.
Rousseau, J.-J. (1997) [1762]. The Social Contract. In Victor Gourevitch (Ed.), *The Social Contract and other Political Writings*. Cambridge: Cambridge UP.
Sieyes, E. J. (2003) [1789]. In Colin Lucas (Ed.), *The Third Estate*. Cambridge: Cambridge UP.
Sternberger, D. (1990). Verfassungspatriotismus. In *Schriften* (Vol. X, pp. 13–16). Frankfurt: Suhrkamp.
Tamir, Y. (1995). *Liberal Nationalism*. Princeton UP: Princeton.
Tönnies, F. (2010) [1887]. *Community and Civil Society*. Cambridge: Cambridge UP.
Walzer, M. (1987). *Interpretation and Social Criticism*. Cambridge/Mass. and London: Harvard UP.
Wehler, H.-U. (2001). *Nationalismus. Geschichte, Formen, Folgen*. München: C. H. Beck.

Michael Becker is a Professor at the Institute of Political Science and Sociology, Julius-Maximilians-University, Würzburg. He received his PhD 1991 at Johannes-Gutenberg University at Mainz and did his Habilitation at Otto-Friedrich-University at Bamberg in 2002. Between 2003-2005 he was Substitute Professor at the Universities of Bamberg, Landau and Konstanz. Since 2007 he is Professor for Political Science at the Institute for Political Science and Sociology at Würzburg University. His Fields of Research are Modern and Contemporary Western Political Philosophy, Constitutional Democracy; Modern Indian Political Thought. Since 2013 he has been Guest Professor at Indian Universities (Delhi, Chandigarh, Mangalore). He participates in the DAAD sponsored "Indo-German-Partnership" (IGP) and is a Member of the BMBF sponsored "International Centre for Advanced Studies—Metamorphoses of the Political" (ICAS-MP) (https://micasmp.hypotheses.org/).

Major Publications: Rechtsstaat und Demokratie (co-editor), Wiesbaden 2001; Verständigungsorientierte Kommunikation und rechtsstaatliche Ordnung (Habilitation), Baden-Baden 2003; Politik und Recht (special issue of Politische Vierteljahresschrift) (co-editor), Wiesbaden 2006; Politische Philosophie (co-author), Paderborn 2006 (4th ed. 2017); Grundstrukturen der Politik in der Bundesrepublik Deutschland, Opladen 2011, Politischer Liberalismus und wohlgeordnete Gesellschaften (ed.), Baden-Baden 2013.

Chapter 3
The Paper-Thin Covering of Constitutional Democracy

Amir Ali

Abstract This paper suggests that constitutionalism serves as a very ineffective covering to democracy, indeed that it is paper-thin. It can very easily be torn apart by some of the more erratic swings of democracy, especially in its more populist moods. The paper then goes on to reflect on the absence of democracy in many parts of the Muslim world and the supposed incompatibility between Islam and liberal democracy. However, there does seem to exist in many Muslim lands, a deep commitment towards constitutionalism. One of the major concerns of the paper then becomes to reflect over the reasons for this kind of constitutionalism sans democracy. There is also prevalent a strain of hostility towards the idea of nationalism, as being divisive of the potential unity of the worldwide Muslim *ummah* or community of believers. The preoccupation with constitutionalism in Muslim lands has led to the increasing centrality of the *shariah,* understood as a rather fixed and rigid legal code. It also surveys the enthusiastic bout of constitution writing that happened in many Muslims countries in the late nineteenth and early twentieth century. The paper ends on a rather gloomy note on the prospects of democracy.

3.1 Introduction

The compound or hyphenated term 'Constitutional-Democracy' immediately leads one to reflect on the various other terms that democracy is prefixed and yoked with, for instance, liberal democracy, social democracy and industrial democracy. The prefixing of a term to democracy and thereby yoking the two together seems to suggest that somehow the democracy part of the hyphenated term has to be reined in, constrained, contained. By doing so it will be steered, channelized, perhaps directed by the term that does the prefixing. In our case the steering, channelizing and containing is done by constitutionalism. The undesirable excesses that democracy is sometimes prone to giving rise to, can be contained and handled by the austere provisions of

A. Ali (✉)
Centre for Political Studies, Jawaharlal Nehru University, New Delhi, India
e-mail: amirali.jnu@gmail.com; amirali@mail.jnu.ac.in

© Springer Nature Singapore Pte Ltd. 2020

A. Roy and M. Becker (eds.), *Dimensions of Constitutional Democracy*,
https://doi.org/10.1007/978-981-15-3899-5_3

constitutionalism. A further reflection that can be brought in is that, somehow democracy seems to suffer from a certain recalcitrance and that this induces the need for the prefixing and yoking that has just been mentioned.

The often turbulent and violent ructions that democracies tend to experience are way more powerful for them to be contained by the subtleties and intricacies of constitutionalism. This fragility of constitutionalism is best captured by invoking a line from the nineteenth century Urdu poet of Delhi, Mirza Ghalib where he says *Kaghazi hai paire han*. The implication of quoting Ghalib is to suggest that the constitutional covering or attire of democracy is paper-thin. This paper-thin constitutionalism is likely to be torn apart by the mood swings that democracies across the world seem to have gone through, most markedly over the last four to five years. The mood swings refer to the tendency among electorates in many countries to return electoral decisions of a rather shocking and it must be said, often bombastic nature. One has in mind, the rather shocking Brexit referendum of June 2016, followed in quick succession by the equally shocking Trump triumph across the Atlantic in the US later that year. In this list can be included the victory of Rodrigo Duterte in the Philippines in 2016 as well as the Turkish referendum of April 2017 that has given enhanced executive powers to President Erdogan, powers to appoint a sizeable number of the judiciary, and to continue doing so possibly until the year 2029. Erdogan followed this up with a resounding victory in the presidential election in June 2018. The bad state of democracy has prompted commentators to query whether we are living through another phase of the dreaded decade of the1930s (Mason 2016).

The idea of democratic ructions and the futility of its paper-thin constitutional attire in containing it can be compared with the notion of 'unstable constitutionalism', which is the title of an edited volume by Tushnet and Khosla (2015). What this paper will attempt to explore is the possibility of democratic ructions and a fragile constitutionalism giving rise to intense conflict and violence in societies across the world. This point about the links between democracy not respecting the fragile limits of paper-thin constitutionalism, and leading to intense conflict and violence is a point that needs to be made with some emphasis, for the simple reason that for at least three decades now, since the collapse of the Berlin wall, there has been a tendency of uncritically singing paeans of glory to democracy.

3.2 An Unstable Compound of Nationalism and Religion

Since the fall of the Berlin Wall, there has been a tendency for democracy to become almost completely aligned with the idea of free markets to the extent that democracy and free markets have become almost coterminous. In India, the country's largely successful democratic experience, barring the aberration of the emergency in the mid 1970s, was further embellished by the adoption of free market liberalization from 1991 onwards. This alignment of free markets with democracy has also been accompanied by the rise of a rather aggressive nationalism which may sound rather ironical in the era of globalization that was inaugurated as the twentieth century came to a close.

One source of democratic ructions and unstable constitutionalism arises from an unstable compound of nationalism and religion, a compound that has the distinct tendency to just as easily come together as to decompose. The unstable nature of this compound, it is suggested, arises from an anomalous positioning of religion vis-à-vis the public sphere, especially in countries where secularism is contested and remains an unsettled question. A restrictive notion of secularism frowns upon its presence in the public sphere, making religion take cover in the private sphere, where it remains subdued only to be lured into an in-between but altogether more assertive position by a resurgent nationalism in the public sphere. To reiterate, the unstable compound is created by religion and nationalism. The implications of this unstable compound are distressing to say the least for constitutionalism.

This frowning upon of religion's presence in the public sphere could be found in a more extreme form in Turkey where the Kemalist Republic introduced an almost authoritarian secularism that was backed by the military. In post-independence India, by contrast, the secularism of the Nehruvian consensus may not have been authoritarian but it seems to have ruffled the feathers of Hindu nationalists to the extent that a great deal of their anger is directed at almost every single aspect of Nehru's considerable legacy and in particular his supposedly secular antipathy towards the Hindu majority. Mark Tushnet and Madhav Khosla observe that the constitutional framework may be subject to different kinds of instability when institutions cross their respective boundaries to disturb the equipoise of the division of labour on which constitutions rest. They note that the obvious example is the military and a less obvious one might be institutions of civil society, especially religion, that are protected by constitutional rights. It may be observed that the military example holds in the case of a country like Turkey and that the civil society example of religious organizations tending to disturb the constitutional balance would very much hold in the case of India (Tushnet and Khosla 2015: p. 7)

3.3 The Public Presence of Islam

Having made the observations regarding the paper-thin constitutional attire of democracy and further noted the horrors that democracy is capable of giving rise to, it is time to flag what will be the major theme and concern of this paper. This is the public presence of Islam. Someone like S. Sayyid would argue that with the advent of the Kemalist republic in Turkey and its superseding the Ottoman empire, the 'Islamicate public space virtually vanished from the world' (Sayyid 2014: p. 3). The vexed issue of the public presence of Islam assumes salience in the light of the observations made in the previous paragraph, which to reiterate, were regarding the unstable compound that is formed between nationalism and religion. Despite the vexed issue of Islam's public presence, this paper will suggest that there is an unlikelihood of Islam combining with nationalism as there is an inherent antagonism between the two sets of ideas, thereby ruling out their forming any kind of bond or compound. The vexed issue of Islam's public presence, it may be added, has become even more aggravated. If there is a year that can be taken as a turning point, it would be 1979, the year of the Islamic revolution in Iran, which was also the year in which armed men entered the Grand Mosque in Mecca (Caryl 2013).

The Muslim problem can be characterized as a problem that arises from two elements that Muslims seem to lack and which make them acutely the problem they are perceived to be. These two elements are **democracy** and **nationalism**. Both these two missing elements in Islamic societies were increasingly introduced onto the international political scene in the years around the First World War. In other words, what is referred to as the Muslim problem arises especially from these two missing elements, which make it difficult for the vast majority of Muslims to function effectively as modern twentieth and twenty-first-century political actors. It is especially the lack of democracy that will become the further focal point of this chapter and a rather disconcerted Muslim is likely to be constantly reminded of it. The constant invocation of democracy and its lack in Muslim quarters can often be perceived from the perspective of many a disgusted Muslim, as a kind of democratic narcissism on the part of the West.

There is further an element of the evangelical in the Western democratic project, which has played itself out in terms of attempting to *transplant* democracy in parts of the world where it has been missing. It may be added that there is a tendency to also *supplant* democracy in some other parts where it may have sprung roots that may not be entirely desirable to the western evangelical project of democracy.

What does one mean by democratic evangelism? It simply means the desire to advance the democratic project to those parts of the world where it is missing for some reason. The presence of Islam has quite often been understood as the reason for the absence of democracy. Thus there is on the one hand the existence and flourishing of democracy and on the other, the absence or lack of democracy, which implies a certain benighted, almost oriental despotism.[1] It may be added that the absence of democracy and the implied tyranny that this involves leads to a renewed zeal on the part of the democratic evangelist. Further, democratic evangelism takes the form of a replication of carbon copies of democracy. Here the pun on carbon is very much intended to convey the rather unfortunate unfolding of the democratic project in lands of Islam overflowing with petroleum and hydrocarbon resources and is a reference to Timothy Mitchell's excellent analysis in his book *Carbon Democracy* (2011). The evangelical approach to democracy is simultaneously matched in the lands of Islam with what Bassam Tibi (2008) calls a 'shariatization of politics' which has the effect of further jeopardizing the prospects of democracy.

One further point perhaps may need to be made about the presence of Islam and the absence of democracy. There seems to be a certain oppositional logic between democracy, more specifically liberal democracy, and Islam. This oppositional logic

[1]On the transition from tyranny to despotism in European perceptions of Ottoman Turkey between the sixteenth and the eighteenth centuries, see Cirakman and Asli (2001).

reaches possibly its most conciliatory point, when the very negatively framed question of whether Islam can be compatible with liberal democracy is begrudged. What this question implies then is that there is a certain something that needs to be done to Islam in order to make it fit with liberal democracy. In this light, the Arab Spring came as quite a surprise. For some democracy enthusiasts, it was interpreted as the democracy project belatedly but surely extending itself to desolate Arab lands that had long been thirsting for it.[2]

The democracy project with all the evangelism that has been suggested comes attached with it, is also associated with certain essential features. The central elements of this democracy project are individual rights, free markets and commitment to free speech. Combined these central elements are supposed to negate despotism.

Such a construction of democracy conceals what has become or is becoming of the liberal democracy project, which now shows clear signs of unravelling (see Levitsky and Ziblatt 2018). Under the auspices of neo-liberalism there is a certain fundamental transformation that has been effected in democracy. The particularly powerful notion of the market in neo-liberalism has become reflected and replicated in democracy itself. Much as the individual rational actor in the market uses his purchasing power to reveal his preference for a particular good or commodity, the individual voter uses his vote to reveal his preference for a favoured brand of politician, in election campaigns that increasingly have become like advertising campaigns (Schumpeter 2011). The configuration of democracy by economic neo-liberalism has thus resulted in, to use Sheldon Wolin's (2008) term, an 'inverted totalitarianism'. It is interesting to note that before the current wild ructions of democracy, there was a narrow and therefore predictable bandwidth in which democratic verdicts oscillated, this narrow bandwidth being captured aptly in the concept of the Overton window. The Overton window refers to the narrow range of political issues, the raising of which can make electoral victory possible. Any issue outside the Overton window would be considered to exist in a kind of political wilderness that is effectively unelectable. The concept of the Overton window began in the 1990s with conservative and pro-market lawyer Joseph Overton. When certain political ideas exist outside the range, then it is possible for think tanks to nurture these ideas until the time that they are ready to enter the larger public domain. This would indicate a shifting of the Overton window

[2] S. Sayyid (2014) in his book, *Recalling the Caliphate*, notes: 'There are those who see in the so-called "Arab Spring" proof that the long march of democracy has finally reached the "Arab street", thus confirming the universal validity of the democratic form' p. 65. Sayyid further notes: 'According to this view, part of US strategy has been to use apparently popular mobilization to try and weaken regimes that the US considers to be hostile. Those who would hold this view focus on popular mobilization in the former Soviet Union—the rose revolution of Georgia and the orange revolution in the Ukraine—that weakened Russian hold over the region, as well as the abortive cedar revolution in Lebanon and the Green Movement in Iran. They point to the level of material support the United States has given to those involved in these mobilisations as an indication of US conspiracy. They also point to the way in which Syria and the Baathist regime is being threatened with a regime change and also the US silence that has allowed Saudi arms to put down an uprising in Bahrain while supporting those in Syria and Libya' (pp. 82–83).

(see Astor 2019). Such democratic verdicts had a staid, almost stage-managed quality to them with the electorate largely becoming indifferent and apolitical, perhaps as a result.

To add to this element of the neo-liberal market replicating itself within democracy, there is the need to further consider the manner in which the technocratic has superimposed itself on liberal democracy. Increasingly technology and the social power associated with it, referred to as technocracy rules many contentious aspects of society outside the court of the political.[3] What this has done is to rule many arenas of conflict that would ordinarily be understood as political arenas of democratic contestation as now no longer being in the realm of the political.

3.4 The Muslim No to Nationalism

An initial focus on the beginning of the twentieth century, more specifically the period around the First World War will reveal the ways in which it was felt by a number of prominent Muslims intellectuals that nationalism went against the grain of the Islamic world. As nationalism spread especially to the parts of the world, that would, with its help become decolonized, the spectre of pan-Islamism was raising its head, surveying in a disapproving manner the carving up of lands, especially Muslim ones, on the lines of secular nation-states.[4] There was a tendency of frenzied despair in most of these intellectuals and this arose from political developments which consistently signalled the almost irreversible decline of Muslim power, prestige and influence in the face of European powers such as the British and the French. The end of the First World War brought about the final fall of the tottering Ottoman Empire, the seat of the caliphate itself and for many centuries an embodiment of Muslim prestige and power. The final fall of this vast empire resulted in the creation of a number of

---

[3]This is what Yuval Noah Harari (2016) has to say about the prospects of democracy in his much talked about book *Homo Deus: A Brief History of Tomorrow*, which is on the disastrous ramifications of technology:

Liberal habits such as democratic elections will become obsolete, because Google will be able to represent even my own political opinions better than I can. When I stand behind the curtain in the polling booth, liberalism instructs me to consult my authentic self and choose whichever party or candidate reflects my deepest desires. Yet the life sciences point out that when I stand there behind that curtain, I don't really remember everything I felt and thought in the years since the last election. Moreover, I am bombarded by a barrage of propaganda, spin and random memories that might well distort my choice (p. 394).

[4]Christopher De Bellaigue (2017) in his book *The Islamic Enlightenment. The Modern Struggle Between Faith and Reason: 1798 to Modern Times*, notes: Beginning at the turn of the century the word 'pan-Islamism had become a portmanteau to explain the political solidarity that seemed to extend across the Muslim lands in opposition to imperialism'. Further referring to the phenomenon of pan-Islamism he notes: 'This "community of interests" had arisen at the same moment that an impulse to divide the world into smaller and smaller, secular units—nations bound by language, history and cultures—had spread from Europe and America to the Muslim lands. Clearly there would have to be some kind of truce or accommodation between the two, or they would turn on each other (pp. 202–203).

nations and nationalisms that emerged out of the rubble of the behemoth that had been knocked down (see Brubaker 1996). Another instance of Muslim humiliation that came in the form of a rising nationalism was the famous and much talked about Balfour declaration of 2 November 1917, indicating a British commitment to the Jewish nation of Israel.

This early phase of the twentieth century imparted a certain valency to the concepts of democracy and nationalism. In contrast to the valency that was lent to these concepts, there was a sense of humiliation and resentment that brewed across the Muslim world. As a result, the momentum of these two concepts was something that the lands of Islam were simply unable to acquire, making them miss the twentieth century political bus, as it were. As these concepts were gaining momentum, large parts of the Muslim world between the Balkan wars of 1912–1913 and the ultimate abolition of the Ottoman caliphate in Turkey in 1924 were preoccupied with the attempt to maintain and protect that very same caliphate.

The developments indicated above, and the turmoil that they would ultimately lead to are reflected in three prominent and well known Muslim intellectual and political figures, Jamaluddin Aghani (d. 1897), Muhammad Abduh (d. 1905) and Rashid Rida (d. 1935). The first two of these figures were active before the actual outbreak of the First World War and the last one Rashid Rida, lived through these strife-torn times and expressed profusely his ideas through the journal, *Al Manar* or 'the lighthouse'. In these three figures and also some others that will be mentioned in the course of this paper, there is a tendency to abstain from nationalism and democracy by expressing wariness towards the two ideas. However, most of them seemed to pour themselves profusely into constitutionalism. What we witness then is a sort of constitutionalism sans democracy. Recall at this stage, the point made at the very beginning of this paper when it was noted that constitutionalism that accompanies democracy by containing and enveloping it is akin to fragile paper-thin attire.

The lesser influence of nationalism and the pre-eminence that pan-Islamism was increasingly coming to enjoy can be seen especially in Jamaluddin Afghani and his disciple Muhammad Abduh in the form of the short lived, but highly influential journal *Al Urwa al-Wuthqa* or 'The Firmest Bond' that was brought out during Afghani's sojourn in Europe. 'The Firmest Bond' was a reference to the Ottoman Empire and the need for it to remain the centerpiece of worldwide Islamic unity.

It seems that the crucial decade and a half leading to the First World War was a period rife to some extent with democracy and most certainly with nationalism. There were enhanced possibilities of their combining to form a potent political compound. Somehow in the Islamic world there was always a break or check on the expansion and proliferation of nationalism. It is quite remarkable that even in the case of Iran, which can be characterized by its exceptionalism with respect to the rest of the Islamic world, there is a tendency to temper or play down nationalism among thinkers such as Ahmed Kasravi and Mehdi Bazargan (Fathi 1993; Barzin 1994). Among Iranian *ulama* such as Sayyid Muhammad Tabatabai and Ayatollah Ruhullah Khumaini himself in his 1943 work *Kashf al-asrar*, there is a feeling that the system of nation-states divides the Islamic community on the basis of language and ethnic culture, in addition to being founded on secular law. This persistent case against nationalism was made again by Ayatullah Murtada Mutahhari (d. 1979) in a 1970 work in which he declares that Islam unites Muslims and nationalism divides them (Martin 1992).[5] The Islamic antipathy towards nationalism can perhaps be gauged from the fact that Turkish nationalism arose only with the demise of the Ottoman Empire and the rise of Kemalism (Tezcur 2007).[6]

A number of secular Arab nationalisms flourished in many Arab lands especially in the middle decades of the twentieth century, specifically the six decades between and including the 1920s and the 1970s. The collapse of these secular Arab nationalisms was to be replaced in the last two decades of the twentieth century, especially with more virulent right wing Islamist political tendencies. It may be observed here that the twentieth century is bracketed by two decades at the beginning and two decades at the very end, by a resurgent political Islam. As suggested the middle six decades of the twentieth century tell us the story of secular nationalisms in which figures such as GemalAbdal Nasser flourished with his high point being the nationalization of the Suez Canal in 1956. Similarly in Iran the nationalist, Mohammed Mossadegh was deposed by a coup in 1953.

3.4.1 The Muslim Yes to Constitutionalism

In stark contrast to the way in which there was almost an abstinence from nationalism and something of wariness towards democracy, one notes across the Muslim world, a tendency to readily accept with some degree of enthusiasm, the idea of constitutionalism. While there was no sanction for constitutionalism in the basic code of the Quran and the Hadith, it is quite interesting to note the readiness with which the idea of constitutionalism has been accepted. Constitutionalism as an idea is of modern provenance and it has therefore been immaterial to the development of Islamic *fiqh or* jurisprudence for the very simple reason that it was just not there in the one millennium of Islamic *fiqh* that developed before the idea of constitutionalism made its entry into the modern discourse of politics. Khan and Ramadan (2011: 113) define Islamic constitutionalism in the following manner: 'The concept of Islamic constitutionalism refers to modern constitutions in Muslim nations, written texts that contain succession rules, federation structures, the supremacy clause, fundamental rights, and economic ideology, such as socialism or free markets'.[7]

---

[5]The 1970 work in question by *Ayatullah Murtada Mutahhari is Khadamat-i mutaqabil-i Iran wa islam* (p. 354).

[6]Tezcur notes on page 489: 'Religious loyalties endangered the ideological foundation of the Republic, as the notion of the "Turkish nation" irreversibly replaced the "Islamic *umma*" as the source of authority'.

[7]L. Ali Khan and Hisham Ramadan further note: 'One reason why the idea of the written constitution has been immaterial to the development of Islamic law is the ever presence of the Basic Code. During the centuries, the Basic Code has served Muslim Empires and communities as the written constitution' (p. 113).

The major instances of constitutionalism, in terms of arguing in favour of the idea and actively engaging in the writing of constitutions, happened increasingly from the late nineteenth century and gained momentum from the beginning of the twentieth century. One of the more prominent and early instances of the Muslim world taking readily to the idea of constitutionalism was the 1876 Ottoman Constitution. This 1876 constitution was a culmination of the Tanzimat Reform movement that began in 1839 (Mardin 2009). The founding statement of the Tanzimat reforms is often considered to be the Gulhane Decree issued by Sultan Mahmud II in the year 1839 itself. Therefore this early constitutional experiment was preceded by a significant period of 'Islamic constitutionalist' thinking.

An instance of this constitutionalist thinking was a work by an Egyptian official of the state of Mehmed Ali, Khalifa ibn Mahmud, in the form of a translation of the Scottish Enlightenment historian William Robertson's work *A View of the Progress of Society in Europe* (1769). Khalifa ibn Mahmud in an appendix to the translation took issue with William Robertson's description of the Ottoman Empire as an 'Oriental despotism'. He critiqued Robertson by drawing significantly from the arguments of an 1825 work by the Sicilian political writer Alfio Grassi, *Charteturque* or Turk Charter. What is further significant is that Khalifa ibn Mahmud was himself a protégé of a figure, no less than Rifa'a al-Tahtawi, who was according to Peter Hill, one of the first figures among the Arab literati to show a sustained interest in European constitutions. He offered a translation of the Charteconstitutionelle of the 1830 Revolution and shortly after this he wrote two newspaper articles comparing two Portuguese constitutions. The Sicilian political writer Alfio Grassi, upon whose work Khalifa ibn Mahmud drew significantly, can be considered one of those freethinkers of the Enlightenment who were particularly sympathetic towards Islam and believed that the Prophet Muhammad was a great law giver (Hill 2017).[8]

While the first instance of constitutionalism in the form of the 1876 Ottoman constitution may have faltered rather quickly, the enthusiasm for constitutionalism in the Muslim world was to however experience widespread interest from the very beginning of the twentieth century. A prominent instance was the Iranian Constitutional Revolution of 1905–1909 when Shiite clerics such as Mirza Hasan Na'ini, a leading *mujtahid* (juriconsult) of Najaf (1860–1936) lent the weight of their religious authority to the writing of a constitution. The enthusiasm towards constitutionalism did not go uncontested and Sheikh Fazlullah Nuri, one of the most learned *mujtahids* of Tehran opposed the idea of constitutionalism as it was considered to go against the grain of Islamic law (Martin 1986).[9] Despite Fazlallah Nuri's considerable opposition to the Constitutional movement in Iran, it is remarkable to see the success of the movement manifesting itself in the setting up of the Majlis in September 1906. There was in Iran around the time of the Constitutional Revolution in the first decade

[8]On the reverence for the Prophet Muhammad as a great law giver see also Humberto (2012), *Islam and the English Enlightenment, 1670–1840*.

[9]Martin (1986) notes on page 181 that around the time of the Iranian Constitutional Revolution beginning in 1905, Shaikh Fazlallah Nuri 'declared constitutionalism (*mashruta*)to be seditious and contrary to the shari'a (*mashru'a nist*).

of the 20th century, almost a binary opposition between constitutionalism and absolutism, with Mirza Hasan Na'ini favoring constitutionalism and Sheikh Fazlullah Nuri supporting traditional absolutism. The first *mujtahid* to take up the issue of constitutionalism extensively was Sayyid Muhammad Tabatabai who in two letters and a speech in events leading to the Iranian Constitutional Revolution of 1906 made the case 'to persuade the Shah to adopt, if not a full constitutional government, then at least a form of government based on a European model which would be both more just and more efficient than the traditional system in Iran' (Martin 1992: 348).[10]

There was a revival of interest in constitutionalism among the *ulama*(religious scholars) in the period of the Mossadegh government of the early 1950s. Notable in this regard was Ayatullah Mahmud Taliqani (d. 1979) who tended to go back to the earlier arguments of Mirza Hasan Na'ini, in addition to which he argued for an ethical element in constitutionalism as it eliminated self-love among people. Despite the seemingly more ethical element introduced here, constitutionalism remains for Taliqani as it was for Na'ini a means to an end and not an end in itself. There is a further disdain for nationalism to be found in Taliqani as well, which is very much in line with the disdain for the doctrine that has been noted in a number of Iranian *ulama* (Martin 1992: 353).

If one casts a comparative glance across the world, it is interesting to note that in 1905 the Russian Empire became a constitutional state and that in the First and Second Russian Dumas (1906, 1907) there was among the Muslim members a significant number of them who were *mullahs* and had a *madrasa* (religious educational institution in Islam) education (Reichmuth 2007: 164).

Around the same time as the constitutional developments in Iran were taking place, Stefan Reichmuth notes a bout of constitution writing activity in Morocco, with three extant constitutional proposals in what he refers to as a 'critical period of modern Moroccan history' in the years around 1908.[11]

---

[10]Martin (1992) further notes again referring to Sayyid Muhammad Tabatabai on page 348 that, 'He was sufficiently pragmatic to realize that it was not possible to introduce full constitutional government in Iran during that period, and adopted a gradualist approach, which aimed, not at an elected assembly with full powers, but what he called a *majlis-i 'adalat*, a council of justice'.

[11]The first of these was written in 1906 and goes back to 'Ali b. Znibar who was a Moroccan from Sale. A second version was published in four editions of the journal *Lisan al-'arab* between 11 October and 1 November 1908. *Lisan al-'arab* was a journal that came out from Tangier and founded by two Lebanese emigrants who lived in the city. The third version was published later and its authorship was for long unknown, this being established as late as the early 1980s when authorship was attributed to 'Abd al-Karim Murad, a largely unknown figure. Reichmuth (2007) informs us that Murad belonged to a prominent Sayyid family from Tripoli and was born around 1860. Murad lived his life in a number of places, spending his time as a teacher in Medina, before moving onto West and North Africa. The different parts of West Africa that he travelled in were Sierra Leone, Ivory Coast and southern Nigeria. He is then purported to have moved to Fez in Morocco, which he left in 1908 and travelled back to West Africa to be found first in French West Africa (Senegal, Ivory Coast, Dahomey). After being expelled from here to Morocco in 1912 he is found back in West Africa, this time British West Africa in Sierra Leone, Lagos and finally settling in Kano to the north, where he died in 1926. In between he is supposed to have visited Amir Shakib Arsalan in Lausanne in Switzerland in 1922' (pp. 165–166).

The acceptance of constitutionalism in the Muslim world would receive a major fillip with the decolonization of many Muslim nations in the middle of the twentieth century. Significant among these would be Pakistan, carved out of British India and where the Constituent Assembly in March 1949 passed the Objectives Resolution which became the foundation of the future constitution of Pakistan. It made a reference to Islam as the 'Religion of the State' and made a commitment to enshrine 'the principles of democracy, freedom, equality, tolerance and social justice as enunciated by Islam' (quoted in Toor 2011: 33). Saadia Toor notes that the passing of the Objectives Resolution created uproar in secular circles as it signalled a decisive shift to the right. It also made references to the desirability of making the *sharia* the basis of law making. This happened just after Jinnah's death and was a complete negation of his vision of a secular and democratic state that he had spoken about in his inaugural address to the Constituent Assembly when he suggested that the religious beliefs of citizens were something that did not concern the state. Toor also notes how the Objectives Resolution created a number of committees that were established to draw up the constitution on the basis of the Objectives Resolution. One of the more important of these committees was the Basic Principles Committee (BPC) that in its interim report of 1950 suggested that the head of the state should be a Muslim and that a board of *ulema* or religious scholars be created to ensure that no law 'repugnant to Islam' should be passed (Toor 2011: 207 endnote 23).

However, the most perverse effect of this readiness to take to constitutionalism would be in terms of what Bassam Tibi understands as the tendency to now start viewing the *sharia* itself as the source of constitutional law. Tibi notes that the *sharia* is mentioned in only one verse in the Quran and even here it is understood as a morality and not as law (Tibi 2008: 101). Tibi's argument extends to suggest that the 'shariatization of politics' is a simple straightforward route to totalitarianism, making the project of democracy that much more endangered in the Islamic world.

The commitment to constitutionalism in the form of viewing the *sharia* as the source of constitutional law has a subtle, yet profound effect on Muslim societies across the world. The *sharia* is now seen less as an exemplary moral path that was trodden by the Prophet Muhammad. Instead it is now viewed with the fixity of a written code. As a result, the term *sharia* law has now become a staple of heated media discussions on Islam. It may be added that these discussions create far more heat than light on the issue. There seems to be a horror across Europe especially, that with increasing Muslim population levels across the continent, *sharia* law is likely to be enforced. The average man on the street is likely to have an extremely caricatured view of *sharia*, understanding it to be mostly about stoning adulterers to death and chopping off the hands of thieves.

Serif Mardin goes to the extent of suggesting that the secularizing and centralizing thrust of the Tanzimat Reforms (1839–1876) resulted in completely upsetting the intricacy and balance of the Islamic legal structure. Mardin notes how the Tanzimat Reforms resulted in an elimination of the office of the *kadi*, a position that combined in it both administrative and judicial functions. Even the *ulama* were gradually displaced from some of the crucial positions that they had occupied. All this happened as the Young Ottomans supported the Tanzimat Reforms and their continuing commitment to Islam was evident in their gestures towards incorporation of elements Islamic in the modern political set up that they wanted to establish (Mardin 2009: 256–261).

The desire among Muslims to lead a more Islamic life in the alienating circumstances of modernity is indeed quite intriguing. Its most obvious form assumes a desire to reassert the *sharia* and its centrality in the lives of Muslims. The *sharia* that is sought to be reasserted, quite often is also one that needs to be protected, almost like putting it in a box, in which it remains unsullied from the corrosive effects of modernity, yet can serve as a continuing source of guidance to Muslims. In this protective encasement, it can prevent them from going astray from the true path of Islamic faith. Scott Alan Kugle in his article 'Framed, Blamed and Renamed' argues that the Islamic or *sharia* law that is cherished by Muslims in South Asia is a law that is something of an oxymoron. He refers to it as Anglo-Muhammadan law in which British principles of jurisprudence overlay and hegemonised the Islamic component of the law to result in the *sharia* becoming a static and reified entity. The irony of Muslim revivalism and political assertion is that it seems to rally around a rather colonized notion of the *sharia*, that has already been divested of its initial flexibility to be replaced by a rigidity and ossification (Kugle 2001).

As a last and final point for this section, one can end by speculating over why Muslims were so willing and enthusiastic to take to written constitutions. Perhaps the answer lies in the fact that written constitutions paralleled the certainty and fixity of the word of God found in the Quran. The cry that the 'Quran is our constitution' has been heard many times resounding across the Islamic world. Yet the readiness to rely on the written may be a particular bane of the modern times that Muslims find themselves struggling to cope with. There is a superiority that the spoken word, the *viva-voce* has over the written word and that is in the fact that the spoken word is written in the hearts and souls of men, while the written word is perhaps, despite is apparent fixity, written transiently on pieces of fragile paper. These ideas are conveyed by Socrates to a young and impressionable Phaedrus in Plato's dialogue that has been named on this particular character (Hackforth 1952). It is a lesson that Muslims might want to learn and yet at the same time go on affirming the centrality of constitutionalism.

3.5 Political Islam as an Overflowing of the Containers of Liberal Democratic Politics

At the outset of this paper, it was suggested that any hyphenated term with which democracy is suffixed has the tendency of trying to contain and constrain the unpredictable in democracy. This paper in the beginning has suggested that there is almost a futility in constitutionalism trying to prevent a bad case of democracy breaking out from its paper-thin constitutional envelope or covering, especially when democracy is itself going through one of its wilder and more recalcitrant populist phases.

In this last section of the paper, political Islam will be viewed as a phenomenon that arises from an overflowing of the vehicles and containers of liberal democracy. There is thus a parallel that is drawn between political Islam understood as a phenomenon that emerges when the narrow channels and dykes of liberal democracy are burst and blown apart by its sheer populist appeal, with the manner in which democratic ructions were experienced in the form of Brexit, Trump in the US, Duterte in the Philippines, etc. that were mentioned at the beginning of this chapter. Political Islam tends to tear apart the constrictions that it experiences in liberal democracy by invoking the authority and popularity of the *sharia*. This invocation of the authority and popularity of the *sharia* tends to have great traction among Muslim majority societies.

As examples of this possibility of Islamist parties threatening to undo the restrictions of liberal democracy one can cite the examples of the FLN victory of Algeria in late 1991, Muhammad Morsi's victory in Egypt in 2013 and the series of electoral triumphs that Recep Tayyep Erdogan has won over the last two decades of his dominance of Turkish politics. In all these three countries mentioned, the military has at some point or the other had to intervene in order to supposedly restore the balance away from the Islamist parties that were threatening to dominate electorally.

Gunes Murat Teczur in a consideration of the cases of Iran and Turkey brings out some interesting points of contrast and similarity. He suggests that in both countries there can be found 'ideological constitutions' that were committed to preventing the vagaries of democracy from overturning the constitutional and political order. The difference, however, lay in the fact that in the case of Iran, the imperative of the ideological constitution was to guarantee the continuity of the Islamist constitutional order of the 1979 Iranian constitution and in the case of Turkey to maintain exactly the opposite, the secular order of the 1982 Constitution. There can be noted here an element of guardianship that steps into play to prevent democracy from charting choppy waters that are disapproved of by the constitutional set up. The supervisory guardian institutions that come into play in either country are also different. In the case of Iran it was the hierocracy (clerical power holders) and in the case of Turkey it was the military and the judiciary (Tezcur 2007).[12]

The point about political Islam emerging from an overflowing of the constricted channels and containers of liberal democracy would suggest that there is a serious issue of incompatibility between Islam and liberal democracy. There are then aspects in the practice of Islam that would make it difficult for it to coexist with liberal democracy and those asking the question of how Islam can be made compatible with liberal democracy would seem to have a valid point. Bassam Tibi has enumerated some of these as violation of individual human rights, the intolerance towards minorities,

[12]In line with the recalcitrant aspect of democracy that paper has talked about a number of times, this is what Tezcur has to say about the element of the unpredictable in democracy:

Democratic politics are by definition unpredictable and may bring to power groups of suspect loyalty in the eyes of the guardians. Majorities might be swayed by populist politicians who seek to aggrandize their power while disregarding the ideological goals of the regimes. Guardians perceive themselves as the only force capable of containing and eliminating these "internal threats" before they irreversibly erode the revolutionary legacy (p. 482).

denial of equality to them and also intolerance towards Muslims who leave the faith. The larger point that Tibi makes is that the return of the sacred as he calls it with a renewed emphasis on the *sharia* as a source of constitutional law poses a threat to democratic constitutionalism and also to the principle of secularism (Tibi, 2008).[13]

The prospects of democracy in Islamic societies are not particularly bright. They are not very bright in the established liberal democracies of the West for that matter. In both cases, viz., democracy in Islamic societies and the liberal democracies of the West, a parallel has been made in this paper in terms of people's democratic aspirations expressed in electoral verdicts failing to be contained in the narrow channels of democracy. The difference, however, lies in the fact that in many successful liberal democracies there was an extended period of time since the Second World War when there was a smoothness with which it functioned. There were political, economic and technological factors behind this smoothness in the operation of liberal democracy for a longish stretch of around seven decades. Five decades after the end of the Second World War, when the Cold War ended and the Berlin wall fell, there seemed to be a confidence, almost a swagger in the manner of liberal democracy as Francis Fukuyama predicted that it would now spread to the rest of the world. In the early 2000s, a series of colour-coded democratic revolutions in three former republics of the Soviet Union, Georgia in 2003 (Rose), Ukraine in 2004 (Orange) and Kyrgyzstan in 2005 (Tulip) seemed to suggest that the confident swagger of democracy was not misplaced.

The onset of the Arab Spring should have confirmed that the March of democracy had finally arrived in the lands of Islam. The Arab Spring while giving rise to an initial and fleeting ecstasy, quickly lapsed into a rather premature autumn. Shortly after this moment, the confidence of the democratic footstep began to falter in the very heartlands of liberal democracy, Western Europe and North America, prompting the fear among many that we may be witnessing the imminent collapse and death of democracy. Hamid Dabashi in his book *The Arab Spring* takes a far more optimistic view of the occurrence of the phenomenon and the direction that it will take. He believes that the sheer extent of the Arab Spring that began from Tunisia in December 2010 and rapidly spread to many other countries in its eastward advance will give rise to a counter revolutionary force from the US, Saudi Arabia, Israel and the Islamic Republic of Iran, in which these just mentioned countries will inevitably fall as 'They are old, they are decrepit, they are remnants of a dreadful political imagination that is already dead'. Dabashi observes:

> Entrenched as the Islamic Republic and Saudi Arabia may be, and determined as the US and Israel may be to keep the Saudis in power and dismantle the Islamic Republic in their own terms, these two theocratic and tribal banalities have been deeply affected, troubled and traumatized by the democratic uprisings. (Dabashi 2012: 14)

---

[13]Tibi (2008) notes that 'today's shari'a is a call to construct an Islamic state with an alleged shari'a as its constitution. The important questions are whether shari'a is really a constitutional law and how consonant the call for Islamization is with the envisioned democracy' (p. 96).

The prospects for constitutionalism and democracy do not look particularly bright as the second decade of the twenty-first century slowly draws to a close. The challenges to upholding democracy today seem to be as difficult in the less economically advanced countries as they are in the advanced liberal democracies.

References

Astor, M. (2019). How the politically unthinkable can become mainstream. *New York Times*, 26 February.

Barzin, S. (1994). Constitutionalism and democracy in the religious ideology of Mehdi Bazargan. *British Journal of Middle Eastern Studies, 21*(1), 85–101.

Brubaker, R. (1996). *Nationalism Reframed: Nationhood and the national question in the new Europe*. Cambridge: Cambridge University Press.

Caryl, C. (2013). *Strange Rebels: 1979 and the Birth of the 21st Century*, Basic Books, New York.

Cirakman, A. (2001), 'From tyranny to Despotism: 'The Enlightenment's Unenlightened Image of the Turks', *International Journal of Middle East Studies*, Vol.33, No. 1(Feb.), pp. 49–68.

Dabashi, H. (2012). *The Arab Spring: The End of Postcolonialism*. London: Zed Books.

De Bellaigue, Christopher (2017) *The Islamic Enlightenment. The Modern Struggle Between Faith and Reason: 1798 to Modern Times,* W.W. Norton, London.

Fathi, A. (1993). 'Ahmad Kasravi and Sayyed Jamal Waez on Constitutionalism in Iran', *Middle Eastern Studies*, Vol.29, No. 4 (Oct), pp. 702–713.

Garcia, H. (2012). *Islam and the English Enlightenment, 1670-1840*. Baltimore: Johns Hopkins University Press.

Hackforth, R. (1952). *Plato's Phaedrus, with an introduction and commentary*. Cambridge: Cambridge University Press.

Harari, N. Y. (2016). *Homo Deus: A Brief History of Tomorrow*. London: Vintage.

Hill, P. (2017) 'Ottoman Despotism and Islamic Constitutionalism in Mehmed Ali's Egypt', *Past & Present*, Volume 237, Issue 1, 1 November, pp. 135–166.

Khan, L. A., & Ramadan, H. (2011). *Contemporary Ijtihad: Limits and Controversies*. Edinburgh: Edinburgh University Press.

Kugle, S. A. (2001). Framed, Blamed and Renamed: The Recasting of Islamic Jurisprudence in Colonial South Asia. *Modern Asian Studies, 35*(2), 257–313.

Levitsky, S., & Ziblatt, D. (2018). *How Democracies Die: What History Reveals About Our Future*. New York: Viking.

Mardin, S. (2009). Heaven and the Administration of Things: Some Remarks on Law in the Tanzimat Era. In H. Islamoglu & P. C. Perdue (Eds.), *Shared Histories of Modernity: China, India and the Ottoman Empire*. New Delhi: Routledge.

Martin, V. (1992). 'Trends in the Shi'i Response to Constitutionalist Ideology in Iran', *Journal of the Royal Asiatic Society*, Third Series, Vol. 2, No. 3 (Nov.), pp. 347–361.

Martin, V.A. (1986). The Anti-Constitutionalist Arguments of Shaikh Fazlallah Nuri, *Middle Eastern Studies*, Vol. 22, No. 2 (April) pp. 181–196.

Mason, P. (2016, August 1st). Are we living through another 1930s?, *The Guardian*, London.

Mitchell, T. (2011). *Carbon Democracy: Political Power in the Age of Oil*. London: Verso.

Reichmuth, S. (2007). The Arabo-Islamic Constitutional Thought at 1907: 'Abd al-Karim Murad (d. 1926) and his draft constitution for Morocco. In S. A. Dudoignan, K. Hisao, & K. Yasushi (Eds.), *Intellectuals in the Modern Islamic World: Transmission, transformation and communication*. London and New York: Routledge.

Sayyid, S. (2014). *Recalling the Caliphate: Decolonization and world order*. London: Hurst & Company.

Schumpeter, J. (2011). *Capitalism*. Socialism and Democracy: Adarsh Books, New Delhi.

Tezcur, G.M. (2007). Constitutionalism, judiciary and democracy in Islamic societies, *Polity*, Vol. 39, No. 4 (Oct.), pp. 479–501.
Tibi, B. (2008). The Return of the Sacred to Politics as a Constitutional Law: The Case of the Shariatization of Politics in Islamic Civilization. *Theoria: A Journal of Social and Political Theory*, No. 115, Politics and the Return of the Sacred (April), pp. 91–119.
Toor, S. (2011). *The State of Islam: Culture and Cold War Politics in Pakistan*. London: Pluto Press.
Tushnet, Mark, & Khosla, Madhav (Eds.). (2015). *Unstable constitutionalism: Law and Politics in South Asia*. Cambridge: Cambridge University Press.
Wolin, S. S. (2008). *Democracy incorporated: Managed democracy and the specter of inverted Totalitarianism*. Princeton: Princeton University Press.

Amir Ali is with the Centre for Political Studies, Jawaharlal Nehru University, New Delhi. Previously he taught at the Department of Political Science, Jamia Millia Islamia University, New Delhi and was Agatha Harrison Memorial Visiting Fellow at St. Antony's College, Oxford (2012–14). He has written a book on South Asian Islam and British Multiculturalism (Routledge, 2016). His research interests are in political theory, group rights, multiculturalism and British politics.

Chapter 4
Ernst-Wolfgang Böckenförde on Law, Religion, and Democratic Models of Secularism

Mirjam Künkler and Tine Stein

Abstract The chapter reviews aspects of the work of one of Germany's foremost legal scholars in the post-war era: Ernst-Wolfgang Böckenförde (1930–2019), who served as professor of law and as judge on Germany's Federal Constitutional Court. He contributed like few others to discussions about the central normative frameworks of post-war German constitutional democracy, the relations between state and society, and the role of religion in democracy. Unlike Jürgen Habermas, he did not believe that participation in shared democratic processes was sufficient to create cohesion and a "we-consciousness" among the citizenry. Instead, he insisted that society had to also continuously work towards creating and sustaining a shared democratic culture so that agreement could be reached on the things that lie beyond the ballot box. The chapter reviews Böckenförde's democratic theory, which evolved significantly out of his criticism of the Catholic Church's views on democracy prior to the Second Vatican Council (1962–1965). It also compares his views on democratic models of secularism with those of Indian theorist Rajeev Bhargava's to suggest that, in the final analysis, differences between the two thinkers stem to no small extent from the fact that Böckenförde, unlike Bhargava, is a theorist of freedom more than belonging.

4.1 Introduction

This volume addresses the central normative frameworks within which constitutionalism in the Indian and German traditions may be understood. The constitutions of the two countries share certain characteristics. For one, they have similar longevity. The (West) German was promulgated in 1949, the Indian in 1950. Both established federal parliamentary democracies and both were thought of by their respective framers as more than just documents about how the political order would function: rather, they were viewed also as transformative documents, laying the basis for the transformation

---

M. Künkler (✉)
The Netherlands Institute for Advanced Study, Amsterdam, The Netherlands
e-mail: mirjam.kunkler@nias.knaw.nl

T. Stein
University of Göttingen, Göttingen, Germany

© Springer Nature Singapore Pte Ltd. 2020

A. Roy and M. Becker (eds.), *Dimensions of Constitutional Democracy*,
https://doi.org/10.1007/978-981-15-3899-5_4

of politics and society.[1] In the German context, the principle of human dignity was accorded central importance, and its interpretation in constitutional jurisprudence has been a major pivot of numerous Federal Constitutional Court judgements.

A central figure in the German context is Ernst-Wolfgang Böckenförde (1930–2019), a legal scholar, historian, and former federal constitutional court judge who shaped post-WWII German thinking about the state and democracy like few others. There is hardly a central topic in post-war German legal and political thinking on which he did not make major interventions, and because Böckenförde not only published as a scholar but was also a prominent voice as a public intellectual, some of his concepts have acquired household currency among the German public.[2]

From the viewpoint of Indian-German constitutional comparison, three topics appear particularly relevant: first, Böckenförde's criticism of the Catholic Church as subscribing to an instrumental view of electoral democracy (supporting democracy where the Church could benefit, but not defending it when endangered by illiberal forces) is key to understanding his democratic theory, and in particular his view of the role of religion in democracy. Second, while Böckenförde argues that no democratic state can impose core values or worldviews on its citizens without violating the very ideas of freedom, human rights, and equality on which it is based, he does see a role to play for religion and other worldviews in society: in feeding the ethos of individual citizens and in motivating citizens to work towards the common good. Finally, his model of the secular state as one of "open encompassing neutrality" rather than strict separation offers revealing contact points, but also contrasts, with the Indian political theorist Rajeev Bhargava's thinking on the topic. Bhargava has argued that the Indian constitution of 1950 provided essentially for a model of "principled distance" between the state and the multiple religions present in Indian society. Like Böckenförde's "open encompassing neutrality", the notion of "principled distance" allows for more intermingling between religion and the state than the notion of a wall of separation does. At the same time, different from Böckenförde's approach, "principled distance" is not based on treating all religions equally, but on responding to each of their specific needs contextually, which necessarily implies prioritizing one over others in certain contexts. The German constitution of 1949, by contrast, is based on the religious neutrality of the state which prohibits the prioritization of one religion over others, as well as of religion over other worldviews. Böckenförde in much of his work outlined what this religious neutrality entailed for the question of religious law, religion in education, and the presence of religious symbols in public

---

[1]That not only India but also Germany should be thought of as bearing features of transformative constitutionalism is argued by Hailbronner (2017).

[2]These concepts include "chain of legitimation", the constitution as an "ordering frame" (Rahmenordnung), and "gateway concepts", among others. Reflective of his ability to coin concepts for wide societal use, Böckenförde was only the second legal scholar ever awarded the Sigmund Freud Prize for excellence in academic prose.

life. Before discussing these three areas of research, a synopsis of Böckenförde's life will be offered with a view particularly to his career as a legal scholar.[3]

4.2 Böckenförde—A Biographical Synopsis

Böckenförde grew up in the Central German town of Kassel with seven siblings. His father was a forester and his mother a housewife. Among the books he said that formed him were Dante's *Divina Commedia* and writings by the Austrian novelist Adalbert Stifter and the German poet Reinhold Schneider (a Catholic anti-war writer). Apart from that, his family's library included many works of philosophy, economics, sociology, and law, and a subscription to the Catholic intellectual monthly magazine *Hochland*.[4]

At the age of 13 years he had a tram accident, as a result of which he lost half of his left leg. Partly as a consequence of this accident, he did not travel much in his life and unlike some of his colleagues of similar academic stature, such as Robert Alexy or Dieter Grimm, did not spend long sojourns at foreign universities. His travels led him frequently to Austria, Italy, and Poland, but seldom further afield, the only exception being a trip to Pakistan and the USA, respectively, and an extensive lecture tour to Japan which he undertook after retiring from the Federal Constitutional Court and the university in 1996.[5]

Böckenförde's studies were unusual in that he decided to pursue not only one, but two university degrees, which he then also followed up with two doctoral dissertations in two separate disciplines, law, and history, followed by a habilitation in law. Both doctoral dissertations were published by the academic publisher Duncker & Humblot, the publisher of Hans Kelsen, Carl Schmitt, and Rudolf Smend decades earlier, and both monographs founded their own book series. In his doctoral dissertation in law of 1956, Böckenförde examined the public understanding of law, tracing the differentiation between formal and substantive notions of law from the nineteenth century to the Weimar Republic. Against the background of conceptual history, he then showed what the changing meaning of concepts could reveal about changing political constellations, in this case the relationship between monarchy and popular sovereignty. He did so through the prism of the statutory basis requirement

[3]The authors are the editors of the English publication of many of Böckenförde's articles: Böckenförde (2017, 2020). The authors have also published four special journal issues on various aspects of Böckenförde's work: See Künkler and Stein (2018a, c, e, 2020a).

[4]Hochland was a Catholic cultural magazine which published contributions by authors regardless of their denomination and was viewed sceptically by the Catholic Church for its independence, critical spirit, and anti-denominationalism.

[5]Despite his lack of sojourns abroad, his works have been translated widely, inter alia into Italian, Polish, Japanese, Korean, and English, as well as to a lesser extent into French, Portuguese, Spanish, Czech, Slovenian, Russian, and Swedish. For an overview of these translations and their reception, see Künkler and Stein (2020b). During his trip to Pakistan, the German Embassy organized for him to deliver a lecture at a Pakistani Research Institute, comparing German and Pakistani Federalism.

for encroachment (*Gesetzesvorbehalt*): the idea that the executive may not encroach upon the citizens' fundamental rights unless the legislature passes a law permitting such encroachment. With the introduction of the legal concept of the statutory basis requirement for encroachment, the balance between monarchy and popular sovereignty had shifted in favour of the latter.[6]

In his history dissertation of 1960, Böckenförde offered a review of nineteenth-century German scholarship on constitutional history. He examined the major conflict lines and models of constitutionalism that emerged over the course of the century and how the concept of "constitution" evolved from a mere juridical contract into a political category, transforming the meaning of a political community which bound itself legally.[7]

Both dissertations historicized concepts of law across time—they applied a historical-critical hermeneutic to unlock insights into changes in the meaning of concepts as a result of changing power constellations. This remained a major theme in Böckenförde's work throughout his career.

Returning from Munich to Münster, Böckenförde completed his habilitation[8] in Law in 1964 on "Organizational Power in the Realm of Government. An Inquiry into the Public Law of the Federal Republic of Germany".[9] In the same year, he was appointed professor of public law in Heidelberg, where he stayed for five years until moving on to the newly founded University of Bielefeld, and then later to Freiburg (1977–95), where he remained until his retirement. Over the course of these appointments, he served as professor of Public Law, Constitutional History, Legal History, and Philosophy of Law.

During his time in Münster, while working on his doctorate in law, Böckenförde became part of the Collegium Philosophicum, a discussion circle convened by the philosopher Joachim Ritter.[10] Here he gained much of his philosophical formation and met colleagues who would accompany him intellectually throughout his life. The Collegium exposed him to intensive discussions about Georg Wilhelm Friedrich Hegel and Hegel's notion of an ethical state, a theme which influenced much of Böckenförde's subsequent thinking. The collegium gave birth to one of the great

[6]Böckenförde (1958).

[7]Böckenförde (1961).

[8]To become eligible for a professorship in Germany, it used to be the case that an applicant needed to have a doctorate and a second major work, usually in the same discipline, i.e., the habilitation (combined with the venia legendi, the authorization to teach the subject at the university level). Nowadays a second book is widely regarded as equivalent to the formal habilitation, although many scholars still seek the formal acquisition of a habilitation as well. To have two doctorates like Böckenförde is rather unusual and testifies to his broad intellectual interests.

[9]Böckenförde (1964).

[10]Joachim Ritter, professor in Münster, was one of the most influential German philosophers of the post-war period, who edited the "Historisches Wörterbuch der Philosophie", a standard work in the discipline of philosophy.

projects of the humanities in post-war West Germany, the *Historical Dictionary of Philosophy*, to which Böckenförde contributed two entries.[11]

Another colloquium that exerted great influence on Böckenförde's development as a legal scholar was a summer seminar, held at Ebrach, a village in Upper Franconia, which the legal scholar Ernst Forsthoff convened on an annual basis.[12] Only a select number of scholars and students were invited, and Böckenförde and Carl Schmitt were regular participants. Some of the lectures given in Ebrach were later published in a *Festschrift* for Forsthoff, including Böckenförde's groundbreaking article on "The Rise of the State as a Process of Secularization" as well as Schmitt's "The Tyranny of Values".[13]

During his career, colleagues like Reinhart Koselleck shaped the evolution of Böckenförde's thought. While at the University of Heidelberg, Böckenförde and Koselleck co-taught a seminar, and both were also members of the working group on social history in Heidelberg, which understood social history primarily as an alternative to the focus on individual elite actors. Both Böckenförde and Koselleck later moved to the newly founded University of Bielefeld, where Koselleck further pursued his programme of *Begriffsgeschichte* (conceptual history), culminating in the *Geschichtliche Grundbegriffe* (basic historical concepts), a magnum opus to which Böckenförde contributed an article.[14] That Böckenförde shared an interest in *Begriffsgeschichte* is hardly surprising, given that his first doctorate on 'Law and Law-making Power' had at its basis a similar line of inquiry: how do concepts emerge and evolve, and how do they at one point take on a new implied meaning that is no longer questioned?

As a professor, Böckenförde became an influential teacher and mentor: eight scholars wrote their habilitation under his guidance, a comparatively high number (among them the world-famous author Bernhard Schlink ("The Reader"), who later became professor of law in Berlin). All of those who clerked for Böckenförde in Karlsruhe went on to assume judgeships at high courts later in their careers, as did several of his doctoral students.[15]

---

[11]'Normativismus' in: *Historisches Wörterbuch der Philosophie*, edited by Joachim Ritter and Karlfried Gründer, Vol. 6. (Basel/Stuttgart: Schwabe 1984), Sp. 931 f.; Ordnungsdenken, konkretes. In ibid, Sp. 1311–13; (Böckenförde 1993).

[12]Ernst Forsthoff (1902–74) was a German scholar of constitutional and administrative law, teaching over the course of his career at the universities of Frankfurt am Main, Hamburg, Königsberg, Vienna, and Heidelberg. Like Carl Schmitt (Forsthoff's mentor) and many other German legal scholars, he welcomed the Third Reich and worked on an ideological justification of the totalitarian state. But unlike most other legal scholars, Forsthoff distanced himself from the regime still during the Nazi period and was banned from teaching in 1942. Unlike Carl Schmitt, he was ultimately permitted to resume teaching in the Federal Republic and returned to his professorship at the University of Heidelberg in 1952. Forsthoff was a leading author of the Constitution of Cyprus and served as the president of the Supreme Constitutional Court of Cyprus from 1960 to 1963.

[13]Buve (1967).

[14]Brunner et al. (1978).

[15]The German court system has three main categories of courts: ordinary, specialized and constitutional courts. Ordinary courts deal with criminal and most civil cases. They are organized in four tiers from the municipal to the regional, Länder and federal level, where the Federal Court of Justice

Böckenförde was unusual in that he combined normative orientations which at his time were associated with different sociopolitical communities in Germany. On the one hand, he was a devout Catholic and active in the lay organizations of the Church.[16] But while most Catholics until the 1980s would have associated themselves with the Christian Democrats (the party of the chancellors Konrad Adenauer, Helmut Kohl, later Angela Merkel), Böckenförde had joined the Social Democratic Party in 1967 (the party of the chancellors Willy Brandt, Helmut Schmidt, and later Gerhard Schröder). And while Böckenförde no doubt was a statist (like Carl Schmitt), he combined this with a strong liberal orientation. On the one hand, he regarded the state as the guarantor of societal peace, but on the other hand he was always apprehensive of state encroachment into citizens' private lives. In the late 1970s, for example, when West Germany was shaken by a number of murders, kidnappings and assaults committed by leftist terrorists (most notoriously, the Red Army Faction), he made a name for himself by writing extensively in defense of the rights of even those who reject the democratic state. "It is important," he noted, "that the so-called enemies of freedom do not lose their rights. They must be restrained, but must not be placed outside the guar-antee of freedom."[17] And elsewhere he commented "the order of freedom must set itself apart from the order of unfreedom also—and especially—by the methods of its defense."[18]

On the constitutional court, where he served from 1983 to 1996, Böckenförde contributed to several pathbreaking decisions, including on asylum, abortion, nuclear disarmament, conscientious objection to military service, taxation, and party financing. With 11 dissenting opinions, he was one of the highest dissenters in the court's

(Bundesgerichtshof) is the court of final appeal. The specialized courts are subdivided into five legal fields: administrative, labour, social, fiscal, and patent law. With the exception of the patent and finance courts that operate only at one level and two levels, respectively, the specialized courts are organized hierarchically on three tiers: on a local, a *Länder*, and a federal tier. Issues at stake in administrative cases are government policies that may harm the legal interests of individuals, for instance plans for land use that infringe on property owners' rights. Labour cases deal with relations between employees and employers. Finally, social courts deal with cases relating to the welfare state and its system of social insurance. A constitutional court exists in each of the sixteen Länder (with different designations) and on the federal level with the Federal Constitutional Court.

[16]He was an advisor to the executive committee of German Catholics, the most important institution of lay Catholicism in Germany. Its tasks include organizing the biennial Catholic *Kirchentag* (church day), discussing pending issues with the German conference of bishops, and representing lay Catholicism in public. He was also one of the founding members of Donum Vitae, a Catholic organization offering prenatal consultancy, including to those planning to undertake an abortion. Such prenatal consultancy is mandatory for those wishing to undertake an abortion (which has been de-criminalized for the first trimester). The creation of Donum Vitae caused a serious conflict with the Vatican, which accuses the organization of indirectly enabling the state's legally tolerated abortion regime.

[17]Böckenförde (2017, Chapter 17, p. 386).

[18]Böckenförde (2017, Chapter 3, p. 100).

history.[19] Extraordinarily, in two cases, his minority opinions became the bases for later majority decisions.

Böckenförde's writings have received wide reception in the academic world. Aside from four *Festschrifts*, several monographs and edited volumes have been published about his work.[20] He has received numerous prizes and awards, as well as five honorary doctorates, three in law and two in Catholic theology.[21] More than 80 of his articles have been translated into foreign languages, and his work enjoys extensive reception in Italy, Poland, Japan and Korea.

4.3 Böckenförde as an Inner-Catholic Critic

Böckenförde's earliest academic writings on law, religion, and politics consist of four key works that demonstrate his sharp analyses of the Catholic Church and of its views on natural law. In his article "The Ethos of Modern Democracy and the Church" (1957), written before the Second Vatican Council (1962–65), he vehemently criticized the Catholic Church's stance on democracy and human rights and called on

[19]In two of his dissenting opinions, his social-democratic leanings come particularly to the fore. One was his take on party financing, where he argued that a law that made donations to political parties deductible for juridical persons, including corporations, violated the equality principle of the Basic Law's Article 3, as would deductible donations by natural persons at a level exceeding the median income. He also dissented in the case regarding the net wealth tax where the majority had ruled that the fundamental right to property, in connection with other basic rights, imposed a general upper limit on taxation. In the majority's view, the cumulative burden of all income and net wealth taxes must not exceed fifty percent of net imputed earnings. Although he strongly defended the right to property otherwise, Böckenförde did not subscribe to the view of a constitutionally mandated upper limit on taxation. In his academic writings, Böckenförde explicitly and implicitly lamented that Article 14 (2) Basic Law, according to which "property entails obligations; its use shall also serve the public good" did not find sufficient reflection in the public regulation of private property.

[20]The *Festschrifts* are Grawert (1995), Wahl and Wieland (2002), Enders and Masing (2006), Masing and Wieland (2011). The edited volumes are Große Kracht and Große Kracht (2014), Mehring and Otto (2014). The monographs are Manterfeld (2000), Falk (2006), Pavelka (2015). Apart from numerous obituaries that were published following his passing in February 2019, the Verfassungsblog in May 2019 convened a review with ten commentaries on Böckenförde's legacy.

[21]Böckenförde received honorary doctorates from the Law Schools of the Universities of Basel (1987), Bielefeld (1999), and Münster (2001), and from the Faculties of Catholic Theology of Bochum University (1999), and Tübingen University (2005). In 1970 he became a member of the North-Rhine Westphalian Academy of Sciences and in 1989 corresponding member of the Bavarian Academy of Sciences and Humanities. He has received the Reuchlin Award of the City of Pforzheim for outstanding work in the humanities (1978), the order of merit of the state of Baden-Württemberg (2003), the Guardini Award of the Catholic Academy in Bavaria for work in the field of the philosophy of religion (2004), the Hannah-Arendt Prize for Political Thought (2004), the Sigmund Freud Prize for scholarly prose (2012), and the Grand Cross of Merit (2016), one of the highest tributes the Federal Republic of Germany can pay to individuals for services to the nation. Böckenförde was Knight Commander of the Pontifical Equestrian Order of St. Gregory appointed by John Paul II. (1999).

it to embrace the principles of religious freedom and secular authority as part of modernity.[22] In the second, "Natural Law against the background of Today" (1958), he developed a comprehensive critique of the church's adherence to natural law thinking, which, he suggested, had caused Catholics to confuse specifically Catholic interests with the public good as such.[23] In the third, titled "German Catholicism in 1933" (1961), he provided the first inquiry into the Church's calamitous relationship with the Nazi regime.[24] The article was the first work to be published in post-war West Germany that forced the Church to face the demons of the past and caused such an uproar that the Church saw itself compelled to convene a commission of historians that would examine the accuracy of Böckenförde's claims. In the fourth article, "Religious Freedom as a Mandate for Christians. A Jurist's Thoughts on the Discussions of the Second Vatican Council" (1964/1965),[25] Böckenförde plead for the acceptance among Catholics of a religiously neutral state, which would imply also that natural law be confined to the realm of the ethical but not be placed at the basis of state law.

As Böckenförde disclosed late in his life, he was dismayed to see that for many years the Catholic Church appeared to view him as a dissenter, even at times as an opponent, when what he sought to be was an engaged voice "from within" for the sake of truth and reform.[26] All four of the mentioned articles were targeted at

[22]Böckenförde (1957). Published in English in Böckenförde (2020, Chapter 1).

[23]Böckenförde (1958). His critique was further expanded in an article co-authored with Robert Spaemann "Die Zerstörung der naturrechtlichen Kriegslehre. Erwiderung an P. Gustav Gundlach SJ." In: *Atomare Kampfmittel und christliche Ethik. Diskussionsbeiträge deutscher Katholiken.* München: Kösel, 1960, 161–196. Böckenförde and Spaemann reacted to the influential Catholic social theorist Gustav Gundlach who suggested that the idea of a nuclear war could be justified by Catholic just war theory if such a war was waged to protect a Catholic state. Böckenförde and Spaemann rejected this claim and suggested moreover that the contemporary NATO strategy of massive retaliation contradicted Christian teachings on just war. The ensuing discussion was of particular acuity as the nuclear armament of the Bundeswehr was being considered in the Bundestag at the time. The two young scholars elucidated that according to Catholic teachings, a Catholic soldier could not in good conscience execute any order given in connection with the deployment of nuclear weapons. The exchange caused an uproar both inside the German Catholic church and the German military establishment, and Böckenförde recalls being branded a "lefty" in the context of the debate. Due to the careful argumentation of Böckenförde and Spaemann, however, Gundlach's position was ultimately no longer tenable and he himself ceased making the argument, though he never recanted it.

[24]Böckenförde (1961). Newly translated in Böckenförde (2020, Chapter 2).

[25]Böckenförde (1964/1965).

[26]My "undertaking [...] was initially accompanied more by criticism than approval—let me recall merely the medium-size earthquake that my essay about German Catholicism in 1933 caused among the Catholic-ecclesiastical public. A change in the direction toward respect and in part—though at first still hesitant—approval came with the various contributions on religious freedom, the first of which was written during the debates of the Vatican Council ["Religionsfreiheit als Aufgabe der Christen," 1965], and those dealing with the political mandate of the Church [1969, 1973, 1980/84, 1983]. Eventually there were discussions as between equals, coupled with growing recognition by the discipline of theology." See Böckenförde (2020, Chapter 11).

Catholic audiences, and two were published in a Catholic magazine (*Hochland*).[27] In "The Ethos of Modern Democracy and the Church", published before Vatican II, Böckenförde outlined why Catholics should embrace the secular democratic state for the sake of their own spiritual wellbeing: indeed he argued that the secular democratic state was the *only* political regime in which it was possible to live a truly Catholic life out of free choice and conviction. While by the 1950s the Catholic Church appeared to have formally accepted the empirical reality that many believers lived in democracies that were ruled by majority decisions, the Catholic Church's official position was still that this majority principle could not be valid regarding the issues of particular concern to the church, including family law (in particular questions of marriage, birth control, sexuality) and education. The Church when opportune highlighted its own role as the guardian of morality and natural law operating in the background of political life.

In "Natural Law against the background of Today", Böckenförde examined the disposition of Catholics to the common good in the late nineteenth, early twentieth century. In the aftermath of the *Kulturkampf* of the 1870s,[28] German Catholics had felt excluded from an increasingly liberal public sphere. Compared to other citizens, they were viewed as reactionary and "ultramontane", i.e., harbouring loyalties to Rome rather than their motherland. Throughout the later years of the German Empire and then the Weimar Republic, they lived lives of inner emigration—seeing the Church as their true home and seeking the guidance of the Church for their behaviour towards the state and their fellow citizens. Political action usually meant defending the interests and rights of the Church; it did not mean, as it should have, so Böckenförde, taking the Catholic faith as an ethical inspiration to address issues of public concern. Due to this state of introversion, pious Catholics concentrated on the inner workings of the Church, on religious practice, and on religious education (all *bona particularia* (particular goods) and not common goods), building up the conviction that as long as these arenas were under the aegis of the Church, Catholics could live under any public order. It is out of this (misguided) logic, Böckenförde explains, that parts of the Catholic Centre party and the Prussian Episcopate had rejected in the spring of 1918 the democratization of the inegalitarian Prussian Three-Class franchise, fearing that this would result in a loss of majorities needed to retain current arrangements on the Church and religious schooling. Overall, Böckenförde diagnosed and criticized, instead of seeing public life as a whole, Catholics

[27] This major occupation as an inner-Catholic Critic also applies to his 1967 article on the rise of the state as a process of secularization. Jan-Werner Müller lays this out in great detail in (2018).

[28] The 'Kulturkampf' (culture war) was a struggle of Chancellor Bismarck's government against the Catholic Church concerning the role and power of Catholic institutions in predominantly Protestant Prussia. Bismarck enacted a series of anti-Catholic laws, including the disbanding of Catholic organizations, confiscation of church property, and banishment or imprisonment of clergy. The Kulturkampf was in the long term unsuccessful and the discriminating laws were eventually repealed. However, the term was still used in the Weimar Republic to refer to (factual or putative) discrimination of Catholics, and the example of the resistance exhibited by the Catholic Church during the Kulturkampf was invoked later to ask why it had done so little to resist its suppression by the Nazi regime.

reduced their gaze to particular Catholic interests only. The adherence to natural law thinking removed Catholics from the public square and made them unfit to be democratic citizens, in that it caused believers to prioritize the interests of the church over their interests as citizens of a larger demos.

In "The Catholic Church in 1933" Böckenförde laid bare the assumptions and priorities that had guided the political outlook of the vast majority of Church officials between 1933 and 1945, leading to the effective endorsement of the Nazi seizure of power on the part of the Church.[29] Going through numerous speeches and private letters of Catholic dignitaries and leaders of Catholic associations, Böckenförde concluded that they paved the way for the rise of fascism—not alone and not necessarily or always knowingly, but nevertheless, they did. Böckenförde blamed this to a large extent on their fascination with "organic" theories of society and economy, which fit with traditional Catholic moral theology's reliance on natural law argumentation. The distance of Catholics to the modern state and the fact that the Catholic Church never came to accept modern democracy doctrinally (a step only undertaken later with the Second Vatican Council) caused a narrowing of Catholic leaders' judgment of public affairs. The article was considered so explosive that several of his mentors advised against publishing it, or urged him to wait until he had secured a tenured faculty position.[30] Böckenförde published it nevertheless, and a back and forth between him and several critics ensued, excerpts of which were subsequently published in the same magazine. Ultimately, the Catholic Church felt compelled to convene a special committee of historians to probe the accuracy of Böckenförde's claims and charges. The "Committee for Contemporary History", as it was called, in the end validated Böckenförde's account in all major points. (The Committee expanded its research later and is still active today.).

The three articles sealed what Böckenförde still regards as his major achievements: an internal engagement on part of the German Catholic Church with its own history and a defence of the secular state from within a Catholic perspective: "I still claim credit for this today. I was able to persuade [German] Catholicism that one's own freedom can be defended only as part of the general freedom."[31]

The fourth article, "Religious Freedom as a Mandate for Christians. A Jurist's Thoughts on the Discussions of the Second Vatican Council", was written to inform the ongoing discussions of the Council on the question of religious freedom.[32] The

[29]Böckenförde recalled in 2009: "[In preparation of writing the 1961 article] I sat in the archive [of the Swiss Catholic journal *Ecclesiastica]*. There I came across some things. At first, I couldn't believe what I was seeing. It became surprisingly clear to me that these were exactly the positions that I had fundamentally criticized in my [1957] democracy essay. [...] That is also why I structured the [1961] essay as a case study, in order to spell out and reinforce that the traditional theory of [natural law of] the Church was untenable. [My essay] was not supposed to be only a historical account, but a case study in order to demonstrate something theoretically and systematically by way of historical events." See (Böckenförde 2020), biographical interview.

[30]Künkler and Stein (2017a).

[31]Böckenförde (2020), biographical interview.

[32]The Second Vatican Council (Vatican II) fundamentally redefined the Church's doctrinal position in a number of areas, notably on the issue of religious freedom. As late as 1886, Pope Leo XIII

laity of Catholics had for long de facto accepted living in secular, non-Christian states and sharing equal citizenship with non-Catholics and non-believers. But *de jure* such positions were still untenable. According to the Catholic Magisterium, Catholics were still required to live in Christian states (not just nominally Christian-majority states, but states where political authority was Catholic and where Catholic norms were implemented by state authority). The Second Vatican Council was reconsidering all of this: it was putting longstanding Catholic doctrine to debate. In his article, Böckenförde identified as the Church's key approach to religious freedom the tolerance theory of 1315, reaffirmed by Pope Pius XII as late as 1953, according to which "religious error had no objective right even to exist", and as a consequence religious freedom was something to be tolerated but, in the final analysis, not to be accepted. Böckenförde gave expression to his bewilderment with the position of the church, according to which it claimed freedom of religion for itself but was not prepared to grant this to others. He had particular trouble comprehending this position as a jurist. Applied as such, Böckenförde wrote, the tolerance theory was not a legal principle, but a "power principle".[33]

The election of Pope John XXIII in 1963, a champion of equality who declared "We were all made in God's image, and thus, we are all Godly alike," facilitated a re-thinking on these matters. "De Libertate Religiosa" for the first time grounded religious freedom in the dignity of the human person as such, which by implication would need to be extended beyond Catholics. The church thereby abandoned the goal for Christians to live in a Christian public order and facilitated a vision of Christianity as a "religion of freedom" (Hegel).[34]

Some of Böckenförde's arguments regarding the necessity for Catholics to accept the religiously neutral state for their own good (only a religiously neutral state facilitates embracing faith out of a position of freedom) made it into the Vatican's final declaration on the matter, the encyclical "Dignitatis humanae". While arguing for the supremacy of secular state law over religious law, and against the idea that natural law could lie at the basis of state law, he championed the importance of natural law as a source for ethical reasoning. In other words, religious norms could and should inform the individual's behaviour in private and public, but could not be made mandatory for citizens to follow (as religious law when enforced by the state would necessarily do). Religion, so Böckenförde, can only be embraced fully from a position of a free choice, free from state and societal pressures.

had reaffirmed that only a state based on the Christian faith was truly legitimate and that religious liberty and freedom of conscience were illegitimate deviations from Christian natural law (encyclical "Immortale Dei"). By contrast, in the encyclical "Dignitatis humanae", the Second Vatican Council declared its acceptance of the religiously neutral state.

[33]"A maxim of law applies by its nature universally, not only for me, but also against me. A legal principle that seeks to exclude this mutuality is not a legal principle but a power principle." Böckenförde (2020, Chapter 4).

[34]Hegel (1959).

4.4 Ethos, We-Consciousness, Sense of Belonging

In 1978 Böckenförde penned an article about "The State as an Ethical State", in which he asked, drawing on Hegel's concept of "sittliche Substanz", whether the state should provide a guiding ethos to the citizenry.[35] Böckenförde answered in the negative. In his widely quoted thesis "The liberal, secularized state is sustained by conditions that it cannot itself secure," he pointed to the problem that the modern constitutional state, cannot resort to imposing certain values or worldviews on its citizens without undermining the very liberalism on which it is founded.[36] "Sittliche Substanz" was no doubt crucial for public life, but it had to emanate first and foremost from society.[37]

What are its sources? "Philosophical, political and social movements can strengthen the sense of commonality in the populace and the willingness, to not always look out for one's own benefit only, but to act companionably and in solidarity with others," he wrote.[38] Further, religion can be such a source, but he insisted, only if it is placed into the service of the common good, not of particular religious goals, or the interests of individual religious groups.[39]

The consensus on a society's basic values "of its way of life and its political organization" is based on the implied and trusted agreement about "that which cannot be voted upon" (*das Unabstimmbare*).[40] No state can survive purely on the basis of guaranteeing constitutional liberties: it also needs a genuine democratic political culture, which can only emanate if citizens trust that others will consider them full members of the polity no matter whether they are in the majority or minority at any given time. Unlike Jürgen Habermas, Böckenförde did not believe that joint participation in the democratic process alone is sufficient for this "we-consciousness" to emerge and sustain itself.

Böckenförde describes this we-consciousness also with reference to what sociologist Ralf Dahrendorf has called a "sense of belonging".[41] It consists of the shared

[35]Böckenförde (2017).

[36]Böckenförde (2020).

[37]"It is not the state that must prescribe and make obligatory a way of life; on the contrary, [the democratic state] must be sustained by basic attitudes within society." Böckenförde (2017, p. 384).

[38]Böckenförde (2009).

[39]See Böckenförde (2020). Böckenförde also explained that when religious groups had in the past used the democratic process to promote their own worldviews, this had been at the expense of the quality and longevity of democracy. "The inner strength of a democratic state depends more on the democratic loyalty which different political groups have to each other than on the realization of certain demands of natural law." Ernst-Wolfgang Böckenförde (1973), here p. 102.

[40]Ernst-Wolfgang Böckenförde, "Noch einmal: Das Ethos der modernen Demokratie," in: Ernst-Wolfgang Böckenförde, *Kirche und Christlicher Glaube in den Herausforderungen der Zeit*, 41.

[41]See Ralf Dahrendorf (1992). Freiheit und Soziale Bindungen. Anmerkungen zur Struktur einer Argumentation.: In: Krzysztof Michalski, *Die liberale Gesellschaft. Castelgandolfo-Gespräche 1992*, Klett Cotta. Earlier in his career, Böckenförde had, like Hermann Heller, referred to this as societal (or relative) homogeneity, but due to the multiple misunderstandings this created, later shifted to the terms "we-consciousness" and "sense of belonging".

visions of how to live together that bind the people to one another, that prompt them to work towards a common good. Böckenförde borrows the idea and the concept of homogeneity from the social-democratic legal scholar Herman Heller, who described it thus:

> In fact, the real intellectual basis of parliamentarism is not the belief in public discussion as such, but the belief in a common ground for discussion, and therefore the chance of fair play for the domestic political opponent, with whom agreement is believed to be possible to the exclusion of brute force.[42]

This we-consciousness is a marker for societal cohesion. It is in perennial need of re-construction and in democratic politics needs to be created in society (through communication, participation in shared activities, exchange, etc.) and cannot be imposed by the state.[43] One might point out that societal cohesion, or we-consciousness, can emerge in multiple ways: it may mean a "sense of belonging" created by similar ethos, a single stream of ethics and consciousness that connects us to each other in a singular humanity.

Or it may mean a sense of co-existence, which is a belief that there are different ethics we have, but we agree to co-exist without believing in, or even trying to develop through dialogue, any notions of common ethic. It is more of a tolerance of others' ethics rather than an agreement with them. It is a co-existence of multiple humanities.

Böckenförde certainly subscribes to a co-existence of multiple humanities as it is a sign, in his view, of a democratic society that it can accommodate different worldviews. But precisely because of this diversity, it is important that society continuously work towards creating agreement on the things that cannot be voted upon. Without the societal processes that force people to engage across the multiple divides of divergent worldviews, democracy will erode from within. Modern democratic life requires a commitment that binds people to one another. After all, it means (in his view) agreeing to pay high taxes so as to alleviate poverty in society and to enable everyone to live a life in dignity. It means being incorruptible, for that would contribute to an erosion of public order. And of course, it means in the ultimately analysis to be willing to die for one another in the case of war. All of these very severe, indeed existential, concessions, require a strong bond with others who are members of the same political community.

Ethos, ethics, *Sittlichkeit* have been recurrent themes in Böckenförde's work. He has written not only about the ethos of the state, but also the ethos of democracy, the ethos of order, the ethos of the church, and the ethos of lawyers.[44] In the end, every democracy can only be as good as the public ethos (created by societal forces) that sustains it.

[42]Heller (1992[1928]), here p. 427.

[43]See Künkler and Stein (2018f).

[44]See Böckenförde (1957, 1958, 1978, 1981, 1988, 1995, 2010, 2001).

4.5 State, Secularity, and Open Encompassing Neutrality

Böckenförde's writings on religion and state offer a conceptual starting point for thinking about models of secularity also outside the context of the Federal Republic of Germany: new challenges and societal fault lines emerge as longstanding democracies are becoming increasingly diverse in religious terms, while more and more citizens disconnect themselves from identification with the religion of their ancestors. Böckenförde argues in favour of a model he calls "open encompassing neutrality" of the state toward religion: an amicable and liberal separation of religious and political authority, defined, among other aspects, in a manner that accommodates positive religious freedom (the freedom to profess a religion) as much as negative religious freedom (the freedom not to profess a religion).[45]

Böckenförde conceives the relationship between law, politics, and religion in the frame of fundamental rights: he regards freedom of conscience and religion not only as one of the key human rights, but as the most important human right, as it enables one to distinguish between good and evil, and to act accordingly. Religious freedom means for Böckenförde the right to have or not to have a religious faith (freedom of belief), to affirm this faith privately or openly and to advocate or not advocate it (freedom to profess), to exercise or not exercise one's religion publicly (freedom of worship), and to join or not join together in religious communities (religious freedom of association).[46] The correlate to these individual rights is the open and overarching principle of the state's religious and ideological neutrality. This principle entails, first and foremost, a prohibition for the state to justify law on religious grounds. Furthermore, it entails the dissociation of political authority from religious authority, and requires of the state to not privilege religion over non-religion and one religious faith over another.

In his article "The Secularized State: Its character, justification, and problems in the 21st century" (2007b), Böckenförde explicitly contrasts his concept of open encompassing neutrality with that of distancing neutrality. The latter "tends toward consigning and confining religion to the private and private-social sphere. [...It] shapes the legal system in a purely secular way and turns away religious aspects as irrelevant and private." Occasionally, he invokes the French model in this context. Open encompassing neutrality, by contrast, "additionally accords [religion] room to develop in the public sphere, for example in the school, educational institutions, and in what is summarily referred to as the public order—though, of course, it does so without any form of identification. [...It] seeks to create a balance, in that affirming and leading a life in accordance with religion, to the extent that it is compatible with the secular goals of the state, is permitted also within the public sphere by the legal

---

[45]Alfred Stepan's model of the "Twin Tolerations" is largely congruent with this view, but in Böckenförde the legal manifestations of this relation between religion and state are thought out in much greater detail. Alfred C. Stepan (2001).

[46]Böckenförde (2007a, pp. 439 ff, here 442). See furthermore Böckenförde (1970, 2020, Chapter 6). Also Sacksofsky (2018).

system and is incorporated into the latter."[47] While distancing neutrality champions negative religious freedom (the freedom not to be religious), open encompassing neutrality, he argues, aims for a balancing of negative and positive religious freedom, in particular the right to live one's life in accordance with one's religion's tenets.

So what does open encompassing neutrality entail? In practice, the rights and interests of the religious and non-religious need to be weighed on a case by case basis. With regard to the presence of religious symbols in public spaces, Böckenförde distinguished between courtrooms and classrooms. Regarding the display of crucifixes in courtrooms, Böckenförde argued that they could be perceived by individuals as an infringement on their negative freedom of conscience and should therefore be removed. As Aline-Florence Manent has explains, since courtrooms are places "where the authority of the state is wielded, the state's symbolic endorsement of a specific religion over others could be perceived as intimidating and potentially coercive by religious (or atheist) minorities."[48] In courtrooms, where the state engages in a sovereign activity (*Hoheitsfunktion*) distancing neutrality towards religion ought to be applied.

Schools, however, unlike courtrooms, are not, Böckenförde argues, institutions of the state as an entity of power, but intermediary institutions that connect state and society. Public schools are a "means through which the state fulfils its duty of civic education, not indoctrination." This allows for a qualitatively different regulation of the presence of religious symbols, namely one of open encompassing neutrality that enables citizens to show themselves as religious or non-religious beings at their own pleasing, including in wearing religious garb.[49]

Böckenförde applied his argument to the deliberative processes of public life, too. In the 2000s, Jürgen Habermas famously argued that citizens could express religious reasons in public deliberation, an argument that Böckenförde had already developed in the 1960s. But Habermas also introduced a *translation proviso* for political processes at the parliamentary level where, he argued, religious arguments would need to be translated into secular rationality in order to count. Böckenförde examined the possible tension between religious and secular commitments in a 1999 article titled "As Christian in the Office of Constitutional Judge," in which he looked back on his years on the constitutional bench. In this office he was exclusively bound by the law and the *bonum commune*—the common good of the entire citizenry. Particularist concerns or interests, such as those of a Catholic, had no place in the inner deliberative process, Böckenförde wrote. This was the logic he had applied as a judge on the constitutional court. Interestingly, unlike with other oaths during his career, he insisted on taking this particular oath of office on the bible. He invoked God here to help him find the strength to keep religion out of his reasoning while serving on the constitutional bench.[50] Böckenförde explained that as a public official one is

---

[47]Böckenförde (2020, Chapter 8).

[48]Manent (2018).

[49]Sacksofsky (2018).

[50]See Böckenförde (2020, Chapter 11). Distinguishing the swearing-in as professor from that of the constitutional judge (both civil service positions), he comments in the biographical interview

accountable to the entire demos and as such cannot allow oneself to formulate positions based on a particularist identity. Religion can and should inform the individual ethos, but religious reasons cannot guide a decision-making process whose results apply to all citizens, regardless of their inner convictions.[51]

4.6 Open Encompassing Neutrality and Principled Distance

The Indian political theorist Rajeev Bhargava has proposed a model of secularism which he describes as an alternative to the "Western model", by which he appears to have in mind predominantly the US-American model.[52] In contrast to the "Western" model of "a strict wall of separation", Bhargava proposed a model of "principled distance" which, he has argued, was the predominant model in post-colonial India in the best of times.[53]

How do Böckenförde's and Bhargava's models compare? Are they guided by similar normative considerations? Are the ways in which these models are translated into policies and institutional design comparable? Where do they differ most significantly?

Bhargava's model has three major pillars. He writes that unlike the French model of laicité, his does not force a privatization of religion.[54] In other words, it does not insist that religion be evacuated from public life and religious practice banished to the private sphere. This is also a significant element of Böckenförde's model of open encompassing neutrality. Both Bhargava and Böckenförde appear to regard the French model of laicité as too restrictive. It privileges negative religious freedom at the expense of positive religious freedom. For example, both regard the requirements

(chapter 16 in the same volume) "[as constitutional court judge I swore with religious affirmation] [b]ecause I believe that especially this entirely independent and unchecked office depends on the morality of the individuals who exercise it. That is why I consider it legitimate that the religiously neutral state in this case lays claim to a person's inner powers of commitment, even if this is formally voluntary. The oath for regular civil service positions does not have this specific meaning. That is also why I left out the religious affirmation when I was sworn in as a professor.".

[51] For further details on the implications of this position, see Künkler and Stein (2020c).

[52] Upon closer examination, the model which Bhargava describes as the Western model appears to apply to the model of the United States predominantly, as most other Western states in fact have not erected a "wall of separation" between religion and state. The famous formulation stems from the 1947 US Supreme Court ruling Everson vs Board of Education. Incidentally, since the 1990s numerous judgments have chipped away at this "wall," so that today the model does not even apply to the United States of America anymore. Some observers characterize the current model of religion-state relations rather as one of equal liberty.

[53] Bhargava (2011).

[54] Bhargava (2006). Bhargava identifies different numbers of pillars in different writings on the Principled Distance Model. Sometimes, he lists as a separate pillar the provision of exemptions for religious organizations that these receive through special clauses in legislation or in court judgments. Since exemptions are nearly universal to all models of religion-state relations, we do not regard these as particular to the Principled Distance Model and do not discuss them here.

of teachers to refrain from wearing religious symbols (such as the headscarf) as unjustified. Böckenförde considers headscarf bans even a violation of a person's right to religious expression.

But Bhargava extends this principle to imply also that it allows "for the state-administered application of religion-based personal law," as is the case in India, as well as Israel and Indonesia, for example. This is a proviso which Böckenförde would most likely reject. Religion-based personal law always necessarily implies discrimination on the basis of religion, beginning with the question of whom such law applies to and who decides on the boundaries of that religion. Further, if a state administers religion-based law, it makes itself complicitous in applying religious truth with the power of the state, which includes its repressive and penal apparatus. Such a notion appears to fundamentally violate Böckenförde's notion of the democratic state as religiously neutral.

A second principle of Bhargava's "principled distance model" is that "all religions are treated equally, although the state is empowered to interfere in case of any discrimination in the name of religion, in the case of female genital mutilation, for example."[55] Böckenförde would go along with the general idea that the state's interference in religious matters is justified when human rights are being violated in the name of religion. But he would insist that such interference was not only justified but was indeed required. Thus, he would go much further than Bhargava in regarding the state as the primary guarantor of the citizens' human rights. Bhargava appears to be more ambiguous on the point, leaving open the possibility that a state would tolerate such violations in the name of granting religions some autonomy over their own affairs. In fact, since to date all religion-based personal law that is applied in India discriminates on the basis of gender, Bhargava's first principle would demand such toleration by the state and conflict with Böckenförde's view that a state is required to interfere in the case of human rights violations (including gender equality).

Bhargava also connects with this second principle the equal right to state support, in the form of state-administered public holidays based on the religious calendar, and state subsidies for religious schools. Here Böckenförde would largely concur. In fact, he called for the institution of a Muslim public holiday in Germany, in light of the fact that many Christian holidays are publicly recognized, but so far no Muslim holiday at all, despite the sizable Muslim population in the country.[56]

Third, Bhargava posits that his model includes a weighing of values. "The state must keep a principled distance from all public or private and individual-oriented or community-oriented religious institutions for the sake of the equally significant-and sometimes conflicting-values of peace, worldly goods, dignity, liberty, equality, and fraternity in all of its complicated individualistic and non-individualistic versions."[57] While other systems prioritized a particular value, such as "equal treatment, equal

---

[55]Berman et al. (2013, p. 84).

[56]Böckenförde (2009).

[57]Bhargava (2016).

liberty, or equality of individual citizenship", the Indian state weighed these considerations when making demands on religious communities.[58] As a judge, Böckenförde was cognizant of the fact that supreme constitutional norms would occasionally conflict in a given case. Different from the court's position in the famous German *Lüth* decision of 1958, Böckenförde did not believe that the court could orient itself along "an objective order of values". He insisted that no such order existed and that every case required a weighing of various norms. A crucial exception to the idea of weighing, however, is the principle of human dignity, which according to the Basic Law (Article 1) is inviolable. Time and again, Böckenförde vociferously rejected Article 1 interpretations which appeared to relativize the absolute supremacy of human dignity in German law and jurisprudence.[59] But already with regard to Article 2 (the right to life and physical integrity), Böckenförde engaged in implicit weighing when considering the question of abortion. Would the right to life also apply to unborn life, and if so, from which point onward? From the point of the development of the nervous system in the embryo? Or much earlier with nidation? Or from the very moment of conception? Böckenförde eventually argued that it would need to be the third option, the moment of conception, for all others appeared to be ultimately arbitrary. But if Article 2 protected the unborn life from the moment of conception, abortion could not be considered lawful at all at any point in time. Here Böckenförde conceived a Solomonic compromise (later adopted in a 1992 abortion decision of the Constitutional Court) whereby abortion would indeed be unlawful, but would not be criminally prosecuted if conducted in the first trimester and after ethical counselling.[60] This compromise consisted of a weighing of considerations in light of the fact that a blanket prohibition, which had existed in West Germany until 1974, generated a large number of unofficial abortions conducted clandestinely and in often dangerous circumstances. The widespread ignoring of the prohibition on abortion eroded the rule of law. It also created situations where mothers were not in a position or did not wish to keep their children and offered them for adoption. Either situation would be traumatic for mother and child and could not be conducive to societal wellbeing, Böckenförde noted. Judging from Böckenförde's lines of argumentation on thorny normative issues (with the exception of the norm of human dignity), it appears that he, like Bhargava, would support the idea that "the commitment to multiple values and principled distance means that the state tries to balance different, ambiguous, but equally important values."

Religious communities vary in their demands for exemptions, which is conditioned, among other things, by the nature of their religion. While most potential conflict lines between Hindu religion(s) and the state fall into the realm of ritual (e.g., considering the special status of cows and strongest prohibitions against the consumption of beef), in Islam they concern to a large degree personal status (e.g., polygamy, guardianship) and commercial affairs (inheritance, prohibition of interest). As Künkler and Shankar have noted, religions are *differentially burdened* by the

[58] Ibid, p. 172.

[59] Böckenförde (2003, 2020, Chapter 14).

[60] Böckenförde (2020, Chapter 13).

state based on the areas of people's lives they aspire to regulate.[61] In light of this differential burdening, Bhargava suggests that the state should not aspire to always take *equal* distance as the supreme point of orientation, but instead a *principled* distance to all religions.

Of course, courts in most democratic states have dealt with applications for exemptions from religious groups, and have necessarily dealt with these cases differently. But whereas for the United States, Eisgruber and Sager, for example, argue that Equal Liberty appears to have emerged as a guiding principle in most of the relevant high court jurisprudence,[62] Bhargava would argue that there should not be one principle guiding the considerations of legislatures and courts but rather "contextual reasoning". Since Bhargava does not elaborate further on which criteria courts ought to consider in their "contextual reasoning", Böckenförde would likely not go along with this part of the model. The lack of criteria would make law less predictable and in the long term erode the public's confidence in the courts as neutral arbiters of societal conflict. While each court case requires careful contextual consideration, Böckenförde would nevertheless insist that the sources of law and the methods of interpretation be broadly agreed upon in a given jurisdiction so that similar cases will lead to similar outcomes. To embrace Bhargava's argument in favour of contextual reasoning, Böckenförde would likely ask for further elaboration and clarification on what would establish the possible boundaries of this type of reasoning.

4.7 Conclusions: Between Belonging and Freedom

Ernst-Wolfgang Böckenförde (1930–2019) was one of Europe's foremost public law scholars and a major commentator on issues of diverse theoretical and practical import, ranging from legal theoretical debates about the rule of law and constitutional democracy, the state of exception, and the place of values in grounding the law, to normative discussions about the deployment of nuclear missiles, the regulation of abortion, asylum, EU enlargement, counter-terrorism, genetic engineering, and the capitalist globalized economy. It is difficult to pigeonhole Böckenförde on a left-right continuum. He appears progressive in some ways (e.g., he does not regard dual citizenship as posing a problem of divided loyalties) and conservative in others (e.g., people need to be grounded in families, and states need to mold their students in schools). As we have laid out elsewhere,[63] Böckenförde writes as a social democrat, a Catholic, and a political liberal. It is not only these plural normative commitments that make Böckenförde an unusual thinker. It is also the originality of his theoretical contributions towards understanding, legitimizing, and criticizing the democratic constitutional state that make him invaluable for contemporary political theory.

---

[61] On differential burdening and models of secularism, see Künkler and Shankar (2018).

[62] Eisgruber and Sager (2010).

[63] Künkler and Stein (2017a, b).

A key idea in Böckenförde's work is that democracy requires "implicit agreement about those things that cannot be voted upon". At a most basic constitutional level, these are the unamendable clauses of a Constitution—they are not subject to electoral majorities, they are "off the agenda", they cannot be contested. Beyond those constitutional clauses, there are wide-ranging conventions which we assume others in the polity will abide by. Böckenförde underlined time and again the fact that legal provisions are only as strong as the democratic culture that sustains them. No democratic state can create or uphold "the implicit agreement about those things that cannot be voted upon" by means of coercion. In his widely quoted 1967 thesis "The liberal secularized state is sustained by conditions it cannot itself secure," he pointed to the problem that the contemporary democratic state, as a necessarily secularized state, cannot resort to imposing certain values or worldviews on its citizens without undermining the very liberalism on which it is founded. The rule of law and democratic procedures, so Böckenförde, cannot be sustained in the long term unless they are carried out by people who consider themselves part of the same demos and work towards a shared democratic culture.

As an inner-Catholic critic, Böckenförde spent significant energies early in his career to show how the Catholic church's practices of embracing the democratic process to further its own worldviews (e.g., calling from the pulpit on voters to elect particular candidates, trying (unsuccessfully) to meddle in the curriculum of state schools), had undermined the ability of Catholic believers to open themselves fully to democratic citizenship. A democratic culture, to Böckenförde, significantly depends on citizens' ability and desire to work across religious, economic and political divides to create a we-consciousness, to find agreement on those things that lie beyond the ballot box and motivate citizens to work towards the *common* good, not to prioritize the interests of particular groups if that went at the cost of other citizens' rights.

A state that is not neutral in religious and other worldviews by definition favours those sharing the worldview such a state promotes and is therefore, in the ultimate analysis, incompatible with democratic politics. But a state that *is* neutral in religious and other worldviews need not impose a strict separation between religion and state, as some of the world's constitutions do. Instead, it may be based on an open or amicable separation of politics and religion, which does not prioritize freedom from religion at the cost of freedom to religion. Precisely because of the neutrality of the state in religious matters, it is important to be as sensitive to positive freedom of religion as to negative freedom. For this reason, for example, Böckenförde rejects headscarf bans for teachers.

With his view that a secular state need not insist on the privatization of religion, but instead can and should still find space for religion in public life (as long as this does not violate the state's neutrality), Böckenförde's conception of a secular state features certain overlaps with that of the Indian political theorist Rajeev Bhargava. Both believe in certain forms of accommodation and both recognize that different religions require different arrangements.

Different from Bhargava, Böckenförde would not only argue that the state is *empowered* to interfere in cases of discrimination that are undertaken in the name of religion (as Bhargava does), but that the state is indeed *required* to do so. Böckenförde would also not share Bhargava's view that the administration of religious personal law by the state is compatible with democratic politics and human rights, unless citizens are able to easily opt out of religious law without facing potential political, social, economic, or cultural disadvantages. In the end, Böckenförde's view of the democratic state is one in which the equal rights of citizens are not up for debate or relativization, while Bhargava's views leave open arrangements of religious autonomy which are likely to shield these religions from state intrusion even if they discriminate on the basis of religion, class/caste, ethnicity, or gender.

This difference between the two stems in no small part from the fact that, in the final analysis, Böckenförde is a theorist of freedom rather than belonging: "One's own freedom can be defended only as part of the general freedom," he wrote in 2007. Arguments for rights and freedoms framed in the context of a particular community can only be sustainable in the long term if one is willing to grant these same rights and freedoms to other communities in the same political space.

As Böckenförde tried to show in his article on "German Catholicism in 1933", Germany learnt this lesson the hard way. His comment on religious freedom can be applied also to issues of diversity: All rights in a functioning democracy must be mutual, for "a legal principle that seeks to exclude this mutuality is not a legal principle but a power principle."

Acknowledgments Parts of this text draw on Künkler and Stein (2017a), and Künkler and Stein (2018a). The authors thank Vineet Thakur for excellent comments, and Mirjam Künkler thanks the Center for Law as Culture in Bonn for providing her with an inspiring and convivial intellectual environment where parts of this text were written.

References

Berman, B. J., Bhargava, R., & Laliberté, A. (Eds.). (2013). *Secular states and religious diversity*. Vancouver: University of British Columbia Press.

Bhargava, R. (2006). The distinctiveness of Indian Secularism. In T. N. Srinivasan (Ed.), *The future of secularism* (pp. 20–53), Oxford University Press.

Bhargava, R. (2011). States, religious diversity, and the crisis of secularism. In *OpenDemocracy*. Retrieved March 22, 2011, from http://www.opendemocracy.net/rajeev-bhargava/states-religious-diversity-and-crisis-of-secularism-0.

Bhargava, R. (2016). Is European secularism secular enough? In Jean Cohen & Cécile Laborde (Eds.), *Religion, secularism, and constitutional democracy* (pp. 157–181). New York: Columbia University Press.

Böckenförde, E.-W. (1957). Das Ethos der modernen Demokratie und die Kirche. *Hochland, 50*(1), 4–19.

Böckenförde, E.-W. (1958). Noch einmal: Das Ethos der modernen Demokratie. *Hochland*, *50*(5), 409–421.

Böckenförde, E.-W. (1961). German Catholicism in 1933. *Cross Currents, 11,* 283–304.

Böckenförde, E.-W. (1964). *Die Organisationsgewalt im Bereich der Regierung. Eine Untersuchung zum Staatsrecht der Bundesrepublik Deutschland.* Berlin: Duncker & Humblot.

Böckenförde, E.-W. (1964/1965). Religionsfreiheit als Aufgabe der Christen. Gedanken eines Juristen zu den Diskussionen auf dem Zweiten Vatikanischen Konzil. In *Stimmen der Zeit, 90*(9), 199–212.

Böckenförde, E.-W. (1970). The Basic Right of Freedom of Conscience. In Böckenförde, E.-W. (2020). *Religion, Law, and Democracy: Selected Writings*. M. Künkler, & T. Stein (Eds.). Oxford: Oxford University Press.

Böckenförde, E.-W. (1973). Kirchliches Naturrecht und politisches Handeln. In F. Böckle & E.-W. Böckenförde (Eds.), *Naturrecht in der Kritik* (pp. 96–125). Mainz: Matthias-Grünewald-Verlag.

Böckenförde, E.-W. (1978). *Der Staat als sittlicher Staat*. Berlin: Duncker & Humblot.

Böckenförde, E.-W. (1981). Ethische und politische Grundsatzfragen zur Zeit. In *Herder Korrespondenz*, Heft 7, Juli 1981, pp. 342–348.

Böckenförde, E.-W. (1988). *Schriften zu Staat, Gesellschaft, Kirche*, Bd. I: Der deutsche Katholizismus im Jahre 1933. Kirche und demokratisches Ethos. Freiburg: Herder Verlag.

Böckenförde, E.-W. (1993). Rechtsstaat. In J. Ritter, & K. Gründer (Eds.), *Historisches Wörterbuch der Philosophie* (Bd. 8, pp. 332–342). Basel/Stuttgart: Schwabe.

Böckenförde, E.-W. (1995). Staatliches Recht und sittliche Ordnung. In H. Fechtrup, F. Schulze, T. Sternberg (Eds.), *Aufklärung durch Tradition. Symposion der Josef Pieper Stiftung zum 90. Geburtstag von Josef Pieper* (pp. 87–107). Münster: LiT-Verlag.

Böckenförde, E.-W. (2001). *Recht, Sittlichkeit, Toleranz*. Ulm: Humboldt Studienzentrum.

Böckenförde, E.-W. (2003). Die Würde des Menschen war unantastbar. In *Frankfurter Allgemeine Zeitung* (FAZ), 204, 03.09.2003, (pp. 33–35).

Böckenförde, E.-W. (2007a). Bekenntnisfreiheit in einer pluralen Gesellschaft. In Ernst-Wolfgang Böckenförde: *Kirche und christlicher Glaube in den Herausforderungen der Zeit. Beiträge zur politisch-theologischen Verfassungsgeschichte 1957–2002*, 2nd ed. LiT-Verlag.

Böckenförde, E.-W. (2007b). *Der säkularisierte Staat. Sein Charakter, seine Rechtfertigung und seine Probleme im 21*. Jahrhundert, Munich: C.F. v. Siemens Stiftung.

Böckenförde, E.-W. (2009). Freiheit ist ansteckend. *die tageszeitung*, p. 4.

Böckenförde, E.-W. (2010). *Vom Ethos der Juristen*. Berlin: Duncker & Humblot.

Böckenförde, E.-W. (2017). *Constitutional and Political Theory: Selected Writings*. M. Künkler, & T. Stein (Eds.), Oxford: Oxford University Press.

Böckenförde, E.-W. (2020). *Religion, Law, and Democracy: Selected Writings*. M. Künkler, & T. Stein (Eds.). Oxford: Oxford University Press.

Brunner, O., Conze, W., & Koselleck, R. (1978). Organ, Organismus, Organisation, politischer Körper. In *Geschichtliche Grundbegriffe. Historisches Lexikon zur politisch-sozialen Sprache in Deutschland* (Vol. 4, pp. 561–622). Stuttgart: Klett-Cotta.

Buve, S., (Ed.). (1967). *Säkularisation und Utopie; Ernst Forsthoff zum 65. Geburtstag*. Stuttgart: Kohlhammer, Series: Ebracher Studien.

Eisgruber, C. L., & Sager L. G. (2010). *Religious Freedom and the Constitution*, Harvard University Press.

Enders, C., & Masing, J., (Eds.). (2006). *Freiheit des Subjekts und Organisation von Herrschaft. Symposium zu Ehren von Ernst-Wolfgang Böckenförde anlässlich seines 75. Geburtstages* (Der Staat, Beiheft 17). Berlin: Duncker & Humblot.

Falk, J. (2006). *Freiheit als politisches Ziel. Grundmodelle liberalen Denkens bei Kant, Hayek und Böckenförde*. Frankfurt a. M.: Campus.

Grawert, R. (Ed.). (1995). *Offene Staatlichkeit: Festschrift für Ernst-Wolfgang Böckenförde zum 65*. Geburtstag, Berlin: Duncker & Humblot.

Große Kracht, H.-J., & Große Kracht, K. (Eds.). (2014). *Religion - Recht - Republik. Studien zu Ernst-Wolfgang Böckenförde*. Paderborn: Schöningh.

Hailbronner, M. (2017). Transformative Constitutionalism: Not only in the global South. *American Journal of Comparative Law, 65*(3), 527–565.

Hegel, G. W. F. (1959). *Vorlesungen zur Philosophie der Religion* [1821–31] (Vol. 2, p. 2017). Stuttgart: Glockner.

Heller, H. (1992 [1928]). Politische Demokratie und soziale Homogenität. In Hermann H. (Ed.), *Gesammelte Werke*, 2nd edn. (Vol. II, pp. 421–433). Tübingen: Mohr Siebeck.

Künkler, M., & Shankar, S. (2018). Introduction: A Secular Age beyond the West. In M. Künkler, & J. Madeley, S. Shankar (Eds.), *A Secular Age beyond the West. Religion, Law and the State in Asia, the Middle East and North Africa* (pp. 1–32) Cambridge University Press.

Künkler, M., & Stein, T. (2017a). State, Law, and Constitution: Ernst-Wolfgang Böckenförde's Political and Legal Thought in Context. In Böckenförde, E.-W. (2017). *Constitutional and Political Theory: Selected Writings* (pp. 1–35). M. Künkler, & T. Stein (Eds.), Oxford: Oxford University Press.

Künkler, M., & Stein, T. (2017b). Böckenförde's Political Theory of the State. In Böckenförde, E.-W. (2017). *Constitutional and Political Theory: Selected Writings* (pp. 38–53). M. Künkler, & T. Stein (Eds.), Oxford: Oxford University Press.

Künkler, M., & Stein, T. (Eds.). (2018a). Ernst-Wolfgang Böckenförde on Law and Religion. *Oxford Journal of Law and Religion, 7*(1), 1–123.

Künkler, M., & Stein, T. (2018b). Ernst-Wolfgang Böckenförde: Inner-Catholic Critic and Advocate of Open Neutrality. *Oxford Journal of Law and Religion, 7*(1), 1–12.

Künkler, M., & Stein T. (Eds.). (2018c). Statism, Secularism, Liberalism–Ernst-Wolfgang Böckenförde beyond German Law. *German Law Journal, 19*(2), 137–460.

Künkler, M., & Stein T. (2018d). Statism, Secularism, Liberalism–Böckenförde's Contributions to German Staatsrechtslehre in the Light of Contemporary Challenges within and beyond the State. *German Law Journal, 19*(2), 137–160.

Künkler, M., & Stein, T. (Eds.). (2018e). Democratic Pluralism, Social Cohesion and Individual Ethos in the Secularized State—the Political Thought of Ernst-Wolfgang Böckenförde. *Constellations. An International Journal of Critical and Democratic Theory, 25*(2), 181–241.

Künkler, M., & Stein, T. (2018f). Carl Schmitt in Ernst-Wolfgang Böckenförde's work: Carrying Weimar constitutional theory into the Bonn Republic. *Constellations: An International Journal of Critical and Democratic Theory, 25*(2), 225–241.

Künkler, M., & Stein, T. (Eds.). (2020a). *Die Rezeption der Werke Ernst-Wolfgang Böckenfördes in international vergleichender Perspektive, Beihefte zu "Der Staat"*, Band 24, Duncker & Humblot (pp. 5–267).

Künkler, M., & Stein, T. (2020b). *Die Rezeption Ernst-Wolfgang Böckenfördes in international vergleichender Perspektive, Beihefte zu "Der Staat"*, Band 24, Duncker & Humblot, (pp. 9–30).

Künkler, M., & Stein, T. (2020c). Böckenförde on the Right to Life, Human Dignity, and its Metapositive Foundations. In Böckenförde, E.-W. (2020). *Religion, Law, and Democracy. Selected Writings*. (Mirjam Künkler and Tine Stein, eds.), Oxford University Press.

Manent, A.-F. (2018). Democracy and Religion in the Legal and Political Thought of Ernst-Wolfgang Böckenförde. *Oxford Journal of Law and Religion, 7*(1), 74–96.

Manterfeld, N. (2000). *Die Grenzen der Verfassung: Möglichkeiten limitierender Verfassungstheorie des Grundgesetzes am Beispiel E.-W. Böckenfördes.* Berlin: Duncker & Humblot.

Masing, J., & Wieland, J. (Eds.). (2011). *Menschenwürde–Demokratie–Christliche Gerechtigkeit. Tagungsband zum Festlichen Kolloquium aus Anlass des 80. Geburtstags von Ernst-Wolfgang Böckenförde*. Berlin: Duncker & Humblot.

Mehring, R., & Otto, M. (Eds.). (2014). *Voraussetzungen und Garantien des Staates. Ernst-Wolfgang Böckenfördes Staatsverständnis*. Nomos: Baden-Baden.

Müller, J.-W. (2018). What the Dictum really meant and what it might mean for us. *Constellations: An International Journal of Critical and Democratic Theory, 45*(2), 196–206.

Pavelka, P. (2015). *Bürger und Christ. Politische Ethik und christliches Menschenbild bei Ernst-Wolfgang Böckenförde.* Fribourg: Academic Press and Freiburg: Herder.

Sacksofsky, U. (2018). Ernst-Wolfgang Böckenförde's Oeuvre on Religious Freedom applied to recent Decisions of the European Court of Human Rights. In *German Law Journal, 19*(2) (Special issue—Statism, Secularism, Liberalism Ernst-Wolfgang Böckenförde Beyond Germany) 301–320.

Stepan, A. C. (2001). The World's Religious Systems and Democracy: Crafting the Twin Tolerations. In A. C. Stepan (Ed.), *Arguing Comparative Politics* (pp. 213–253), New York: Oxford University Press.

Wahl, R., & Wieland, J. (Eds.). (2002). *Das Recht des Menschen in der Welt. Kolloquium aus Anlass des 70. Geburtstages von Ernst-Wolfgang Böckenförde*. Berlin: Duncker & Humblot.

Mirjam Künkler (Ph.D. Political Science Columbia University) is Research Professor at the Netherlands Institute for Advanced Study. Her books include *Democracy and Islam in Indonesia* (with Alfred Stepan), Columbia University Press, 2013; *A Secular Age Beyond the West* (with John Madeley and Shylashri Shankar), Cambridge University Press, 2018; *Female Religious Authority in Shi'i Islam: Past and Present* (with Devin Stewart), Edinburgh University Press, 2020; *The Rule of Law and the Politics of the Judiciary in Contemporary Iran* (with Hadi Enayat), Cambridge University Press, 2020. She used to teach Near Eastern Studies at Princeton University for many years, where she also co-directed the Luce Program on "Religion and International Affairs". She sits in the editorial boards of international journals in comparative politics, Islamic Studies, the Sociology of Religion, and Law.

Tine Stein (Dr. phil. University of Cologne, Habilitation Free University Berlin) is Professor of Political Theory and the History of Ideas at the University of Göttingen. Among her research interests are the democratic constitutional state and its normative bases, the relation between politics, law and religion, as well as the relation between politics and nature. She is a member of the Supervisory Board of the Heinrich-Böll-Stiftung and of the scientific advisory council of the publication series "Notions of the State" (Staatsverständnisse) of Nomos Publishers. Her publications include *Himmlische Quellen und irdisches Recht*, Campus: Frankfurt 2007; *Endlichkeit. Zur Vergänglichkeit und Begrenztheit von Mensch, Natur und Gesellschaft*, ed. with Anja Franke-Schwenk and Andreas Bihrer, transcript: Bielefeld 2016; *Recht und Politik. Das Staatsverständnis von Ulrich K. Preuß*, ed. with Claudio Franzius, Nomos: Baden-Baden 2015.

Chapter 5
Constitutional Democracy and Indian Secularism: Considerations from the Perspective of Democratic Antinomies

Oliver Hidalgo

Abstract Regarding the relationship between religion and politics, this article is based on a conception of democracy as a permanent struggle of contradicting and thus conflicting principles. This complex structure of antinomies stretches a discursive framework within which we can differentiate legitimate political demands from extreme ones being incompatible with a democratic constitution. Furthermore, as getting unequal attention in different cultures and societies, these principles help us to understand the coexistence of diverse—Western and Non-Western—but not less available and legitimate political directions as well as to estimate their contributions to theory and practice of democracy. Against this background, the contribution supports Rajeev Bhargava's interpretation of Indian secularism. Concerning the complex relationship between religion and politics, Bhargava's analysis works as an indication and illustration of how to meet this challenge as it can be interpreted as an accurate balance of conflicting principles the approach of democratic antinomies extracts on the scale of religion and democracy.

5.1 Introduction

A constructive comparison between constitutional democracy in Germany or Europe on the one hand and India on the other first of all benefits from an unbiased point of view. It enables the estimation of Western and Non-Western contributions to theory and practice of democracy as widely equitable attempts to realize a complex political idea without neglecting the integrity of the concept of democracy itself. In this respect, my contribution wants to show to what extent we have to understand democracy basically as a permanent struggle between contradicting, and therefore conflicting principles such as plurality versus social harmony, liberty versus equality, individual and collective claims. These principles, because of getting quite unequal

O. Hidalgo (✉)
Department of Politics, University of Münster, Münster, Germany
e-mail: Oliver.Hidalgo@politik.uni-regensburg.de

University of Regensburg, Regensburg, Germany

© Springer Nature Singapore Pte Ltd. 2020
A. Roy and M. Becker (eds.), *Dimensions of Constitutional Democracy*,
https://doi.org/10.1007/978-981-15-3899-5_5

attention within different cultures and societies, might help us to explain why Western and Non-Western democracies are (and must be) similar and dissimilar at the same time. Against this background, we may not only gain a sound basis to compare the characteristics and peculiarities of German/European and Indian democracy concerning a crucial aspect as religion but also consider a very general discernment from political theory and the history of political thought: that it is among the most important features of democracy to offer a wide scope of options that different countries and societies could use in order to develop their own and particular convergences to the universal conception of democracy without falling in danger to become arbitrary.

My main argument concerning the theory of democracy is that the abovementioned conflicting principles constitute democracy as a complex structure of *antinomies*. These antinomies stretch a discursive framework that can function as a measure to distinguish legitimate political struggles from extreme political demands exceeding the limits of democracy, in particular regarding the general relationship between democracy and religion. Hence, on the basis of the concept of democratic antinomies, we can differentiate these (religious or political) positions which are compatible with a *democratic constitution* from those which are incompatible with the authentic institutionalization of democracy. Proceeding from this theoretical framework, I want to reconstruct as well as to discuss especially the thesis of Rajeev Bhargava estimating the Indian idea and practice of secularism as a convenient paradigm for religious accommodation which accepts a public role of religion in politics and society without going beyond the necessary boundaries of a democratic constitution. To demonstrate this, I will go forward in three steps: first, I want to introduce my antinomic theory of democracy which I take from the Western history of political thought (Chap. 2); second, I will show what this theory generally implies with regard to the relationship between democracy, politics and religion (Chap. 3); and third, I am going to underpin why Rajeev Bhargava's particular approach to secular democracy in India can be seen as a possible interpretation of religious accommodation under the democratic antinomies approach (Chap. 4).

5.2 A Theory of Democracy in the Light of Western History of Political Thought

In different times and spaces of history, the concept of democracy has been associated with some very opposing ideas. Thus, the countless patterns, (sub-)types and varieties of democratic decision-making processes have led at least to the common distinctions between liberal and republican, direct and representative, consensus and majoritarian,[1] market and social democracies, as well as to the appearance of special participatory, deliberative, grassroots and agonistic forms or to the opposition between Western and Non-Western democracy (e.g. Eisenstadt 1999; Cunningham

[1] For this distinction see particularly Lijphart (1999), Chaps. 2 and 3.

2002; Dunn 2005; Held 2006; Tilly 2007; Diamond 2008; Schmidt 2010). Nevertheless, this observation should not confirm the popular prejudice that democracy can mean 'everyone and everything' (Sartori 1992, p. 11). Instead, the evident coexistence of many divergent democratic systems suggests that democracy itself might consist of significant paradoxes, aporias and contradictions. In fact, the conceptual history of democracy proves that the overwhelming success of the concept is most of all due to its ability to subsume very contrary ideas and realities under its semantic field, whereas each antithetical component implies a similar level of legitimacy:

- liberty versus equality (1)
- representation versus popular sovereignty (2)
- the principles of quality and quantity concerning democratic decision-making (3)
- plurality versus social homogeneity (4)
- individual versus collective claims (5), and, finally,
- universality versus particularity (6).[2]

Actually, a lot can be said about each of these six democratic antinomies. However, merely a brief sketch of my relevant theoretical considerations is possible in this context. Most of all, it has to be explained why liberty and equality remain contradictory although liberal doctrines as these ones by Ronald Dworkin (Dworkin 1981a, b; 1987), Rawls (1971) and others usually claim to combine both ideals as the ineluctable normative fundament of democracy. Nonetheless, a 'real' or 'essential' equality could only be achieved by repression because a free society must necessarily evoke social differences, inequalities and hierarchies. That is also why liberals tend to reduce equality to a political or legal *status* and give priority to liberty, while social democrats conversely prefer equality against liberty. Indeed, democracy means both liberty *and* equality, but on the other hand there is a never-ending struggle between the *left* and the *right* political camp for the necessary extensions and boundaries of both concepts and also the adequate balance of them. The same may be said about the rather evident antinomies between people's sovereignty and representation, individual rights, and collective duties, or also the quantitative principles of participation and majority rule on the one hand and the need for qualitative or normative measures to guarantee a particular output of political decision-making on the other. Democracy always means *both* and is only 'complete' if not neglecting any one of these components, although it is very obvious that democracy is not able to solve the inevitable and consequential tensions and paradoxes.

[2]For a comprehensive theoretical and genealogic reconstruction of these six pairs of conflicting principles as pillars of a discursive framework of democracy see Hidalgo (2014), Chap. 3. Most relevant to prove and to illustrate the antinomic character of democracy are the works of Alexis de Tocqueville (liberty vs. equality), Jean-Jacques Rousseau, Joseph Schumpeter and Benjamin Barber (people's sovereignty vs. representation), Hans Kelsen, Claude Lefort, Jacques Rancière, Jacques Derrida, Niklas Luhmann (quantity vs. quality), Carl Schmitt, Hermann Heller (homogeneity vs. heterogeneity), John Rawls, Robert Nozick, Michael Sandel, Charles Taylor, Michael Walzer, Richard Rorty (individual rights vs. collective claims), Friedrich Nietzsche, Jean-François Lyotard, Gayatri Spivak and Ernesto Laclau (universality vs. particularity).

Hence, since current democratic systems (have to) show high affinities to all of these norms and principles, we can state that democracy basically means nothing else but the juxtaposition of disparate characteristics that can be deduced from the aforementioned opposites: liberal society *and* social state (1); the influence of lobby groups *and* the principle *one man, one vote*; the legislative power of parliaments *and* public debates, elections or referenda (2); majority rule *and* the rule of law (3); the pluralism of opinions or lifestyles *and* a collective identity of the people (4); civil rights *and* the duty of solidarity (5); and last but not least, the paradox that every democracy is both similar and dissimilar to other democracies because of reflecting always a *particula*r will of the people (6).

The keyword that can conceptually grasp these special characteristics of all democracies is as already stated 'antinomy'. With the concept of democratic antinomies, we are able to state that democracy consists of several unsolvable contradictions. Moreover, it is due to its antinomies that democracy shapes an infinite number of disagreements, disputes and conflicts, since there is never the one and only democratic position but at least a few alternatives on how a particular question can be treated and decided. In addition, the democratic antinomies stretch a unique framework in which different political decisions are available by emphasis, for example, liberty *against* equality, the individual *against* the community, quality *against* quantity or vice versa. As long as these political demands show respect for the (normatively equivalent and only temporarily renounced) other side of the opposition, the democratic character of the political process or debate is maintained *in toto*. The latter is the case if a political demand or decision does not abolish or *sublate*[3] the opposition itself by pursuing extreme objectives or denying the general entitlement of opposing views. Therefore, democracy means also a permanent struggle to bring or to keep its extremes into a dynamic balance.

With regard to the history of democratic theory, the democratic antinomies approach confirms—on the one hand—Gallie's (1956) classical statement that *democracy*—like *justice* or *arts*—is among the 'essentially contested concepts' which lack some unique standards for both a commonly accepted definition and a consistent discursive practice. On the other hand, the concept of democracy shows at least clear contours of its boundaries, which means that it is unmistakable what all controversies within democracy are about. Consequently, the democratic antinomies approach is against both a minimal concept of democracy[4] and the idea that the concept of democracy is only 'boundary contested' (Lord 2004, p. 12). Proceeding from this assumption, I will attempt to demonstrate henceforth why the democratic antinomies approach is able to guidę us, for instance, in order to understand the complex relationship between democracy and religion.

---

[3]Accordingly, Hegel's philosophical concept of *sublation* designates an alternative draft to the democratic antinomies approach. Instead of overcoming the stages of conflicting democratic principles in order to emerge a higher rational unity, democracy stands and falls with the maintenance of its intractable contradictions.

[4]As is generally known, we can find such a minimalist institutional and procedural conception of (liberal and pluralistic) democracy in the works of Robert A. Dahl. See Dahl (1971, 1989, and 1998).

5.3 Politics and Religion in the Shadow of Democratic Antinomies

The orientation we can draw from the democratic antinomies approach to evaluate both the risks and chances of religion in modern societies basically follows the three deep tensions between quality and quantity (3), plurality and collective identity (4) and between individual rights and community responsibilities (5).[5] In line with this, we can figure that religion and religious convictions might support each of these opposing sides of democracy but likewise be directed against each one. While in democracy, religious freedom belongs to the fundamental rights of the individual, it can be seen at the same time as a bulwark against individualism, and therefore as an important resource for social capital, solidarity and collective duties (5) (Bellah et al. 1985; Putnam 2000). Furthermore, the empirical plurality of religions in modern societies could be estimated as both an authentic expression of the rule of the (heterogeneous) people *and* a serious threat to social harmony or the necessary *overlapping consensus* (4) (Rawls1993, pp. 134–149). Finally, a political role of religion in democratic societies possibly means a qualitative boundary of majority rule and people's sovereignty by strengthening human dignity, but—on the other hand—a majority rule dominated by religion/a certain religious community may also become a huge problem for minority rights and the inviolability of the person (3). The latter one is also called the 'commitment problem in emerging democracies' (Kalyvas 2000), since it is uncertain if a religious party, once in power, will subject itself to democratic control anyway if having complied with the emerging democratic order before.

Apparently, it depends on the matters and modalities of *how* religion and politics are combined, whether religion implies a risk or rather a chance for democracy. As a matter of course, this is the reason why—since the era of Western enlightenment—an institutional and mental separation of state and church is assumed as inevitable precondition of all democracies. However, due to the fact that a religious community is never an only private association but always an organization with political impact, the liberal idea to divorce the religious from the political sphere in a very strict sense, remains just a fiction. Instead, *the twin tolerations* argument by Stepan (2001) that democracy requires religious leaders to accept the authority of elected officials, while, in return, state authorities have to allow both freedom of private religious worship and democratic participation of religious groups in civil and political society, is rather

[5]This statement does not involve an irrelevance of the three further antinomies—liberty versus equality (1), people's sovereignty versus the political principle of representation (2) and universality versus particularity (6)—in this context. Instead, it should be evident that religion can function as both a legitimation of natural law and gender hierarchy *and* a transcendental confirmation of social and democratic equality (1). The same ambivalence can be observed concerning the role of religion as an entitlement of universal values *and* as an eventual fundament for a kind of segregating religious identity (6). At last, the main challenge for every religious accommodation in democracy is the imperative to refer to the (ethical) authority of religion only in a way that does not violate the validity of people's (political) sovereignty (2). However, since all of these additional aspects are deeply linked with the subsequently discussed issues, the selected focus is supposed to be justified.

adequate to correspond with the complexity of religion and politics in democratic systems.

Even beyond arguing with the general need for twin tolerations, the democratic antinomies offer us a concrete benchmark for judging the various connections between religion and politics we are observing. Since in democracy the necessary arrangement between the adherents of different religions includes 'non-believers' in the religious sense, there is not only a peaceful coexistence of different religious communities at stake. In consolidated democracies, there is, in fact, a balance between the plurality and conflicting interests of religious and secular groups on the one hand and—on the other hand—the general consensus that the results of democratic struggles and the procedures of democratic decision-making have to be accepted not only by the superior but also by the inferior: Because democracy *is* conflict, but only a kind of conflict that shows respect to the interests of *all* citizens and does not degenerate into a 'tyranny of majority' in the sense of James Madison, Alexis de Tocqueville, and John Stuart Millor a hegemony of one (religious) group over the other(s) (3). Hence, if a shared foundation of values and a common democratic identity are missed, the hasty implementation of elections would even force existing ethnic, cultural, social and religious antagonisms, as Paul Collier has pointed out in his book *War, Guns, and Votes. Democracy in Dangerous Places* (2009). This relevant *synchronicity* between consensus and conflict in democracy (4) is supplemented by an additional balance between the individual right to belief—what one person thinks is true—and the right of the community to define such boundaries of religious freedom in order to prevent the trust in God and in the truth of revelation from undermining democratic principles as people's sovereignty and the rule of law (5).

As a preliminary result, we can state that democratic antinomies are able to function as a criterion for distinguishing these connections between religion and politics as far as they are compatible with democracy (e.g. religion as a pre-political resource for guiding citizens in civil society; civil religion; religious parties on the basis of the democratic constitution and the rule of law) from those not being compatible (e.g. theocracy, God's political sovereignty and religious governance; political religion in the sense of Voegelin (1938/1996) and Aron (1944) and others). Moreover, with the application of the democratic antinomies approach, it is not only possible to rate and to classify these political systems dominated by religion which are apparently anti-democratic but also to become aware of much more differentiated processes revealing the dangerous and sometimes suicidal tendencies of democracy itself. Hence, the criterion to make a distinction between authentic democracies and only superficial ones is always the question if the antinomic character within the range of democratic principles is respected or denied and if the affinity of a political system to these opposing principles is balanced or just one-sided.

In rethinking the analytical and normative framework of democracy based on the conceptual measure of democratic antinomies, it becomes also plausible to understand why it is still an open question for all Western (and Non-Western) democratic theory and political practice if and where required—to what extent secularism is or is not a precondition for the implementation of a democratic constitution. In this regard, we are able to observe very different ideas and conceptions of secularism in Western societies: the *laïcité* in France, the state churches in England and Scandinavian countries as Norway, Sweden, Denmark and Iceland, the strict institutional separation of religion and politics in former British colonies as the United States of America, Canada, Australia and New Zealand, the only partial separation between state and church in consensus democracies as Germany, Austria, Belgium and Switzerland and many further hybrid models (for instance, in Spain, Italy and Portugal).[6] This empirical variation reflects and suggests that—although the theory of democracy usually demands the neutrality of the state in religious matters—there is actually no one and clear democratic principle to organize and to institutionalize the relationship between religion and politics, state and church. Instead, in order to solve this problem, Western societies apparently use the wide range of options offered by the conflicting, antinomic principles of democracy by stressing *either* the political role of religions for the community *or* the (negative) freedom of individuals (5); *either* the need for a public consensus supported by religions as a resource of moral orientation *or* vice versa the plurality of values and religious convictions (4); and last but not least *either* the quality of religion to define (universal) metaphysical boundaries to the democratic power of disposition *or*, in contrast, the specific role of majority religions to shape the 'national character' of one country and to designate a (particular) common identity that is usually directed against immigrant and minority groups who belong to a different religious association (3). Proceeding from this, it is very relevant to enter a higher level of comparison now, and therefore to ask about the role of religion in Non-Western countries. By doing so, we are probably able to confirm the thesis that the democratic antinomies approach does not only provide categories to understand the diversity of Western democracies but also the parallel conformities *and* differences between Western and Non-Western democracies.

5.4 The Case of India: Secular Democracy and Religious Accommodation?

To give one example of the relevance of democratic antinomies in order to operationalize the comparability of Western and Non-Western democracies, I will refer to Rajeev Bhargava's interpretation of Indian secularism and its possible relevance for Western societies. In an essay published in 2006 in a volume concerning the *future of secularism* in India, Bhargava (2006, p. 20) discussed the 'distinctiveness' of secular reality in India. In the original paper first presented in 2004 at the Political Theory Colloquium at Queens University in Kingston, Bhargava (2010, p. 63) called Indian secularism rather precisely as both an 'alternative' to Western theory and practice of secularism *and* a 'trans-cultural ideal'.

---

[6]An overview of the various state–church relations in Western democracies is presented in Minkenberg (2003).

The umbrella of Bhargava's argument consists of three major preliminaries: First, with the term 'distinctiveness', Bhargava does not have a 'unique' form of secularism in India in mind. For Bhargava (2010, p. 65), the 'elementary formal constituents of secularism are the same throughout the world', which leads him to the following definition: 'Broadly speaking, secularism, anywhere in the world, means a separation of organized religion from organized political power, inspired by a specific set of values'. In this respect, the distinctiveness of Indian secularism implies just a specific and interestingly different way of interpreting and relating the basic constituents of secularism. Indeed, this is why the distinctive character of Indian secularism does not make it non-universalizable at the same time. The second preliminary emphasizes that secularism is not a 'doctrine with a fixed content' but 'has multiple interpretations which change over time'. In consequence, there are both Western and Non-Western contributions to secularism, whereby 'the secular idea has developed over time transnationally'. In this regard, Bhargava (2010, p. 67) thinks that today 'secularism in the single-religion societies of the west is beginning to be challenged not only from religious believers within but also from recently emigrated believers of other religions. This new multi-religiosity is threatening to throw western secularism into turmoil'. As a result, the 'constitutional history of India' with its special way of secularism traditionally dealing with the plurality of religions and never being 'understood to mean the blanket exclusion of religion from the state' might have the supplemental 'potential to shape the future of western secularism' (ibid., p. 68). However, the third and last preliminary ultimately insists: 'In India everything has begun to be seen in terms of an irritatingly dichotomous grid that divides the social world into two groups, the western modern and the indigenous traditional'. This had led into a certain (and completely wrong) 'pattern' of thinking: 'If secularism is modern, they believe, then it must be western' (ibid.). In contrast to this, Bhargava considers Indian secularism as a particular alternative to the Western understanding of the secular with the potential of being a paradigm for Europe in the future.

At the end of his essay, Bhargava (2010, pp. 96–105) returns to these three preliminaries stressing that the Indian model of secularism has hitherto been underestimated. In between, he develops his argument, explaining what makes Indian secularism so remarkable:

> Indian secularism is distinguished from other versions by five features. First, its explicit multi-value character. Second, the idea of principled distance that is poles apart from one-sided exclusion, mutual exclusion and strict neutrality. Third, its commitment to a different model of moral reasoning that is highly contextual and opens up the possibility of multiple secularisms, of different societies working out their own secularisms. Fourth, it uniquely combines an active hostility to some aspects of religion with an equally active respect for its other dimensions. Finally, it is the only secularism that I know that attends simultaneously to issues of intra-religious oppression and inter-religious domination. In my view, these are path-breaking features of any model of secularism. (Bhargava 2010, p. 69)

With regard to these five features, I will not go into detail now. What should be evident, is that Bhargava appreciates the political role of religions in India instead of both demanding a strict 'wall of separation' between religion and politics along the lines of the US model *and* underestimating the dangers of a too deep intertwining, that is, a mutual alliance between both spheres. According to his view, a secular state that ends all religious hegemony, (intra-religious) oppression and (inter-religious) domination must not be confused with a completely unpolitical role of religion and a denying of its politically positive dimensions. Concerning this matter, he ascertains that anti-religious secular states are in danger of turning into amoral states that usually are imperial and autocratic (ibid., p. 76). Moreover, it should be added that the multi-value-character that is mentioned to describe the 'distinctiveness' of Indian secularism is formed by several coherent normative pillars: peace with justice and toleration, religious liberty, citizenship identification, passive citizenship benefits (as physical security, a minimum of material well-being or privacy) and, lastly, active citizenship rights that demonstrate the recognition of all citizens as equal participants in the public domain (ibid., p. 77–79). The guarantee of these characteristic values is assumed to distinguish India even from those states that have formally established multiple religions and churches, since this might support peace, toleration and also equality between all religious communities but fail to secure the same for non-religious people as well as non-religious liberties of all individuals (ibid, p. 73). Thus, it is up to a secular state to separate religion and politics 'for the sake of extensive' or even a maximum of 'religious liberty and equality of citizenship' (ibid, p. 83).

Proceeding from these assumptions, it becomes clear why Bhargava does not only argue against a *theocracy* (that is a state that has a union with a particular religious order)[7] or against states with a singular or multiple constitutional *establishments* of religions or churches (which means that one or several religions or churches are officially granted and legally recognized but without the sacerdotal order being able to govern). Apart from that, Bhargava polemizes against an anti-religious secular state, since he assumes religion as an important source to shape citizenship identification and to function as a normative basis of political culture and activity as well as religious liberty as a fundamental individual (and collective) right[8] that would not be ensured under anti-religious conditions. Instead, he prefers a 'value-based secular

[7]For Bhargava (2010, p. 70), a rather accurate definition of theocracy would be a 'state' that 'is governed by what it claims are divine laws directly administered by a priestly order claiming divine commission'. As major historical examples of such (anti-democratic) theocracies, he mentions ancient Israel, certain Buddhist regimes in Japan and China, the Geneva of John Calvin, the Papal States and the Islamic Republic of Iran. Moreover, Bhargava refers to the *Catholic Encyclopaedia of Religion* and its idea of theocracy 'as a form of political government in which the deity directly rules the people or as the rule of priestly caste'. In this sense, the political rule of Brahmins in India in accordance with the Dharmashastras could be called 'theocratic' (ibid., no. 3).

[8]In this context, Bhargava (2010, p. 77f.) distinguishes three important dimensions of religious liberty in a secular state: first, the (intra-religious) right 'to criticize, revise, or challenge' dominant interpretations of a religious heritage; second, that such religious liberty 'is granted non-preferentially to all members of every religious community'; and third, that all 'individuals are free not only to criticize the religion into which they are born, but at the very extreme, to reject it and further, given ideal conditions of deliberation, to freely embrace another religion or to remain without one'. Particularly, the last condition is identified as the main problem in states with multiple establishments of religions or churches.

state' which shows disconnections between state and religion at three levels—political objectives, institutions and public policy—without neglecting that—especially at the third level—there is some space for a not strictly privatized role of religion in democracy (ibid., p. 75). For Bhargava, the paradigm for such a value-based secular state with a just 'principled' distance from religion beyond strict neutrality or a one-sided exclusion of religion[9] can be observed in India. To grasp this given model, he presents a chart which implicitly illustrates the difference of Indian secularism from all contemporary theocracies (as the Islamic Republic of Iran or the monarchy in Saudi Arabia) as well as to all states with established religions or with only partial institutional disconnections (as, for instance, Germany and Great Britain) and also from anti-religious secular states as the former Soviet Union (Table. 5.1).[10]

The table confirms that—for Bhargava—only the last model of a 'value-based secular state' fulfills all normative requirements on an optimal state-religion order, whereas an anti-religious (and anti-democratic) secular state usually lacks all dimensions of religious liberty as well as a sufficient citizenship identification and active citizenship rights. States with formal multiple establishments of religions and churches (and we could have Germany in mind as an example for this) are quite close to this reference point but nevertheless show one decisive difference: the citizenship identification of non-dominant groups, of religious minorities, atheists, agnostics and sceptics, is supposed to be relatively weak. It is this reason which motivates Bhargava's conviction that Indian secularism might become the right answer to the challenges of multicultural societies in contemporary Europe.

Having presented this brief outline of Bhargava's theoretical approach, I will now attempt to translate his argument into the language of democratic antinomies. First of all, we are able to envisage the parallel validity of the conflicting norms *universality* and *particularity* (6) in Bhargava's considerations giving democracy a general normative orientation beyond cultural imperialism *and* cultural segregation. It is only because he integrated this evident contradiction (or antinomy) in his theoretical analysis, he could constructively combine the 'distinctiveness' and historical context of Indian secularism with its potential to become a universalizable and (trans-cultural) ideal.

Apart from that general association of conflicting principles, Bhargava's approach can be seen as an option to guarantee a maximum of liberty *and* equality (1) in the religious sphere which is supposed to be decisive for the whole democratic system, since 'liberty and equality in the religious sphere are all of a piece with liberty and equality in other spheres' (Bhargava 2010, p. 78). In other words, the

[9]'The idea of principled distance unpacks the metaphor of separation differently. It accepts a disconnection between state and religion at the level of ends and institutions but does not make a fetish of it at the third level of policy and law. [...] Does principled distance also entail that religion intervene in the affairs of the state? In some contexts, it may certainly do so. Religion may intervene in the affairs of the state if such intervention promotes freedom, equality, or any other value integral to secularism'. (Bhargava 2010, pp. 88, 91).

[10]For Bhargava (2010, p. 98f.), however, France does not embrace an anti-religious secular state but a state merely guiding its citizens by the value of 'equal citizenship' while neglecting the idea of secularism as a multi-value doctrine.

Table 5.1 Comparative moral evaluation of secular and religion-centred states

Values	Peace with justice	Religious liberty			Citizenship Identification			Passive citizenship benefits/rights			Active citizenship rights		
Form of state		Dominant groups		Others	Dominant groups		Others	Dominant groups		Others	Dominant groups		Others
		Elites	Others		Elites	Others		Elites	Others		Elites	Others	
Theocracy	A	P	A	A	P	A	A	P	A	A	A	A	A
States with substantive singular establishment	A	WP	A	A	P	P	A	P	A	A	A	A	A
States with substantive multiple establishment	WP	WP	A	WP	P	P	A	P	WP	A	A	A	A
States with formal singular establishment	P	P	P	P	P	P	A	P	P	P	P	P	P
States with formal multiple establishment	P	P	P	P	P	P	WP	P	P	P	P	P	P
Anti-religious secular state	A	A	A	A	P	A	A	P	P	P	A	A	A
Value-based secular state	P	P	P	P	P	P	P	P	P	P	P	P	P

Notes A-Absent; WP-Weakly Present; P-Present
Source Bhargava (2010), p. 82

relation of religion and politics is interpreted as *pars pro toto* of democracy: if liberty and equality are not realized in the religious sphere, this will provoke inequalities and illiberal practices in other spheres as well. In contrast to this, Bhargava'smulti-value secularism permits religious liberty and is likewise linked with the equality of free citizenship. Furthermore, Bhargava's approach can be reconstructed as an acceptance of *both* democratic sides or poles: the *individual* right (to believe or not to believe in a religious truth) *and* the enabling power of religion/religions as a resource for shared social responsibility (5); the plurality of (religious and non-religious values and liberties) *and* the need for a common citizenship identification and also a collective identity drawing upon political and religious convictions (4); the receiving of social state benefits (what means nothing else but to be entitled to remain in 'passive citizenship') and the opposite right (or also the duty) to play an active political role and participate in public discourses and projects (2); finally, the right of majority (and major religious groups) to dominate the political and religious discourse to a certain extent and, on the other hand, the rule of law giving the political and religious minorities the right to question and to criticize this (inter-religious) dominance or (intra-religious) oppression whenever they want to do it (3).[11]

Concerning the fourth and fifth democratic antinomies between plurality and social homogeneity, individual and collective claims, we could add further that Bhargava (2010, p. 85f.) definitely assumes religious identities and communities as a source of political conflicts that have to be tackled by democracy. Thus, the risks and dangers a political role of religions in democracy implies do not lead him to the opinion that there is a disaggregation of religious communities into collections of individuals or even a privatizing of religions necessary. Instead, he thinks that only a fairly equal status of religious communities is crucial for the consolidation of emerging democracies.

In sum, the multi-value set Bhargava identifies as the normative fundament of democracy in general and as an advantage of India's secular system, in particular, does represent—more or less—all the principles we have already identified to be the antinomies Western *and* Non-Western democracies are sharing. And although Bhargava sometimes uses different terms and concepts to evolve his theory of secular democracy, in essential, the (ambivalent) requirements and problems of democracy he addresses in his essay are quite the same as the six opposing normative poles of democracy we have discussed before.

Beyond Bhargava, we might merely stress that he is apparently convinced that the different norms and principles he amalgamates in order to frame democracy as a *multi-value structure* are able to coexist in a rather unproblematic manner. Unlike the democratic antinomies approach, he does not explicitly remark that these values and norms include significant problems, tensions, or even contradictions of democracy itself. But at least implicitly, he acts in concert with this. For instance, when he testifies his acceptance of religious liberty as a *collective* right and therefore a non-individualistic construal of religious liberty (Bhargava 2010, p. 85f.), he stops short of

[11]For the last issue, see once again Bhargava's statement to the first level of religious liberty which has been quoted in note 8.

forgetting that a certain de-politicization of religion is one of the favourite aims of the Indian constitution (ibid., p. 104). Another example that might be able to prove this is, when Bhargava (2010, p. 103) states it would be 'inappropriate to identify secularism with equal respect for all religions',[12] which includes a clear contradiction to some of his statements before and could only be explained by his neglect of essential tensions and oppositions between liberty and equality. Finally, we could (or should) also make it clearer than it has been expressed in Bhargava's essay that, at the end of the day, secular democracy is characterized by the contradictory coexistence of connections and disconnections, differentiations and linkages between religion and politics. This conclusively reveals the juxtaposition of religion and the secular as an important part of the antinomic comprehension of democracy in total. *Both*—the political dimension of religion *and* the secular differentiation and emancipation of the political from the religious sphere—belong to democracy. Ipso facto, this might be the best testimony for Bhargava's thesis that the relation of religion and politics in democracy could be seen as *pars pro toto* of the antinomic democracy itself.

5.5 Conclusion

In general, the democratic antinomies between liberty and equality (1), people's sovereignty and representation (2), quality and quantity (3), plurality and social homogeneity (4), individual and collective claims (5) on the one hand, and our example of religion and secularism in India on the other might enlighten one overarching acknowledgment: all of these conflicting principles irrevocably lead to democracy's main contradiction between universality and particularity (6). In this respect, it can be illustrated that the polarity between Western and Non-Western concepts is a completely consistent result of the historical and contemporary discourse about democracy itself. Moreover, since every Western or Non-Western democratic system that represents not only a fraudulent labelling has to show high affinities to all of the aforementioned conflicting norms, we can deduce the juxtaposition of the aforementioned disparate characteristics as relevant indicators of *all* democracies. With democratic antinomies and the corresponding unique normative framework in mind, we can notably demonstrate that the coexistence of Western and Non-Western perspectives towards democracy is nothing but the inevitable consequence that, *within* this framework, very different political aims and directions are available and legitimate at the same time. Hence, Western and Non-Western societies are definitely allowed to set their own 'democratic' priorities: in favour of liberty *or* equality, the individual *or* the community, plurality *or* social harmony, the principle of quantity

[12]As an example, Bhargava (2010, p. 90f.) discusses (and accepts) the fact that, in India, some laws interfere with Hinduism. In this respect, he argues that 'the relevant consideration in their evaluation is not whether they immediately encompass all groups but whether or not they are just and consistent with the values undergirding secularism'. In other words, it is the democratic legitimacy of such laws which is assumed to be decisive. Along with this argument, similar (substantial) laws for Muslims or other religious groups in India are suggested to be redundant.

or quality etcetera. As long as Western and Non-Western democracies show no less than respect for both sides of the antinomic oppositions, the democratic character of the respective system, political process or debate is not in danger. So once again we can assess that the normative measure for all (Western or Non-Western) democracies is to be able to avoid an abolishment of their constitutive antinomies and therefore to keep the political extremes into a dynamic balance. The latter demands first and foremost, that, in accordance with the six democratic antinomies, different social objectives, opposing views and not the least, disputing political camps and parties not only exist in a concrete society but are politically and institutionally represented there as well, in a way that offers the political opposition as the current minority to assume one day the reins of government as a possible majority in the future.[13]

In this respect, and as far as we may be convinced of Rajeev Bhargava's analysis of India's constitution, the distinctiveness of Indian secularism could be seen as an almost perfect indication and illustration of how to meet this main challenge of democracy concerning the complex relationship between religion and politics. The value-based secular state Bhargava affirmatively describes not only provides a positive arrangement between different religious groups as well as between 'believers' and 'non-believers' in a religious sense but can also be interpreted as such an accurate balance of pertinently conflicting principles the democratic antinomies approach extracts on the scale of religion and democracy. Apart from that, it is still to be clarified to what extent the theory has actually been implemented into an efficient political practice. Despite the secular and religiously tolerant Indian constitution, religious conflicts and violence, especially between Hindus and Muslims but also with involved atheists, Christians and Sikhs, signify an unaltered part of modern India. However, the main question in this regard is certainly not what could be done in order to adjust the constitution to this problematic political reality but rather if there is reason to fear that someday the constitution of India may not work anymore in order to mitigate these still existing religious conflicts at any rate. As a real paradigm for religious accommodation, the secular democracy in India is definitely a success story. But as the history of political thought (as located here in democratic antinomies) suggests: the story of democracy itself is still open.

References

Aron, R. (1944). L'avenir des religions séculières. *La France libre, 4*(8), 210–217.

Bellah, R. N., Madsen, R., Sullivan, W. M., Swidler, A., & Tipton, S. M. (1985). *Habits of the heart. Individualism and commitment in American life*. Berkeley: University of California Press.

Bhargava, R. (2006). The distinctiveness of indian secularism. In T. N. Srinivasan (Ed.), *The future of secularism* (pp. 20–53). New Delhi: Oxford University Press.

[13]For this understanding of democracy as an oscillation between government and opposition, which is obviously due to the democratic antinomies approach, see exceptionally Luhmann (2002, pp. 96–105, 164ff., 269ff.).

Bhargava, R. (2010). Indian secularism. An alternative, trans-cultural ideal. In R. Barghava (Ed.), *The promise of India's secular democracy* (pp. 63–105). New Delhi: Oxford University Press.
Collier, P. (2009). *Wars, guns, and votes. Democracy in dangerous places*. New York: HarperCollins.
Cunningham, F. (2002). *Theories of democracy. A critical introduction*. Oxon/New York: Routledge.
Dahl, R. A. (1971). *Polyarchy. Participation and opposition*. New Haven: Yale University Press.
Dahl, R. A. (1989). *Democracy and its critics*. New Haven/London: Yale University Press.
Dahl, R. A. (1998). *On democracy*. New Haven/London: Yale University Press.
Diamond, L. (2008). *The spirit of democracy. The struggle to build free societies throughout the world*. New York: Times Books/Henry Holt and Company.
Dunn, J. (2005). *Setting the people free. The story of democracy*. London: Atlantic Books.
Dworkin, R. (1981a). What is equality? Part I: Equality of welfare. *Philosophy & Public Affairs, 10*(3), 185–246.
Dworkin, R. (1981b). What is equality? Part II: Equality of resources. *Philosophy & Public Affairs, 10*(4), 283–345.
Dworkin, R. (1987). What is equality? Part III: The place of liberty. *Iowa Law Review, 73,* 1–54.
Eisenstadt, S. N. (1999). *Paradoxes of democracy. Fragility, continuity, and change*. Washington, DC: The Woodrow Wilson Center Press.
Gallie, W. B. (1956). Essentially Contested Concepts. *Proceedings of the Aristotelian Society, 56,* 167–198.
Held, D. (2006). *Models of democracy* (3rd ed.). Cambridge: Polity.
Hidalgo, O. (2014). *Die Antinomien der Demokratie*. Frankfurt am Main/New York: Campus.
Kalyvas, S. N. (2000). Commitment problems in emerging democracies. The case of religious parties. *Comparative Politics, 32*(4), 379–398.
Lijphart, A. (1999). *Patterns of democracy. Government forms and performance in thirty-six countries*. New Haven/London: Yale University Press.
Lord, C. (2004). *A democratic audit of the European Union*. Basingstoke: Palgrave Macmillan.
Luhmann, N. (2002). *Die Politik der Gesellschaft*. Frankfurt am Main: Suhrkamp.
Minkenberg, M. (2003). Staat und Kirche in westlichen Demokratien. In M. Minkenberg & U. Willems (Eds.), *Politik und Religion. PVS-Sonderheft 33* (pp. 115–138). Wiesbaden: Westdeutscher Verlag.
Putnam, R. D. (2000). *Bowling alone. The collapse and revival of American community*. New York: Simon & Schuster.
Rawls, J. (1971). *A theory of justice*. Cambridge: Belknap Press of Harvard University Press.
Rawls, J. (1993). *Political liberalism*. New York: Columbia University Press.
Sartori, G. (1992). *Demokratietheorie*. Darmstadt: Wissenschaftliche Buchgesellschaft.
Schmidt, M. G. (2010). *Demokratietheorien. Eine Einführung* (5th ed.). Wiesbaden: VS.
Stepan, A. (2001). The World's religious systems and democracy. In A. Stepan (Ed.), *Arguing comparative politics. Crafting the twin tolerations* (pp. 213–254). Oxford/New York: Oxford University Press.
Tilly, C. (2007). *Democracy*. Cambridge: Cambridge University Press.
Voegelin, E. (1996). *Die politischen Religionen [1938]*. Munich: Wilhelm Fink.

Oliver Hidalgo is a Senior Lecturer at the department of politics, University of Münster, and Professor of Political Science at the University of Regensburg. From 2015 until 2017 he was Visiting Professor of political theory in Münster. His main research topics are the history of political thought, democratic theory, politics and religion, and international political theory. His recent publications include the monograph *Politische Theologie* (2018), the edition of a special issue concerning religion and right-wing populism in the *Journal for Religion, Society, and Politics* (2018), and the article "The Theory of Democratic Antinomies and the Identification of Value Trade-Offs in Political Practice" (*Politics and Governance* 2019 (7): 264–274).

Chapter 6
Mainstream Indian Nationalisms and Its Critique: A Minority and Islamic Perspective

Krishna Swamy Dara

Abstract The dominant form of nationalism in the Indian Independence Movement was propagated by the Indian National Congress. This party which was mostly composed of upper caste Hindu and other dominant sections of Indian society. They articulated a generic conception of nationalism that characterized their preconceptions and interests. This was vehemently opposed by minority leaders. By questioning the assumptions and their covert strategies to protect their class/caste interests in the name of nationalism by the congress they offered different conceptions of Nationalism and some like Iqbal critiqued the very idea of nationalism. Some critiqued the Hindu nationalism as propagated by the Rastria Swayamsevak Sangh (R.S.S). There was also an internal critique amongst the minorities. One major question was: What is the stand a good Muslim should take when it comes to question of Nationalism? Some opposed Iqbal who argued that nationalism was a bane and a false ideology to control Muslims. They saw nationalism more positively and in inclusive terms. This came to called in English Composite Nationalism. This paper attempts to portray the various arguments that were forwarded by various minority leaders against mainstream nationalism and anti-nationalism positions taken by other minorities. It looks at the arguments of Ambedkar who was standing at the crisscross of this heated debates and try to show what was distinctive about his argumentative stance.

6.1 Introduction

A critique of mainstream nationalism (Congress/Hindu) is in vogue in recent times. The so-called Indian nationalism shares some ideological background with Hindu nationalism (Gould 2004). This has been a major concern for minority leaders and intellectuals in the late colonial period be that they are from Muslim background or a Dalit-bahujan background. Dalit-bahujan thinker particularly Ambedkar was also critical of the way Muslim elites played their role in both supporting and opposing national movements. This paper attempts to explore the idea of nationalism and

K. S. Dara (✉)
Department of Political Science at Jamia Millia Islamia, New Delhi, India
e-mail: kdara@gmail.com

© Springer Nature Singapore Pte Ltd. 2020
A. Roy and M. Becker (eds.), *Dimensions of Constitutional Democracy*,
https://doi.org/10.1007/978-981-15-3899-5_6

mainstream congress nationalism and its critique from a minority/Islamic perspective: both Dalit and Muslim. Conceptions of nationalism in India can be classified into four broad rubrics: Composite/Secular nationalism, Islamic/Muslim nationalism, Hindu nationalism, Democratic egalitarian-nationalism. Composite nationalism is the main, official and dominant version supported by the congress and its allies. Islamic nationalism is a commitment to Islamic value and social ethos. Sometimes it is articulated as the interests of Muslims also. The Hindu version of nationalism is also dominant but was not very popular as the secular version. What I would like to call Democratic nationalism is the nationalism that is supported by classes/groups that are historically and social disadvantaged (not just numerically). Kindly note that these nationalisms are not mutually exclusive all the times sometimes there is an inter-sectionality of interests and values amongst these nationalisms. For example, the Islamic nationalism may also share the same values with composite nationalism of the Azad variety. Tamil Nationalism also shares values with the Democratic anti-Brahmin nationalism. In order to understand this, we need to go to their key concept ualizers such as Iqbal, Madani, Azad and Ambedkar. This paper also attempts to engage with their critiques of mainstream nationalisms. This mainstream nationalism is a confluence of many varieties of nationalism. This includes the Hindu or Hindutva version where the argument is that Hindus who are a majority should have a greater say in the country. Then there is the composite nationalism where a framework is evolved where religion will be given importance but no religion will have an upper hand. Gandhi is mostly a supporter of this kind of nationalism. Lastly, there is the secular version where religion will take a backseat or pushed to the realm of private sphere and the state will promote science and reason for national development with a special focus on social justice and welfare. All these version of nationalisms was claimed by the Congress party. This complex composite nationalism is imperative to understand the Indian version of constitutional democracy. The constitution of India attempts to fructify the various versions of nationalism. It balances development and social welfare with cultural and religious needs of its citizens. This paper will attempt to engage with this mainstream nationalism and if possible critiques of each other Islamic nationalism. I will, further, look at idea of territoriality in their conceptions of nationalism/cosmopolitanism. The chapter is broadly divided into three sections. The first section deals with Iqbal's critique of Nationalism from an Islamic perspective and also the Indian Muslim version of composite nationalism. The next section will focus on Maulana Azad's version of composite nationalism which he claims to be compatible with Islam. We will move on to Madani who is also is a defender of composite nationalism and the complex arguments he provides. Lastly, we will deal with Ambedkar who critiques both the Muslim versions and the mainstream congress version of nationalism and offers his own version of nationalism.

6.2 Islam, Iqbal and Nationalism

I will begin with Iqbal's pan-Islamism and his critique of western nationalism. As it is well known that Iqbal critiqued both 'Territorial Nationalism' and 'Composite nationalism' of both Azad and *Muttahida Qawmiyat aur Islam* of Madani, Deobandhi scholar. Nationalism according to Iqbal 'was the greatest enemy to Islam'. (Sevea 2012, p. 10) He says that nationalism was ideology propagated by European and colonial forces to divide the *Ummah* of Islam. He writes, 'European imperialism demanded the break-up of the religious unity of Islam', and that no 'other weapon would serve the imperial interests better than the propagation of the British concept of nationhood' (Sevea 2012, p. 139). Before getting into Iqbal's critique of nationalism as a threat to Muslim *Ummah*, we need to ponder on the idea for a moment. The idea of *Ummah* basically means a community of Muslim believers (Bilici 2006, p. 319). Influenced by the work and ideas of Said-i Nursi (a Turkish theologian and intellectual) Mucahit Bilici defines the *Ummah* as an alternate imagined community like the nation. It (Ummah) belonged to those conception communities that preexisted before the emergence of modern notion of a nation. Although like the nation, it is an imagined community and it differs from the concept of nation in three different ways. 1. Its assumptions about *individual human* beings; 2. The place of *political economic thinking* in its imagination; 3. its *ontological assumptions* (Bilici 2006, p. 319). Important for this chapter is the third assumption. The way this Ummah has conceptualized the self and other is interesting unlike the nation. The self is God and the other of this self is the Ummah. Therefore, the divide is vertical rather than horizontal between God and the believer or group of believers. In the words of Bilici, it is a self-othering community. Bilici writes, 'Human beings (and ummah) as part of creation are expected to believe that all that is positive is from God and all that is negative originates from human beings. Furthermore, in structuralist terms the centre is God; creation is the structure. The relationship between ummah and other communities around (and within) it must be understood in connection with these ontological assumptions' (Bilici 2006, p. 319). Iqbal's critique of nationalism must be understood in the broader intellectual context where Muslim intellectuals are resisting the dominant euphoria of nationalism in early twentieth century. Moreover, Iqbal's 'reference to nationalism as a "weapon" must be studied in the light of his fear that the mere imitation of western political ideals and institutions would lead to intellectual domination' according to Iqbal Singh Sevea in his book titled 'The Political Philosophy of Muhammad Iqbal'.

Although, he was attached to Hindustan he was simultaneously an Islamist. He was committed to Pan-Islamism. In his famous piece titled 'Islam as a political and ethical ideal' he articulates the basic philosophy and goal of Islam. He uses the comparative approach with other religions to demonstrate this. Interestingly, the contrast with Buddhism is very illuminating. As we will see, how Ambedkar will understand Buddhism or possible critique of Islam. Iqbal in this lecture delivered at Aligarh in 1910 articulates his critique of Western notion of nationalism. The lecture was later published with the title 'The Muslim community (a Sociological Study)'. Interestingly, he likes to retain the term 'nationalism' for a particular kind of 'pan-Islamism'. We need to understand his socio-philosophical underpinnings to better understand his critique of nationalism. It is integral to his understanding of nationalism. He begins by arguing that man has evolved by overcoming his natural limitations and environments to realize as 'more perfect vision of himself and impels him to discover the means which would transform his brilliant dream of an idealized-self into a living reality'. Iqbal employs a kind of quasi-Spencerian rational when he writes,

> By the great discovery of the law of Natural Selection he (man) has succeeded in reaching a rational conception of his own history which, before long, appeared to him to be nothing more than an inscrutable series of events dropping out, one by one, from the mysterious womb of time, without any inherent order or purpose (Sherwani 1995, p. 118).

However, discovering a deeper structure and law in history is not the end for man. Man gains an even deeper insight in this rational history (through post-Darwinian thinkers,) and 'other equally important facts of collective life are calculated to work a complete revolution in man's notions of group-life in its social, economic and political aspects. It has been brought to light by recent biological research that the individual as such is a mere abstraction, a convenient expression for facility of social reference, passing moment in the life of the group to which he happens to belong' (Sherwani 1995, p. 19).

Methodological holism runs through all of Iqbal's thought. Even when relating thought (reason) with intuition, in the context of the relationship between philosophy and religion, he tends to side with intuition where he thinks, 'They spring up from the same root and complement each other. The one grasps Reality piecemeal, the other grasps it in its wholeness' (Sherwani 1995, p. 19). Coming back to his argument about that importance of society. He argues that a society is more than the summation of its individuals. He disapproves liberal western individualism, when he says that 'Society has a distinct life of its own, irrespective of the life of its component units taken individually' (Sherwani 1995, p. 19). The individual needs to sacrifice his or her interests for the society as a whole. This argument is very similar to the arguments provided by Tilak, Patel and all other defenders of Hindu social order. In particular, the caste system which is excellent in their view where the social philosophy behind the system is that society is valued more than its component parts functionally. Iqbal writes,

> His thoughts, his aspirations, his ways of life, his entire mental and physical outfit, the very number of days which he lives, are all determined by the needs of the community of whose collective life he is only a partial expression. The interests of society as a whole are fundamentally different and even antagonistic to the interests of the individual whose activity is nothing more than an unconscious performance of a particular function which social economy has allotted to him (Sherwani 1995, p. 119).

This does not mean that Iqbal is a defender of caste system but the social logic that is employed is similar to Hindu casteists for an egalitarian and just society, which he thinks is the main motive of Islam and its conception of society. He writes, 'That the Muslim Commonwealth is based on the absolute equality of all Muslims in the eye of the law. There is no privileged class, no priesthood, no caste system' (Sherwani 1995, p. 140).

Although he rejected western individualism, which he thinks prioritizes individual's interests over society's interests, he is not willing to give up individualism altogether. The religious authorities (ulema) enforced a uniform social life on all Muslims to maintain a coherent social order but it has killed all innovation: a major reason for the stalling of spiritual and intellectual growth in Muslim societies. Iqbal says, 'In an over-organized society the individual is altogether crushed out of existence'. Therefore, individuality needs to be nourished but not at the cost of society.

Islam, for that matter, Quran, lets individuals have their freedom provided they do not violate the laws prescribed by god. In this sense, Quranic philosophy wants the development of individual personality. However, there is a communitarian tendency in Iqbal in his social thought which can sometimes ignore the individuality for the larger individuality of the community. He, at many places appreciates the egalitarian values of Islam when it comes to issues of race, class, language and other ethnic identities. He seems to go back when it comes to Gender relations and closer to the Hindu traditionalists. Talking in relation to the education of the Muslim woman. *'I must however, frankly admit that I am not an advocate of absolute equality between man and woman'* (Sherwani 1995, p. 134). This is typical of most Islamists for Sir Syed Ahmad Khan, Syyid Qutub to Maulana Maududi. There is a deep anxiety that modernity and westernization are challenge to traditional and Islamic gender relations. Familial relations, sexual difference, differential labour between genders should confirm to qur'anic and hadith conceptions. A questioning of this is seen as Jahilliyat (ignorance/or referred to sometimes in the sense of barbaric) and domination of western epistemic hegemony. Iqbal in the same speech writes,

> It appears that Nature has allotted different functions to them (women), and a right performance of these functions is equally indispensable for the health and prosperity of the human family. The so-called "emancipation of the western woman" necessitated by western individualism and the peculiar economic situation produced by an unhealthy competition, is an experiment, in my opinion, likely to fail, not without doing incalculable harm, and creating extremely intricate social problems. Nor is the higher education of women likely to lead to any desirable consequences, in so far, at least, as the birth rate of a community is concerned. Experience has already shown that the economic emancipation of women in the west has not, as was expected, materially extended the production of wealth. On the other hand it has a tendency to break up the Physical life of Society (Sherwani 1995, p. 134).

Although he is willing to allow some cultural and intellectual influences from other cultures particularly modern western ideas but these influences cannot be allowed to override the basic Islamic values and institutions. 'Considering, then the peculiar nature of our community, the teachings of Islam and the revelation of Physiology and Biology on the subject, it is clear that the Muslim women should continue to occupy the position in society which Islam has allotted to her' (Sherwani 1995, p. 134). Iqbal a la Gandhi critiques of modernity although he is at pains to show how medieval Islam contributed to rise of European science and achievements. It is in such deep suspicion of western modernity that Iqbal places his critique of Nationalism as an ideology. Talking about how some young Muslims are enamored by the ideas of west in particularly with nationalist thinking he writes, '*Some of them are, unfortunately, too much dazzled by the glamour of western ideals to realise the difference between Islam which constructs nationality out of a purely abstract idea,* i.e. *religion, and westernism which builds nationality on an objective basis i.e. Country*' (Sherwani 1995, p. 135). His critique is also intrinsic to the overall critique of colonialism and its orientalist view of Muslim societies. He writes, '*The tyranny of imperialism struts abroad, covering its face in the masks of Democracy, Nationalism, Communism, Fascism and heaven knows what else besides*' (Sherwani 1995, p. 298).

Although, he is a critique of western idea of nationalism, he is not willing to give up either the term nationalism or some aspects of it. He pushes the meaning of the term to a more cosmopolitan direction. A kind of pan-Islamic nationalism. Despite the fact that Iqbal's thought is cosmopolitan but this cosmopolitanism is more bounded. In this sense, Iqbal appears more on the side of Afgani, Syyid Qutab and Maududhi. For Iqbal, Islam as a moral and political ideal is universal. It is meant for all of humankind. A Muslim as a part of humanity is committed to the universal values of Islam. Ideologies like nationalism, socialism, fascism and including democracy can distract the Muslim for this Islamic universalism. The ultimate patriotism that a Muslim is allowed to is the patriotism towards Islam. In a Statement on Islam and Nationalism in Reply to a Statement of Maulana Husain Ahmad, published in the Ehsan on 9 March 1938, Iqbal writes,

> The name of the faith which the Muslim community professes is "Din-i-Qayyim" in which term lies concealed a remarkable Quranic point, namely, that it is this religion alone in which is vested the responsibility of sustaining the present and future life of a group of people which surrenders its individual and social life to its system. In other words, according to the Quran, it is the religion of Islam alone which sustains a nation in its true cultural or political sense. It is for this reason that the Quran openly declares that any system other than that of Islam must be deprecated and rejected (Sherwani 1995, p. 309).

The demands of Indian nationalism is therefore problematic for Iqbal because it puts the religious Muslim at odds with his religion. He staunchly opposes any attempts to interpret Islam that supports Indian nationalism. This is exactly what some Maulanas, particularly the Deoband School, see a role Muslims can play in fighting the (Christian) oppressive British Raj. Nationalism for most of the maulana is an oppositional force to colonialism than to arrive at an ideal. Azad and Madani would call this 'composite nationalism'. Composite nationalism is broadly also endorsed by the Congress leaders. It has almost become the official version Congress. Although one cannot rule out its deeper links with the majoritarian Hindu nationalism. It (composite nationalism) has close resemblances with 'secular nationalism' but with greater role for religious beliefs and sentiments. The other radical version of nationalism is the 'Hindu nationalism'. We will come to that later in the paper. Coming back to the idea of composite nationalism Maulana Azad in my view is its best exponent, though Madani has a text which is popular.

6.3 Azad and Madani on Nationalism

Azad, who is trained as a religious scholar unlike Iqbal is willing to explore living with the temporary others, i.e. Hindus. He is also willing to interpret Islam more as a religious and moral ideal and can live with a political setup other than the Islamic. Iqbal thinks a practicing Muslim or a community should live both by the ethical and political ideal of Islam. He is opposed to secularism because it relegates religion to the private sphere. This is one of the great harms that modernity in the name of secularism inflicts on traditional religious societies. Moreover, secularism is Eurocentric and Christian because it takes the European experience and protestant Christian conceptions of religion and religious authority and generalizes to all other religions and societies. In the case of Islam this is even more harmful. Iqbal is at pains to show how Islam is different. Furthermore, its political conception is egalitarian to the core. He takes great pains to show how Islam cannot be understood in the eurocentric, Christian and Western conceptions of religion.

Azad would agree with Iqbal about the uniqueness of Islam but would disagree that Islam and Nationalism are fundamentally opposed or exclusive. In his famous article, in the Al-hilal titled: *Islam and Nationalism* he begins by describing nationalism before he gets into Islam. Optimistically, he writes, 'the concept for a special state of man's collective consciousness and a notion of social order. It distinguishes one group of people from another and makes it possible for a large number of them to come together to lead their lives and undertake their collective responsibilities' (Hameed 1990, p. 51). The concern for social order he shares with Iqbal but the idea of 'collective responsibilities' is in tune with Ambedkar and other modernists. Azad makes distinction between patriotism and nationalism. He writes, 'Patriotism is a maturing of one's allegiance to the city-state. As civilization progresses and expands, habitations and towns grow in numbers, man's contacts become more extensive and the concept of city-state also starts to widen.' (Hameed 1990, p. 51). Allegiance to city-state for him is patriotism and is not necessarily restricted to a religion. Inevitability of patriotism as humans expand and interact with each other is another aspect of Azad's dialectical thinking. Nationalism is the next step to patriotism. What is interesting to Azad is that the geographical origin of the idea is not a necessary element for his appreciation of the idea. He, neither sees it as intellectual hegemony of the west like Iqbal. Azad does not accept the idea of nationalism uncritically as he is at pains to show how nationalism can go wrong and he gives good and lucid arguments to show how it can go wrong. He is simultaneously grounding his arguments as compatible with the values of Islam. This has the dual purpose to show to both Muslims and non-Muslims about the relation of Islam to nationalism.

He qualifies the feeling of nationalism or national pride in two broad categories. Defensive nationalism and chauvinist nationalism. National chauvinism, He writes,

> There are two aspects of chauvinism. The protection of race and nation. And the prejudices of race and nation. The spirit of Islam is opposed to prejudice but not to protection. But the problem is what when such an orbit is formed, though it originated with the spirit of protection, later it turns into prejudice. To being with, a group of people create the orbits of patriotism and nationalism in order to protect themselves from external invasion. This

> is 'defensive nationalism'. Its continuance over a period of time, however, gives birth to feelings of national superiority and patriotic pride, in pale of national defence. 'Defensive nationalism suddenly turns into jingoism'. Not content with its own protection, nationalism want to attack others. (Hameed 1990, p. 55).

The problem is that often good nationalism ends up into chauvinism and jingoism. When this jingoism is combined with racism it becomes very dangerous. *He writes, 'Moreover, the heady wine of racial and national superiority evokes a sense of distinction from others and breed contempt and disdain for them. As a result, violence erupts between different national, and better human sense becomes dormant'* (Hameed 1990, p. 55). The initial purpose and intentions of nationalism become upside down, which must of course be avoided. 'Nationalism, in its simplest form, has existed for ages. But the collective beliefs and ideas that the term brings to mind are the product of the new era of European civilization. It started as a defense for human rights and liberty, but has today, become its greatest threat' (Hameed 1990, p. 55).

Azad goes on to explain how nationalism has become a bane. Before 'the advent of modern times, despotism and unequal distribution were confined to a few hand and a few families; now they were extended to bigger groups. Consequently, the forces against equity and justice were no longer concentrated and centralized as before' (Hameed 1990, p. 56). This conception of nationalism needs to be transcended and the solution is provided by Islam. So instead of pitching nationalism against Islam Azad hierarchizes in a Hegelian fashion as a stepping stone so to say or a dialectical move towards a higher cosmopolitan society as envisioned by Islam. Therefore, it is incumbent upon Muslims to join the nationalist struggle against the British along with the Hindus.

Coming to the conception of Ummah, Azad seems to have a very inclusive and broader conception of it than that of Iqbal and Madani. Azad cites hadiths of the prophet for clarifying his conception of Ummah, which includes all of humanity not just Muslims. He cites, 'The call of Islam was call to "humanism" and "human brotherhood" hence its bias against all prejudices that resulted from racial and national distinctions' (Hameed 1990, p. 49). While Iqbal also believes in the universality of Islam and its conception of human brotherhood he tends keep the Muslim and non-Muslim binary in his conception of the political. In Azad, although the specificities of Muslim culture and politics are recognized, the binary of Muslim/non-Muslim does not play a dominant role. It only plays heuristically but not politically. He is at pains to prove it that it is backed by textual evidence in the Hadith. He cites in Al-Hihal prophet words after his prayers as 'God, our lord and the lord of the Universe; I confess that only you are the lord of the Universe and no one but you. God, our lord and the Lord of the Universe; I confess that Mohammad (peace be upon him) is no more than your slave and messenger. God, our lord and the Lord of the Universe; I confess that all your people are brothers, and whatever differences they may have created among themselves you have created them as one human race' (Hameed 1990, p. 54). In this sense, the conception of Ummah for Azad is another word of 'humanism' and 'Human brotherhood'. It is not exclusionary and is compatible with the politics of composite nationalism. Azad aligned himself with the congress party and politics of

Gandhi most of his political life. A lesser known figure is Madani whose conceptions fall somewhere between Iqbal radicalism and Azad's liberal view of Islam.

6.4 Madani

Now moving on to Madani as said before his book on Composite Nationalism and Islam (*Muttahida Qawmiyat aur Islam*). For those who don't know him, Maulana Husain Ahmad Madani (1879–1957), a theologist and political activist, was one of the longest serving principals of *Darul Uloom*, Deoband: the renowned Islamic seminary of the Indian sub-continent. Darul Uloom, Deoband was founded in 1866 by a group of learned theologians with the purpose of imparting Islamic education among Muslim youth.

Madani justified a kind of secular government for a society comprised of people of different religious backgrounds. Expanding on his idea of pluralism and mutual coexistence, he also expressed the need for Muslims and non-Muslims to continue to work together in the spirit of the 'Constitution of Medina'. It is also called by various names like '*Dustūr al-Madīnahm,Ṣaḥīfat al-Madīnah and Mīthāq al-Madīnah*'. This constitution or covenant was unilaterally drafted by Prophet Muhammad in 622 as a formal agreement between himself and different tribes and communities. The Jews were also included in the Ummah. One needs to understand how the *ulama* are organized and structured to understand the role it played in shaping Islamic and Muslim political thought.

Barbara Metcalf in her book *Islamic Revival in British India: Deoband, 1860–1900* argues that Muslims and "the *ulama* are multi-layered, as evinced by their varied stances on colonial and post-colonial India; the *ulama* have, contrary to popular belief, shown a long-term commitment to democracy and secularism; 'the concept of *jihad* has had a different connotation than how it is perceived today; and, last but not least, the Indian freedom struggle was a collective of different segments of the society, and the *ulama* played no lesser a role" (Rehman 2009). The Ulema played a significant role in shaping and defining the nature of Muslim community in India. It also attempted to answer the question of how Muslims should relate to non-Muslims in a colonial oppressive India.

From Sir Syed onwards the question about whether India was a single nation or a plurality of nations was part of public debates. One such argument was that the Muslims were outsiders and the Hindus as original inhabitants. Sir Syed and Phule argued that every group has come from outside (but for Phule the indigenous what is today referred to as lower castes (Other backward castes plus Dalits.) what matters is not from where and when some group has come but the adoption of India as their home was important and if the English also adopt India as their home they should welcome for Sir Syed.

But interestingly Madani develops and expands the meaning of the term 'original inhabitants' and argues,

'Among various communities residing in India, Muslims alone can legitimately claim they are the original inhabitants of the land. Among all the communities residing in India, only Muslims have firm religious faith that they are the descendants of Adam, the first human aborigine of planet Earth. It is inseparable part of their belief based upon Quranic verses that entire humanity on this earth has originated from Adam. Contrarily, rest of the communities in India; believe in the gradual evolution of Homo sapiens' (Madani 2001, p. 1).

Since the Muslims bury their dead unlike the Hindu who burns their dead the Muslims are more attached to the land than the Hindus. Although there are cultural and religious differences for Madani this cannot preclude the argument that both the groups are Indians and therefore a common nationalism. He says,

'Indians have something in common that remains along with the religious and cultural differences. It is like our human nature does not change just because of variance in our visages, differences in our personalities and traits, and differences in our color and stature. Likewise our religious and cultural differences do not become hurdle in our national partnership. From the point of view of nationality, we all are Indians' (Main 2005, pp. 202–203).

In a machiavellian sense of *civic virtu* it is the responsibility of all in the territory to work for the whole territory. Madani writes, 'If the whole village would not erect embankment during the flood, then the whole village will be destroyed and life would become difficult for one and all' (Main 2005, pp. 202–203). Solidarity between groups can emerge for Madani not because they have to agree metaphysically on issues of law and ethics but the common victimhood can be the unifying force for him. This argument in the colonial context, *Jihad* meant to fight against the British oppression meted out on all Indians. Therefore, speaking to Muslims in particular it is his religious Islamic duty to fight against oppression of both oneself and others. It is 'incumbent upon every Indian to fight against such a barbaric regime and throw off the shackles of slavery'. Religious diversity can be overcome through jointly working hard and through the formation of a national partnership. 'Likewise, whenever the country is in trouble it is the duty of the inhabitants of a country (whether they are Muslims, Hindus, Sikhs, or Parsis) that they should strive hard and jointly to remove it. The duty of national partnership applies equally to all residents' (Main 2005, pp. 202–203).

A kind of overlapping consensus can be achieved between different religious groups, 'therefore differences of religion cannot become any weakness or a hurdle'. He further says 'Members of various religions fulfill their duties in these institutions and feel themselves as composite part of it. This is the meaning of "composite nationalism" here. To read in it any other meaning than this is wrong and inappropriate' (Main 2005, pp. 202–203). Once a common front is established to fight against colonial slavery, there should also be a mutual respect and distance (principled distance) towards each other. Madani is not imagining a society which relegates religion to the private sphere. He writes, 'It is important not to interfere in another's religion—rather all nations (*aqwum*) living in India are free to practice their religion, life by its moral values and act according to their religious traditions'(Madani 2005, pp. 118–120). Not just they can practice their religion but they can and 'should propagate their ideology, follow their culture, promote civilization and protect their personal law' (Madani 2005, pp. 118–120). However, they can promote their civilization and religion with interfering, 'in the personal affairs of other minorities or (In fact) the majority, nor should the majority strive to assimilate the minority into itself' (Madani 2005, pp. 118–120).

6.5 Madani on Muslim Brotherhood

For Madani, the idea of Ummah can be compatible with nationalism unlike Iqbal although there is a deep contradiction in this position. Madani writes, 'Muhammad (ṣallāllāhuᶜalayhiwa-sallam (SAAS)) created a bond among Muslims that is superior to all bonds. In comparison, bonds such as nationalism are pale and colourless. A Muslim, whoever and wherever he is, is the brother of another Muslim and he has right over other Muslims. This bond of *rabita* (relationships) exists only among those who have accepted Islam' (Madani 2005, pp. 118–120). What about those who are non-Muslims, he further writes, 'In the case of those who have not embraced Islam, this bond cannot be established'. However, the good news is that there can be a special relationship between Muslims and non-Muslims but not something that overrides the earlier *Ummaht* but a temporary and pragmatic relationship. He writes, 'They could be part of composite nationalism, but only through the bonds of *nasal* (race), *rang* (colour) and nationality, etc. The question is: Can a Muslim join hands with non-Muslims and become part of the same nation and on the basis of this composite nationalism, can he enter into *siyasate mulki* and forge economic, commercial, agricultural and industrial relations with them? Is there a need of such a thing in India?' (Madani 2005, pp. 102–105). He further adds, 'It is quite apparent that waiting for all Indians to become Muslims in order to enter into such an alliance is wrong and harmful. There is no doubt that Islam combines principles of both ideological and practical reformation' (Madani 2005, pp. 102–105). This pragmatism of Madani is questioned by Arshad Alam by naming it as 'theological anti-pluralism'.

The problem with Madani is that this solidarity built with the Hindus is only temporary and pragmatic. Madani later in the book write, 'while being aware of the truth of their (other religions') falsehood' (Madani 2005, p. 117). Islam is ready to 'cooperate and tolerate' them. This according to Alam does not go well with avowed pluralism. He writes, 'In other words, Madani not only disqualifies and derogates other religions as being false, he is also of the view that, ultimately, Hindustan be Islamised: that the Hindu–Muslim entente (composite nationalism) is only required till the time people of this country do not become Muslims (*Jab Tak Hindustan Ke Tamam Baashinde Mussalman Nahin Ho Jate*). Such a notion hardly augurs well for any kind of pluralism' (Alam 2016). Apart from this Madani also makes judgement about the superiority of Islam over other religions. This attitude is very similar to Iqbal and Ambedkar who take a critical and evaluative stance against religions by which they do show their allegiance. Madani says that 'Islam is not fanatical and discriminatory like Hinduism, that considers the followers of all other religions as *mlecchas* (untouchables) and food touched by them as inedible. In Hinduism, a section of people of its *qaum* is labelled *shudra* (untouchable). It has no place for those who have left its fold' (Madani 2005, p. 116). Islam is in this sense, according to Madani, a very open-minded, unbiased and liberal religion in comparison to Judaism, Madani comes to Buddhism which is insensitive in his eyes because it has no 'specific principle by which his followers could claim to have a distinct identity' (Madani 2005, p. 117). This argument needs to be understood critically because in the Indian political context the dominant argument put forth by Hindu religious plus political leaders is that all religions are either equally true or equally false (Jains). In such a sensitive context claiming finality of truth creates a resentment in the hearts of others. This has been one of the thorny issues in creating a composite yet pluralistic religious culture in India. Hence, Madani's claims for composite nationalism does not go well with neither the hardliner Islamist camp nor the hardliner Hindutva camp. However, coming back to the virtues of Islam that Madani is articulating it is ability to address the individual and also the community.

Islam does not only strive for the reformation of an individual, but also strives to reform society as a whole—irrespective of privileged or underprivileged. Islam focuses on problems universally and permits all sorts of reforms. He writes, 'But the point is whether Islam (the Islamic principles that deal with individual as well as community life and pertain to such issues as God, relationship of God with His creatures and relationships between His creatures) permits that together with non-Muslims, a United Front can be formed on the basis of *wataniyat*, *nasal*, *rang* or language (*zabaan*), etc., to defeat the enemies of Islam and benefit Muslims in political, commercial, agricultural and industrial fields, without compromising on the basic tenets of Islam?' (Madani 2005, pp. 102–105). Remember that this response is primarily aimed at Iqbal who argues that Islam does not support divisive sentiments and politics like race and Nationalism. Madani is responding to the feasibility of Nationalism within Islam's fold.

Madani believes that flexibility is available to Islam and it 'does not denote weakness or giving credence to falsehood, illegitimate behavior and immoral deeds' (Madani 2005, p. 117). Madani argues that his argument has textual evidence from Islam. He says, 'As far as I have studied and followed the verses of the holy Qur'an, I have understood that there is no clear cut categorization of it, i.e. at times it is obligatory, at other times it is desirable, or preferable, or permissible, or even prohibited. Its condemnation is only on the basis that nationalism, in Western parlance today, is applied to those principles that relate to collective human life and that is altogether anti-religion, and thus would be attributed by this particular terminology. However, this meaning of nationalism is neither popular among people, nor would a true Muslim accept it, nor is there any such movement underway. Neither, the Indian National Congress and its volunteers are propagating it. Therefore, raking up this issue to an emotional pitch is an exercise in futility' (Madani 2005, pp. 102–105). Therefore, this relationship with the non-Muslim particularly with the Hindus both an ethical responsibility of the Muslims to fight against British slavery but also a strategic move to secure the political and economic interests for Muslims.

6.6 Ambedkar on Nationalism

Nationalism in India for Ambedkar is riddling with contradictions that until these contradictions are not resolved it works as a hegemonic idea. However, the idea of nationalism is in itself not a bad idea. In his speeches and writings, he claims to be committed to Indian national interests and also is against colonial domination. However, he makes a scathing critique of mainstream congress version of nationalism. Like Jinnah,Periyar and (to some extent Iqbal) his political life can be safely said to be a struggle against congress and its ideology. His view that the congress is an upper caste Hindu-dominated organization is well known. He says, 'Indian Nationalism has developed a new doctrine which may be called the Divine Right of the Majority to rule the minorities according to the wishes of the majority. Any claim for the sharing of power by the minority is called communalism while the monopolizing of the whole power by the majority is called Nationalism' (Ambedkar. States and Minorities, Vol.1). Before going in his critique of Congress Nationalism let us see what he means by nationalism. Like Iqbal, Ambedkar also relies on Renan for his definition of Nationality. Ambedkar attempts to define 'Nationality is a subjective psychological feeling. It is a feeling of a corporate sentiment of oneness which makes those who are charged with it feel that they are kith and kin. This national feeling is a double-edged feeling. It is at once a feeling of fellowship for one's own kith and an anti-fellowship feeling for those who are not one's own kith' (Ambedkar, Pakistan and Partition of India, vol. 8). Note for Ambedkar, it is a 'double edged' feeling. It has both a positive and a negative attitude. What interests Ambedkar is of course its positive attitude towards once closer relations. He goes on to define, 'It is a feeling of "consciousness of kind" which binds together those who are within the limits of the kindred and severs them from those who are outside the limits of the kindred' (Ambedkar, Triumph of Brahmins, vol. 3, 309).Belonging, for Ambedkar, is one of the crucial elements in understanding the sentiment of nationalism. It 'is a longing to belong to one's own group and a longing not to belong to any other group. This is the essence of what is called a nationality and national feeling' (Ambedkar, Philosophy of Hinduism, vol. 3, p. 309). His critique of Hindu Nationalist demand can be understood with the concept of belonging. Hindu nationalists reduce the idea of belonging to two sentiments that of Hindu religion and its territory. In the case of Savarkar, it is Hindu territory. Moreover, it completely misses the point that nationalism can be more than this. It can also be against domination. Specifically, in agreement with Iqbal and Madani, if it is colonial domination. Ambedkar adds to this majoritarian domination and writes, 'The Hindu Nationalist, who hopes that Britain will coerce the Muslims into abandoning Pakistan, forgets that the right of nationalism to freedom from an aggressive foreign imperialism and the right of a minority to freedom from an aggressive majority's nationalism are not two different things' (Ambedkar, vol. 8, p.10).

Within this nationalist context, Ambedkar is also against the dominant binary, popular among Indian circles that the West is materialistic and the east is spiritual. Here he would be in disagreement with Iqbal and Tagore who subscribe to these binaries. Ambedkar says, 'Nay, in the present days of Indian Nationalism—which sadly enough is tantamount to justifying everything Indian—the attitude is likely to be upheld and continued. Note, that of the stock contrasts between the East and the West, thrown in relief by the war, the East is ever eager to give prominence in terms of self-glorification to one—that of its being free from the extreme materialism of the West leading to war and devastation. There is however no justification for setting the West in such a cruel contrast. The East is too prone to forget that materialist we all are; even the East in spite of itself' (Ambedkar, Mr. Russell and the Reconstruction of Society, vol. 1, p. 487).

Coming to one of his main works, a key text in the Indian national debate on 'Pakistan and Partition of India'. Ambedkar attempts to understand the so-called the communal problem and its relation to the national question of Pakistan. As said earlier like Iqbal but more intensely Ambedkar is influenced by Ernst Renan in his views on nationalism and also on Islam. It is important to understand because Ambedkar's arguments both consciously and unconsciously are be shaped by Renan's perspective. We know that Renan is an orientalist and he had a very reductive and dismissive view of Islam and its prophet. Ambedkar seems to have critically accepted Renan's view that Islam is conservative and conflicts with egalitarian values. His critique against gender relations within Indian Islamic society in the 'Pakistan and Partition of India' is well known. The condition of women with special institution of *Burqa* and *Parda* makes Islam unattractive for Ambedkar. Even the institution of slavery which Iqbal says was on the way out and not supported by prophet was not a convincing argument for Ambedkar. For Ambedkar, the truly universal spiritual philosophy belongs to that of Buddhism not Islam. Therefore, Islamic nationalism and pan-Islamism has no attraction to his temperament. There is some criticism that his views are orientalist and uncritical in accepting western categories. I do not agree with it whole although there is some trace in his thought. As a pragmatist, an idea needs to be evaluated both in its ideal form and in its practice for him. In fact, the idea as it is practiced takes precedence over its purely theoretical or textual articulations. However, Ambedkar sees the Muslim question as an important question because of his commitment and concern towards minority rights in a democracy: in particular with the rights of Dalits.

Coming to Ambedkar's more practical concern with Muslims and their idea of Islamic brotherhood he condemns it a divisive force between Muslims and non-Muslims not a unifying force. His critique of Hinduism and its caste system as a dividing force in not restricted to Hinduism only but the same principles apply to other religions as well. By the same yardstick, he has this to say about Islam, 'Hinduism is said to divide people and in contrast Islam is said to bind people together. This is only a half-truth. For Islam divides as inexorably as it binds. Islam is a close corporation and the distinction that it makes between Muslims and non-Muslims is a very real, very positive and very alienating distinction. The brotherhood of Islam is not the universal brotherhood of man. It is brotherhood of Muslims for Muslims only. There is a fraternity, but its benefit is confined to those within that corporation. For those who are outside the corporation, there is nothing but contempt and enmity' (Ambedkar Vol. 8. p. 330). This aspect is important to understand the communal tensions between Hindus and Muslims and the problem of forming a single nation.

The 'defects in Hinduism and in Islam which are responsible for keeping the sore between Hindus and Muslims open and running' (Ambedkar Vol.8. p. 330).

Venkata Dulipala's work titled, '*Creating a New Medina: State Power, Islam, and the Quest for Pakistan in Late Colonial North India'*, is a valuable and interesting contribution in helping us understand the context in which Ambedkar is writing. By 1940s most Muslims in Uttar Pradesh were on the side of the Muslim League. The Deoband Ulema split up. Most important of them is Shabbir Ahmad Usmani who sided with Jinnah and his politics of creating an ideal Islamic state. One of the interesting concepts that Ambedkar analyses are the concept of Ummah. The concept of Ummah at least the way Ambedkar understands is negative and against universal brotherhood. Next, he introduces the distinction between social-self-government and local self-government. He says, 'The second defect[defeat] of Islam is that it is a system of **social self-government** and is incompatible with **local self-government,** because the allegiance of a Muslim does not rest on his domicile in the country which is his but on the faith to which he belongs. To the *Muslim ubi bene ibi patria* [Where it is well with me, there is my country] is unthinkable. Wherever there is the rule of Islam, there is his own country. In other words, Islam can never allow a true Muslim to adopt India as his motherland and regard a Hindu as his kith and kin' (Ambedkar Vol. 8. p. 330). The next question should concern us is about his evaluation of Islam as a religion and value system. His major problem was that although it claims to be egalitarian it is not egalitarian in practice. Particularly Iqbal claims that Islam is a truly universal religion. In fact, he takes the Bergsonian notion of a dynamic religion and applies to his understanding of Islam in his reconstruction of religious thought in Islam. Iqbal in his speech titled Islam as a moral and political ideal compares Islam with Christianity, Zoroastrianism and Buddhism. For Christianity sees man's existence as determined by an original sin which for him is very negative. Zoroastrianism sees that there is good and bad in the world and ultimately the good forces are going to win and Buddhism sees the existence as suffering. All the three above religions see man and his existence negatively. Islam, on the other hand, sees man and his existence in a positive way. Although there is pain and suffering but ultimately they can be overcome through intelligence and god's guidance. Islam was meant to live a life without fear both by natural forces and other human beings. God is the so-called guarantee of man's existence without fear. Iqbal also says, Islam is a religion of equality and he refers to Prophets adopting a slave as his son and marrying him to girl from a rich respectable family. This the way Iqbal also has at many places talks about how equality was in practice. But for Ambedkar, the institution of Slavery in Islamic society is something unacceptable for him. This also contradicts with its idea of *Ummah.* Citing William Muir's 'The Quran and its composition', He writes,

> Take the caste system. Islam speaks of brotherhood. Everybody infers that Islam must be free from slavery and caste. Regarding slavery nothing needs to be said. It stands abolished now by law. But while it existed much of its support was derived from Islam and Islamic countries. But if slavery has gone, caste among Musalmans has remained. There can thus be no manner of doubt that the Muslim Society in India is afflicted by the same social evils as afflict the Hindu Society. Indeed, the Muslims have all the social evils of the Hindus

> and something more. That something more is the compulsory system of purdah for Muslim women (Ambedkar Vol. 8. p. 228).

He also thinks that, 'Muslim politics is essentially clerical and recognizes only one difference, namely, that existing between Hindus and Muslims. None of the secular categories of life have any place in the politics of the Muslim community and if they do find a place—and they must because they are irrepressible—they are subordinated to one and the only governing principle of the Muslim political universe, namely, religion. For Ambedkar, the ideal universal religion is Buddhism as it does not has the limiting concept of Ummah but also can work out of a sociopolitical ideal with his idea of Sangha.

6.7 Conclusion

The critique of 'Mainstream Nationalism' from both Muslim and Dalit groups is that it is undemocratic, hegemonic and rigid. Within critiques from the Muslim side there those who are against the very idea of nationalism both as a western idea and as something that is incompatible with Islam. The more liberal side sees sources in Islam that can accommodate nationalism in a limited sense. For scholars like Iqbal whom we studied in this paper, nationalism is mostly secular nationalism and it relegates religion to the private realm. Therefore is incompatible with Islam and its socio-ethic political ideal. Iqbal also critiques composite nationalism of Azad and Madani. He has his own vision of pan-Islamic nationalism. It is a species of non-secular nationalism which does not limit itself to a particular territory, language or race. Although more dynamic and wide-ranging the conventional one, this conception can become very rigid; and Iqbal's varies depending on the political context. Azad has a very broader conception of the notion of brotherhood in Islam. It includes all of humanity. This enables Azad to cooperate with non-Muslims to fight against imperialism and colonial oppression. His interpretation of nationalism does not see the need for a separate Muslim nationalism to the likes of Jinnah and his supports from the *Deobandi ulema*. Madani, on the other hand, has a more pragmatic approach to nationalism. This like Azad helps him to support the mainstream congress nationalism but oppose Hindu nationalism. However, he seems to have conception of nationalism and its compatibility in a very specific and limited sense. A distinction between Muslim brotherhood (Muslim Ummah) and human brotherhood seems to be emerging in such thinkers. There is also a tension between both these ideals which can be regulated and negotiated for Madani. Not so in the thought of Iqbal and other Islamists. This also prevents from composite nationalism becoming acceptable to Hindu nationalists and Islamic nationalists. It also failed to garner support from majority of Muslims in India. Therefore, the success of Muslim league. This appears to one of the reasons for its failure in the Indian context. Ambedkar makes a very important intervention into this debate. He is important because he appears and claims to have an unbiased view of politics at this time. This does not mean he does not have his values and sympathies. He openly shows this support for the rights of minorities of all kinds. However, he is critical of politics that claims exclusive rights for themselves whether it is Hindus or Muslims. Venkat Dulipala seems to acknowledge the importance of role played by Ambedkar. Therefore, there emerges what can be called a Dalit critique of mainstream nationalism. Dalit critique of nationalism does not have a problem with the very idea of nationalism itself but it is opposed to the way in which it deployed by mainstream congress elites. There is also a critique of Ambedkar against pan-Islamism or the idea of Islamic brotherhood. It is not truly universal in theory and certainly in practice. Moreover, it is un-egalitarian. He concedes to the Muslim demand as a group that they are a nation and therefore defends their nationalist aspiration of Pakistan. He also agrees with the Muslim groups their critique of congress nationalism. To conclude, Nationalism in the Indian context took various forms as it was adopted by numerous but diverse groups to articulate their interests and values. An example of this is apart from the mainstream nationalism there were many minor nationalisms that were shaped by linguistic, regional and cultural specificities. These minor nationalisms continue to challenge the mainstream version to this day.

References

Abu-Rabi', I. (2006). *The Blackwell Companion to Contemporary Islamic Thought.* Malden, MA: Blackwell.

Alam, A. (2016). *Deoband and Theological Anti-Pluralism: A Critique of Husain Ahmad Madani's 'Islam and Composite Nationalism.* New Age Islam. http://www.newageislam.com/books-and-documents/arshad-alam,-new-age-islam/deoband-and-theological-anti-pluralism--a-critique-of-husain-ahmad-madani's-'islam-and-composite-nationalism'/d/106179.

Ambedkar, B. (1990). *Dr. Babasaheb Ambedkar: Writings and Speeches* (vol. 1–17). Mumbai: Education Department, Government of Maharashtra.

Bilici, M. (2006). Ummah and empire: global formations after Nation, in A.-R. Ibrahim (Ed.), *The Blackwell Companion to Contemporary Islamic Thought* (pp. 313–327). Malden, MA: Blackwell.

Dhulipala, V. (2016). *Creating a New Medina: State Power, Islam, and the Quest for Pakistan in Late Colonial North India* (1st ed.). Delhi: Cambridge University Press.

Gould, W. (2004). *Hindu Nationalism and the Language of Politics in Late Colonial India.* Cambridge: Cambridge, UK [u.a.],.

Hameed, S. S. (1990). *Islam and Nationalism. India's Maulana: Abul Kalam Azad*, vol. II, New Delhi: Indian Council for Cultural Relations.

Madani, M. H. A. (2001). *Hamara Hindustan AurUskeFadhail*, tr. by Muhammad Anwar Hussain, *India Our Land and its Virtues*, New Delhi: Jamat-i-Ulama-i-Hind.

Madani, M. H. A. (2005). *Composite Nationalism and Islam.* New Delhi: Manohar Publications.

Metcalf, B. D. (1982). *Islamic Revival in British India*: Deoband, 1860–1900. Princeton, N.J.: Princeton University Press.

Metcalf, B. D. (2009). *Husain Ahmad Madani: The Jihad for Islam and India's Freedom.* Oxford: Oneworld.

Main, M. S. M. (2005). *The Prisoners of Malta.* New Delhi: Manak Publications.

Rahman, M. R., & Metcalf, B. D. (2009). *Husain Ahmad Madani: The Jihad for Islam and India's Freedom.* Hong Kong: Southeast Review of Asian Studies.https://www.thefreelibrary.

com/Barbara+D.+Metcalf%2C+Husain+Ahmad+Madani%3A+The+Jihad+for+Islam+and...-a0213529580.

Sevea, I. S. (2012). *The Political Philosophy of Muhammad Iqbal: Islam and Nationalism in Late Colonial India*. New York, Cambridge University Press.

Sherwani, L. A. (1995). *Speeches, Writings and Statements of Iqbal.*. Lahore: Iqbal Academy Pakistan.

Krishna Swamy Dara is faculty in the Department of Political Science at Jamia Millia Islamia, New Delhi, India. He received his Doctorate from the Department of Political Science at Jawaharlal Nehru University, New Delhi. His thesis titled "The Idea of Minority in Ambedkar's Thought: Equality and Differential Rights" was awarded the best PhD for 2007 by Nirman foundation, India. He completed his Post Doctoral research at the Humboldt University and the Wissenschaftskolleg zu Berlin where he assessed how caste (race), culture and law intersect, especially how the Dalit and African American experience has been in combating legal conservatism in India and the US. He has recently been a visiting professor at the University of Wurzburg, Germany.

His research interests include: Minority Issues, Indian Political Ideas with special emphasis on Minority Leaders and Thinkers; Minorities and Political Psychology with an emphasis on Dalits, Untouchability and the issue of Social Stigma, and Legal Reasoning and Practice in India with special reference to Religious and Social Minorities. He has extensive publications and presentations on the condition of minorities in India.

Chapter 7
Abul Kalam Azad and the Right to an Islamic Justification of the Indian Constitution

Shaunna Rodrigues

Abstract While the examination of the 'background conditions' to ideas that emerged in the Constituent Assembly has become a necessary paradigm for studies on Indian constitutionalism, little attention has been paid to religious justification as an important background condition to the formation of constitutional essentials in India. This chapter questions this secular bias in scholarship on Indian constitutionalism and argues that religious justifications played an important role in shaping the plural political conception contained in the Indian constitution. In particular, it studies the construction and endorsement of constitutional principles by Maulana Abul Kalam Azad. It argues that Azad developed a framework laying out the form and concepts of a justificatory discourse that adherents of Islam could endorse and employ in shaping a political conception for the future Constitution of India. By exploring his formulation of concepts of *tawhīd*, *jihād* and democratic equality, this paper elaborates the discursive strategies that Azad used to align political pluralism with Islamic ideals as they historically developed in South Asia. The paper concludes with a short reflection on why Azad's justification of constitutionalism in India has not retained its discursive power over time.

7.1 Introduction: The Political Azad

What does an Islamic justification for a liberal constitution look like, especially when such an Islamic justification is constructed by a significant minority? This paper seeks to answer this question by turning to the formulation of constitutional aspirations for India from the perspective of an Islamic political thinker—Abul Kalam Azad. It asks how the *plural* political conception that Indian institutions took as foundational to the Indian constitution, for a long time since independence, came to be envisaged and authenticated using arguments emerging from Islam in India.

S. Rodrigues (✉)
Department of Middle Eastern, South Asian and African Studies (MESAAS), Columbia University, New York, USA
e-mail: sr3328@columbia.edu

© Springer Nature Singapore Pte Ltd. 2020

A. Roy and M. Becker (eds.), *Dimensions of Constitutional Democracy*,
https://doi.org/10.1007/978-981-15-3899-5_7

At the heart of this paper is the political thought of Abul Kalam Azad, an important leader of India's anti-colonial movement as well as India's Constituent Assembly. He became politically prominent as the ideologue of the Khilafat Movement in the early 1920s, where he worked closely with Mohandas Gandhi, and an anti-imperial network located across the British empire extending from Egypt to Bengal, to preserve the authority of the Ottoman Sultan as the Caliph of Islam after the collapse of the Ottoman Empire (Minault 1982). After this, he was elected as the President of the Indian National Congress twice, first in 1923, and for the second time from 1940–1946. More significantly, he led negotiations between the British imperial state, the Muslim League, the Indian National Congress and other political groups and leaders in the years leading up to independence and post-colonial constitutionalism in India.

He was also highly respected among various political, religious and academic circles across the British imperial world for his scholarship on Islamic political and theological thought (Douglas 1988). Despite not being educated within the colonial system of education, Azad's thought transcended smaller circles of debate and discussion in the South Asian Islamic world to become relevant among Muslims outside of this region, as well as non-Muslims within the region. The means through which Azad reached out to this wide public readership, besides politics, was his Urdu journal *Al-Hilāl* which was censured under the Press Act of 1914 by the British colonial government. He also authored several books, his magnum opus being the *Tarjumān ul Qurā'n* or his commentary on the *Sūrah al Fātiha* of the *Qurā'n.*

7.2 Azad's Constitutional Aspiration for Independent India

In assessing Azad's thought as a constitutional aspiration for post-colonial India, this paper shifts the focus from the usual framework of studies on Azad, i.e. to study him as a historical anti-colonial and nationalist Muslim figure who valued pluralism as a political ideal. We argue here that Azad's constitutional aspirations were not only seeped in contesting the denial of basic dignity and rights by the imperial state to its subjects. Rather, he went a step beyond many of those who used legislative means to contest the imperial state in India by questioning what he identified as an imperial construction of the political and attempting to restructure this framework. In doing so, he developed an alternative framework laying out the form and concepts of a justificatory discourse that adherents of Islam could endorse and employ to shape a political conception for the future Constitution of India.

In considering the normative imagination of constitutionalism from the perspective of one of independent India's most prominent Islamic thinkers, this paper delves into Azad's preferences, methods and practices of justification, which employed an Islamic worldview in a modern constitutional democracy. These preferences, methods and practices, it argues, demonstrated a strong claim to extend and establish, as normatively desirable for Indian democracy as a whole, a discursive power in the public domain for Islamic justifications of constitutionalism, the rule of law and stable social cooperation across diverse groups in the polity. Thinkers like Azad constituted adherents of Islam as a significant minority who had a right to Islamic justification within India's constitutional democracy.[1]

In order to build this right to Islamic justification, Azad interrogated the boundaries of the political, as established by British imperial rule for India, to argue that it can and should be reconstructed to incorporate ethical, moral and theological arguments emerging from, among other sources of Indian traditions, Islam, on the nature, justification and critique of a unified rule of law for a diverse people. Further, he contended that Islamic arguments also ought to shape imaginaries of self-rule, which would be exemplified in the rule of law that independent India would adopt for itself. In particular, this paper focuses on how he argued for this by rejecting a secular worldview as an inevitable evaluative criterion of the political in a constitutional democracy like India.

Thus, the constitutional aspiration for a post-colonial India that emerged from his anti-colonial thought did not adhere to a constitutional defiance of imperialism, like the political praxis and thought of many other anti-colonialists has been described (De 2015), rather, it emerged from a defiance of imperial constitutionalism altogether. We follow the lexical steps that Azad employed in this defiance of imperial constitutionalism to build a strong constitutional aspiration for Islamic adherents in India through the different sections of this paper.

Part I looks at how he demarcated and established the significance of different *forms* of argument to the political in India. Part II analyses how he conceptualized the political, based on an 'alternative universality' emerging from Islamic sources, by dissembling basic concepts emerging from different forms of argument to justify non-secular but plural political conceptions for constitutionalism in India. Part III assesses how these practices of justification contested the requirement of a secular worldview as a necessary criterion for the evaluation of the political, and therefore also questioned the form of management of populations that a secular worldview enabled for the modern state. Part IV discusses the implications of these Islamic practices of justification for constitutionalism in India.

7.3 Political Liberalism and the Dilemmas of Diversity

In the last century or so normative liberal political theory has taken an unquestionably secular approach when it comes to building political frameworks for constitutional democracies. Prominent liberal and constitutional answers to the question of inadmissibility of religious arguments in public deliberation have varied over a limited range which (i) asserts a principle of religious self-restraint altogether or (ii) demands

[1]In using the term right to Islamic justification, this paper uses and develops Rainer Forst's framework for a right to justification within the contemporary Indian context. See Rainer Forst. (2014) *The Right to Justification: Elements for a Constructivist Theory of Justice,* (New York: Columbia University Press).

that any religious arguments be translated into the vocabulary of 'public reason' in the public sphere (Rawls 1997) or (iii) more recently, accepts a religious argument so long as there is due recognition of the secular aspects and constitutional structure of pluralist constitutional democracies (Waldron 2012). The emphasis in these arguments has been to assume a secular worldview as the necessary evaluative criterion to assess reasons emerging from non-secular epistemes in the public sphere.

The approach towards religion in the public sphere can be seen in contemporary Indian debates on constitutionalism as well. In this discourse, the impartial terrain of the law has been seen as an exemplary secular space of public political reason (Krishnaswamy 2011). The capacity for religious reasons to determine the contours of the political or the law is minimal, even while the law has historically assumed rightful power to structure, determine and change religious convictions (John 2019). This one-way traffic in the influence of foundational aspects of constitutionalism, such as the rule of law, over religion has arbitrated both the regulative functions of religion including various practices and personal laws, as well as cognitive forms of religious conviction itself.[2]

These debates have predominantly treated religion as a fixed conceptual category, i.e. as containing certain criteria and characteristics of religious conviction that different religions either fulfil, or can fulfil once reformed and rationalized by the law. This has led large religions like Hinduism and Islam in India to be treated as internally and epistemically homogenous,[3] rather than containing different forms, concepts and traditions of arguments within themselves. It has also caused the entrenchment and institutionalization of a secular worldview as the only and necessary evaluative criterion towards diverse modes of life categorized under the epistemically homogenous label of religion. In doing so, the law and democratic public reason in India have predominantly employed a justificatory discourse constructed around the conceptual vocabulary of political liberalism, especially concepts such as equal rights.

7.4 Contesting Religion as a Homogenous Category

Abul Kalam Azad's thought provides an excellent framework to question this rationalizing approach that the law and constitutionalism in India takes towards religion. Contesting the public portrayal of 'religion' as a homogenous category, Azad did not follow a strategy of combining different forms of Islamic argument into a single text, speech or pamphlet. Rather, he explicitly employed a discursive strategy which

---

[2]This can be seen in the several cases which use Article 25 (a) and Article 25 (2) (b) of the Constitution of India to structure religion into a core set of essential beliefs. See Ronojoy Sen (2009) "The Indian Supreme Court and the Quest for a "rational" Hinduism", *South Asian History and Culture,* 1:1, 86–104.

[3]Few within the discourse on constitutionalism in India have noticed and pointed out this rationalizing and homogenizing approach towards religion by the law. For an exceptional analysis of this see Mathew John (2019) 'Framing Religion in Constitutional Politics: A View from Indian Constitutional Law', *South Asian History and Culture,* 10, 2,124–135.

distinguished between different forms of (religious) argument such as religious commands from revealed texts, theological or moral doctrines, juridical debates emerging from historical contestations in Islamic law, and references to practices found in religious traditions. He provided the justification and appeal behind distinguishing between these different forms of arguments in the prefaces to his form-specific writing, speeches and praxis. This made him one of the most methodologically conscious and astute political thinkers of his time.

He defended political and social diversity, and Islamic modes of engaging with the same, through sets of epistemologically separate arguments in different texts that he wrote. Using this method consistently, he provided Islamic constructions for a plural political conception that India could adopt through theological arguments in his *Tarjuman-ul-Qurān*, or genealogically constructed arguments in his *Tazkirah*, political theoretical contentions on self-rule and distributive justice in his 1940 Rampur Congress Presidential Address, or *fiqh* or Islamic jurisprudential arguments in his *Jazirat-al-'Arab*.

7.5 Dissembling Multiple Sources of Islamic Arguments

Demonstrating the distinctions between different forms of Islamic argument allowed him to make a variety of Islamic concepts and vocabulary accessible in and to the public, letting both Muslims and non-Muslims engage with them in the variety that they presented. Dissembling Islamic ideas into different forms revealed several bases of political engagement, each with a greater or lesser degree of appeal to India's diverse public. Islamic arguments publicly presented in this way held an appeal not just as (private) moral motivations, but also as multiple sources and forms of moral knowledge which could address problems of collective action. It demonstrated that the debate on religious reasons in public justification itself cannot be worded as such as there was no such thing as a single Islamic argument. Further, it also indicated that some forms of argument could be translated relatively easily in other moral languages, like that of the law. Given this, it also made a stronger case for the acceptability of *an* Islamic argument, if not all *all* Islamic arguments, in the public domain.

In employing this discursive strategy to shape constitutional aspirations for India from an Islamic point of view, Azad demonstrated that an Islamic argument need not be evaluated merely on grounds of being religious or not, but could be made available for deliberative engagement through different typologies of reasons considered to be Islamic. Given this, Islam did not have to be seen in a homogenous way, from the 'outside', but could be accessed in its internal diversity as well. In portraying an Islamic argument in this way, Azad exerted a constitutional aspiration for a more nuanced mode of politics which did not reduce political morality to one master value like secularism or religious self-restraint.

7.6 Questioning the Modern State's Approach Towards Difference

Azad was also one of the first influential Muslim political figures in India to publicly argue for an alliance between Hindus and Muslims against imperial rule and to conceptualize the idea of social solidarity that we see in the Indian Constitution. The public appeal of Azad's Islamic discourse contested the modern British colonial state's approach to difference, later adopted by the Indian multicultural state, that debates occurring within minority religious groups ought to stay and be resolved within those communities, and be predominantly outside the purview of politics, unless violating some fundamental right to be human.[4]

As many have pointed out, this assumption emerged and continued from the characterization and management of populations according to their religion and customs by the British imperial state (Chatterjee 1993; Mamdani 2012; Mantena 2010). It allowed for the secular state to equate positions by a consolidated religious community with a representative element (such as a person, or a set of customs or laws) of the community in public, rather than acknowledging the ethical, legal, political, and knowledge structures which maintain different groups as single religious communities.

Against this assumption of the modern state Azad posited an 'alternative universality', a normative description that Uday Mehta gives to the constitutional aspirations of anti-colonial thought (Mehta et al. 2016), to the modern state's management of difference. This 'alternative universality' emerged around a set of related concepts developed to reconstruct a political domain different from the secular political domain shaped by imperial laws and government in India.

7.7 The Relevance of *Tawhīd*

The first set of these concepts referred to the importance of acknowledging the political as being a part of the unity constituted by different attributes of god in different spheres of life or *tawhīd*.

In his magnum opus, the *Tarjumān-ul-Qur'ān*, Azad argued that one could not attribute god's qualities to any other being. Approaching the idea of god through similitude reduced one's perception of what god can be and restricts one's access to attributes such as god's providence (*rubūbiyat*), mercy (*rahmat*) and justice (*adālat*) (Azad 1962). According to him, drawing analogies of god had led (Western) anthropologists to argue that the idea of god had developed through an 'evolutionary process' of the human mind—through the honing of man's cognitive abilities. Secular epistemology was portrayed as an outcome of this evolutionary process (Ibid 99). But,

[4]For those who have critically assessed the Indian multicultural state along these lines see Gurpreet Mahajan (2012), *Accommodating Diversity: Ideas and Institutional Practices*, (New Delhi: Oxford University Press).

Azad contended, belief in the existence of god could never be an achievement of the human mind because the human mind was bound by its senses and could not comprehend the totality of *tawhīd*, it could only understand different attributes of *tawhīd*. Not accepting this idea of *tawhīd* would be both ontologically and epistemically limiting for man.

The relevance of *tawhīd*, Azad argued, extended to every aspect of human activity including matters of public and political concern. 'If I separate *tawhid* from politics, what will remain? I have deprived my politics of religion but my ideas are themselves the product of religion. How can I separate them?' (Azad 1990a). He made this argument in his journal, *Al-Hilal* as early as 1913 before Gandhi began to use this as a dictum for his own conception of the political. For Azad, the secularizing impulse in the political domain had separated human life into different domains of thought and praxis. While Azad was not averse to identifying and constructing different forms of argument, he also thought it necessary to pay attention to what held these together: the idea of *tawhīd*.

Further, modernity's urge to place everything within the domain of what man knew with certainty, rather than accepting that there are some things over which man cannot have complete knowledge, had led man to a political condition that was debilitating rather than enabling. Thus, state structuring of populations based on anthropological knowledge which attempted to capture all knowledge possible on colonized peoples, had placed the latter into separate religious groups based on characteristics identified as 'social'. This had led to the consolidation of different communities adhering to Islam in India into a political community identified as Muslims, separate from other groups that were categorized as Hindu. However, as Azad pointed out, this totalizing attempt by the modern state to gain knowledge of diverse people did not simultaneously occupy the 'sacred space' through which these groups themselves identified with each other. This 'sacred space' did not necessarily exist through cultural practices, though Azad often wrote about shared practices between Hindus and Muslims. According to him, it lay in a shared acceptance of the idea of *tawhīd* (Azad 1990a).

Despite the secularizing impulse created by the imperial state, he also saw *tawhīd* as being at the heart of the formation of the political. Man's attempt to construct in the state a valued unity between political ideas of justice (*adālat*), affective ideas like mercy (*rehmat*), and economic ideas of building and distributing an abundance of resources, was actually not a secular impulse, but one of constructed similitude with the unity of god or *tawhīd*. In trying to emulate the unity of *tawhīd*, the modern, imperial state employed a metaphor of secularism, but such an order of things, according to Azad, could only be a limited one. Given, this, could a conception of politics that valued its unity in structuring and influencing everything else be, at all a secular one?

In extending a theological concept like *tawhīd* to the question of state unity, his emphasis was more an epistemological one, pertaining to the modes of knowledge through which the modern state came to understand the concepts that shaped the political domain over which it claimed control.[5] A defiance of such an imperial construction of the political, had to begin with identifying the limitations of drawing importance to the unity of the state and its agentic activity.

7.8 Muslims in India and Their Right to Justification

Azad had specific motives in reasserting the political field around the idea of *tawhīd*: Initially, it was to bring Muslims out of what he called their "position of passivity", vis-a-vis the imperial state, and "slavery" to a secular social domain as constructed by this state (Azad 1990b). He simply argued that Muslims ought to make themselves present in the political domain on their own terms. They could not remain silent in terms of their political assertions while their fellow Hindu residents in the subcontinent made a radical political claim of self-rule for all those living in colonial India.

By arguing for the presence of Muslims in the political domain, on their own terms, Azad was asserting that Muslims had a right to justification, that is, the right to reject the imperial state's formulation of political and constitutional essentials, using the multiple vocabularies, practices and ethical inheritances of Islam in India. He asserted this right by first recognizing how relations between political concepts as drawn by the imperial state undercut the ideas fundamental to imaginaries of social cooperation that Muslims valued, such as the idea of *tawhīd.* His primary attempt in doing so was to provide discursive power to, and highlight the burdens of judgement involved in political concepts which draw their significance from accepting the non-secular idea of a unity of god.

This becomes clear in his later *Al-Hilāl* writings: In these, he states that the real purpose of his journal *Al-Hilāl* is to invite his readers to follow *tawhīd* in making sense of the world in order to bring about self-rule. Accepting *tawhīd* as relevant to politics would enable those who accepted the idea of god(s) as an operative epistemic frame in politics to assert this claim in public, and invoke a substantial spirit in them that was not merely religious as secularists understood religion, but political because of the way in which it assumed the space to assert such a theological argument in the public domain (Azad 1990a).

7.9 Pluralism and Self-rule

The implications for those who accept *tawhīd* would be to derive justifications for the political from traditions of thought that valued different conceptions of god. While

[5]Unlike other theorists who use similar arguments on similitude to make vastly differing claims on the nature of sovereignty, etc., with exclusive implications, rather than the inclusive implications of Azad's formulation of *tawhīd.*

Azad argued that the Qura'n and Islam possessed a very refined idea of what he projected as a universal idea of *tawhīd*, he did not limit himself to Islamic sources in constructing this argument. Other traditions ranging from the ancient Greek thought, to Chinese conceptions of god possessed a conception of *tawhīd* as well and these, according to him, needed to be pitched against the secular arguments of liberal imperialism to build an idea of the political.

The case for building an alliance with the Hindus was made stronger by Azad's search for an idea of *tawhīd* in traditions that could broadly be considered Hindu. Although he was critical of the way practices of (Hindu) Brahmanism tried to substantiate *tawhīd* with polytheism, this did not reduce the importance of the epistemic way of thinking centred around *tawhīd* in what was now considered Hindu traditions as well. Drawing on this episteme would undermine the domination of secular ways of thinking that liberal imperialism had brought about and was one of the most important steps towards self-rule (Azad 1962).

Such a conception of self-rule would be important to Muslims in particular as it implied ridding oneself of one's fear of the Hindu majority and building grounds of alliance with them on a conception of the political that did not consider the secular to be primary to it. Commentators on Azad argue that this argument for an alliance was driven by pragmatic concerns more than just a philosophical scheme in Azad's thought. Whatever the intention behind his thought, there was a coherence to the way in which Azad connected self-rule to the concept of *tawhīd* that lent degree of compulsiveness to his construction of this non-secular political domain.[6] This coherence was brought about with his use of the normative and political idea of *Jihād*.

7.10 Azad's Early and Later Formulations and Practice of Jihād

Ayesha Jalal argues that during the decade of the First World War, Azad was perhaps the most celebrated theorist of transnational *Jihād*. He 'was the foremost Indian Muslim intellectual to blend the politics of Islamic universalism with a comprehensive anti-colonial vision derived from a close study of the Quranic concept of *jihād*' (Jalal 2007, p. 99) The effective meaning of *Jihād* in Azad's formulation was to *discursively* formulate political action for Indians as a whole, and not just Muslims alone, while simultaneously questioning how various forms of concentrated power, extending from the religiously dominant *Ulāma* to the pervasive might of the British empire, constantly sought to do so for those who had to adhere to their power. Azad's use

[6]In making this point, we borrow Talal Asad's argument on attributing coherence to a body of thought, i.e. to argue for a form of coherence by which a discourse is held together is not ipso facto to justify or defend that discourse; it is merely to take an essential step in the problem of explaining its *compulsiveness*. See Asad, Talal. *Genealogies of religion: Discipline and Reasons of Power in Christianity and Islam,* (Baltimore: John Hopkins University Press, 2009).

of the term *Jihād* occured close to a century before its instant synonymisation with ideas of religious violence and danger by the dominant vocabulary and operation of laws created by the Global War on Terror. His imagination of the term, especially as one defined in and through the historical circuits of mobility through which anti-imperialism was organized in the 1910s and 1920s, employed different sites and modes of realizing *Jihād* than the stereotypical conceptions of it in the contemporary world.[7]

In his initial years of writing, *Jihād* was used by Azad as a conception of 'internal' struggle, first for his own personality which valued freedom above all else (hence his adoption of the pseudonym Azad, literally meaning 'free', in political life), and then against the 'medievalism' of Islamic jurisprudence (*fiqh*) and customs.[8] According to Azad, the *ulāma* or scholars of Islamic theology and jurisprudence, were not the only ones who could preach the good, and prohibit the wrong, as was traditionally argued within Islamic discourse (Douglas 1988).

Rather, shaping the good and knowing the wrong was the collective duty and struggle (*jihād*) of the people at large rather than the prerogative of consensus among religious scholars. Here, he was departing from the agreement between *Qurā'nic* and *fiqh* scholars on how consensus as a determining principle for those who followed Islam could be employed.[9] Azad's first development of the idea of *jihād*, therefore, was in opposition to the *ulāma*, or Islamic religious scholars of the time. His questioning of the *ulāma* was no secret and he remained, throughout his political career, a well-respected critic of the *ulāma* both in India and elsewhere.

His use of the term *jihād* shifted to the idea of a struggle against the rule of liberal imperialism in the early 1910s, the same time in which he began to see those who identified themselves as Hindus as employing non-secular arguments for self-rule. The imperial state, both in its imposition of an unfair, 'external' rule, and in its enforcement of a secular laws of politics had made the political terrain devoid of the epistemic crossings emerging from different groups in India prior to secularization (Azad 1990b). Under a section titled "A Special Chapter of Indian History" in his journal *Al-Hilāl,* Azad asserted that Muslims in India would, like their non-Muslim

[7]For critical accounts of *Jihād* shaped by the Global War on Terror, see Faisal Devji 2005. *Landscapes of the Jihad, Militancy, Morality and Modernity, Ithaca: Cornell University Press; Darryl Li (2020), The Universal Enemy: Jihad, Empire and the Challenge of Solidarity, Stanford: Stanford University Press.*

[8]In this formulation of both *tawhid* and *jihad,* the influence of Sufism and mysticism, especially that of the Sindhi mystic Sarmad Shaheed on Azad thinking is evident. For more on this see Syeda Hameed, *Islamic Seal on India's Independence*, (Karachi: Oxford University Press, 1998) pp. 46–50. Azad's aversion to the importance of *taqlīd* (unquestioned adherence to the opinions of Islamicjurisprudence/fiqh) was what eventually led to Azad's estrangement from Shībli Numāni, his political mentor in the early 1910s. See Syeda Hameed's Introduction to Azad's edited works in Syeda Saiyidain Hameed eds. *India's Maulana Abul Kalam Azad 1888–1958.* (New Delhi: Indian Council for Cultural Relations, Vikas Publishing House, 1990).

[9]This was one of the central grounds of debate among Muslim political figures in South Asia in the late twentieth and early twenty-first centuries. See Shaikh, Farzana. (1989). *Community and Consensus in Islam: Muslim Representation in Colonial India, 1860–1947* (Cambridge: Cambridge University Press).

contemporaries, have to acknowledge that "The country was groaning under unjust laws. The Hindus (have) launched a *Jihād* against these," and Muslims needed to join them (Azad 2002). *Jihād,* thus, according to Azad, was a struggle which non-Muslims could shape and participate in, and in the Indian context entailed questioning the process of secularization imposed on politics by British imperial power.

In this, Azad was not averse to 'the use of the sword'. However, a physical war to exemplify *jihād* against the imperial state was not suitable, he argued, because the oppression of religious justificatory practices caused by imperial secularization had not explicitly occured through conquest but through the political processes that now structured British India. Given that such oppression took place because of the modern forms of knowledge collection, bureaucratic organization of populations, and the operation of political institutions espoused by the British government across its empire, Azad argued that the means to wage *jihād* had to be the spoken and written word.[10] The process and justification of undertaking *jihād,* therefore, had to be shaped by the 'wrong' that *jihād* was questioning. Unlike *tawhīd,* which Azad treated as an epistemological and theological concept, *jihād* came to be conceptualized by him as an ethical form of praxis against epistemic violence and political rule emerging from it.

Further, Azad created a difference between temporal warfare *(harb)* and *jihād.* While *harb* referred to wars in which human beings were subjugated, *jihād* referred to a struggle to establish peace, freedom and the dignity of man (Azad 1920; Jalal 1994, p. 104). It was different from *harb* because it could not be assessed from the temporal plane alone, but had to be imbued with the idea of *tawhid,* or conducting an act of protest keeping in mind *adālat* (justice), *rehmat* (mercy) and rubūbiyat (providence).

Azad's analysis of the imperial state as an impediment to attaining an ethical idea of good was not based on a racial or religious distinction of the brown man versus the European, or the Muslim versus the Christian/non-Muslim. Rather, it was based on questioning the imperial framework of the political which excluded ethical arguments on grounds of difference. His *jihād* of the 'written word' against the empire became evident through his journals like the *Al Hilāl* and *Al-Balagh*, his writings both in Urdu as well as their translations in English and other languages which he oversaw with care, and the speeches he gave over the course of his political career.

7.11 Common Ground with Non-Muslims

This conception of *jihād* was strengthened because of the way Azad began to formulate the interactions of Muslims with non-Muslims. Explaining the Shar'ia in the light of the *Surah-e-Mumtahina* of the Qur'an, Azad classified two types of

---

[10]The struggle with rejecting violent forms of protest was evident in Azad's own struggle with Gandhi's approach to non-violence, especially in his calling off of the Non-cooperation in the Chauri Chaura movement. For more on this, see Abul Kalam Azad, *Quol-e-Faisal*, in Syeda Hameed, *India's Maulana Abul Kalam Azad.*

non-Muslims: those who do not declare war on Muslims and those who massacre Muslims. He argued that the Qur'an asks Muslims to enter into treaties with the former while severing connections with the latter (Hameed 2014, pp. 94–95). The Hindus, and those who identified as Indians fell into the former category, because of their shared and continued presence in the place that was India. After World War I and the pressure that the British put on the Caliph in Turkey to step down, the British imperial state and its officials fell into the latter category.

The Hindus, he argued, have already paved the way for self-rule of India.[11] Muslims needed to participate in this formative anti-imperial public which was paving the way for their self-rule too. Along with their own internal struggle and adherence to *tawhīd,* Muslims must join Hindus in the struggle to demand political justice from those (British imperial and colonial officials) who forced their own political precepts on them (Hindus and Muslims) (Azad 1990b).

Self-rule was important, according to Azad, as it implied ridding oneself of one's fear of the Hindu majority. Muslims should join hands with Hindus as power did not lie in just a 'numbers game' but in claiming deliberative space in the political domain through a combination of political values like social solidarity, the ability to respond to collective problems and developing a plural moral attitude towards others. At the time at which he was making this argument, very few other Muslim political leaders were engaged in conceptualizing self-rule along the lines of Hindu-Muslim unity. 'The Hindu Muslim issue is an acrobatic feat in which, unfortunately, those who are expected to perform are rarely found in the arena' (Azad 1990a). Thus, *jihād*, for Azad, was an ethical principle which had to be exemplified as much through regulative practices of public politics and faith, *as* the cognitive practices of belief.

7.12 India's Political Domain and Its Overlapping Publics

What was the implication of conceptualizing the non-secular political domain in this way? Azad, was able to speak to two overlapping but differently driven 'publics'. The first was a nationalist anti-imperial public that used principles emerging from the rule of law, as conceptualized by the imperial state in India, in its anti-colonial, independence movement. The main political figures within this public were intent on giving the diverse people of India a self-definition to demand a constitution of their own.

The second was a more complicated 'public'—one that had been consolidated into a single Muslim community through the forms state management practiced by the imperial state—the creation of a census based on religion, the codification of Muslim personal laws, the creation of a separate electorate, the knowledge systems of imperial

[11]Gandhi had already published his tract on *Hind Swaraj* (Self-Rule) in 1908, where he makes his argument that *Swaraj,* the word used for freedom from colonial rule by Indian nationalists at that time needs to translate into self-rule rather than mere home-rule. Azad's position comes very close to Gandhi on this.

bureaucracy—which categorized diverse customs and practices in the subcontinent into large religious categories viewed from the outside rather than within (Cohn 1996; Kaviraj 2010). Azad's publication of the *Al-Hilāl* as a weekly journal was an attempt to bring the Muslim community, which shared in common both epistemic forms of sense-making of the world around them, as well as a constructed and codified form of claim-making vis-a-vis the imperial state, into the first kind of nationalist, anti-imperial public.

Several concerns came to inform the debates which took place among Muslim political thinkers in the period from 1931 to 1946. The foremost among them, however, was the question of what is central to Islam in the subcontinent. Thinkers like Jinnah argued that the most important concern for Islam in the subcontinent was the minority status of Muslims in the region. This concern was predominantly articulated by employing the sociological identity of Muslims versus non-Muslims, without taking into consideration (a) the imperial processes that had gone into creating majorities and minorities, and (b) the difference in ethical frameworks with which different ethnic groups within this consolidated minority Muslim community approached politics, even while there was a larger Islamic epistemic framework which held their religious convictions together. To that extent, many have argued that Jinnah was representing an 'interest group' within the political domain by arguing predominantly for the distribution of economic and political interests to Muslims, rather than paying attention to the varying ethical character, modes of justification, differing traditions customs and customary laws, as well as the regional locations and place-making capacity of Muslims across South Asia.

7.13 Grounds for the Recognition of Minorities

There were many factors that went into Azad's position of rejecting the claim for minority status purely on grounds of numbers pertaining to the calculus of the modern state's sociology of Muslims in India. First, his emphasis on lexically dissembling the form and then basic concepts emerging from Islamic arguments, asserted his explicit intentions to frame a minority as a political group which had the right to justify a political framework for themselves on their terms. His argument for a 'minority' came to be constructed not primarily on the basis of a sociological calculation of a Muslim minority and their interests of distributive justice, but through the construction of an epistemological 'minority' or group that could participate as equals by using Islamic ideas and discursive traditions in India's aspiring deliberative democracy. The constitutional framework discussed below that he proposed for minorities substantiates this point.

Second, his experience of travelling across the Muslim world extending from Egypt to Burma had made him aware of the deep diversity that existed within it, including within South Asia itself. Given this, Muslims, even in India couldn't be seen as possessing a fixed and consolidated set of interests, especially when it came to the distribution of primary goods. Therefore, the modern state's calculus of understanding and providing separate representation, and eventually a separate nation, to a Muslim minority based on numbers could not be the basis of a foundational argument for asserting democratic equality and participation for Muslims.

Rather, Muslims, as a *significant* minority ought to be recognized as they developed discursive and justificatory practices to represent their epistemological, ethical and political positions in a constitutional democracy. On this, Azad shared a position similar to Muhammad Iqbal. For both of them, the most important concern for Islam in South Asia was to recover and reconstruct an Islamic domain of the political from the onslaught of colonial modernity.[12] It was in the manner in which they extended this domain to non-Muslims on which they differed.

7.14 Azad's Constitutional Framework for the Rights of Minorities

Azad took a different position from the Muslim League in the subcontinent on the question of having a separate legislative framework for Muslims to build a political consensus on the frameworks, concepts and primary goods that must drive their collective lives. Rejecting the proposal for separate legislatures, Azad framed his argument for Muslims as a significant minority by constructing a *right to justification* for Muslims in a public domain where they could exist and deliberate as equal citizens with non-Muslims.

From the first major election after the Government of India Act, 1935, till the Partition of the subcontinent into Pakistan, there was an increased public use of terms like majority and minority as essentialized categories, fixed according to the religious communities identified by the imperial state as Hindu and Muslim. Azad held this fixity as responsible for the rise in the demand for Pakistan (Azad A. K. 1988). In an attempt to question the separatism that such fixed categories of majority and minority had given rise to, he proposed a unified constitutional framework that could enable a right to Islamic justification in India.

According to this framework, (i) Any constitution that would be framed for India must contain the fullest guarantees for the protection of the rights and interests of those now politically identified as minorities. (ii) The decision with regard to safeguards for the protection of the rights and interests of the minorities must rest with the minorities and not the constructed majority. (iii) The safeguards must be formulated by minority consent and not by majority vote (Azad 1985).

If the Constitution of India sought to shape and maintain a deeply diverse polity, as many have argued it was, then it had to be defined in a big way by the guarantees it extended to what it recognized as minority communities. The foundational argument

[12] Azad's contemporaries like Muhammad Iqbal engaged deeply with modern Western epistemology in order to develop a reconstructed Islamic critique of the same. For more on this see Iqbal, Muhammad; *The Reconstruction of Religious Thought in Islam.*

Azad was asserting by placing the acceptability of guarantees for minorities in their own hands or consent, was that the justification of these guarantees could also come from the understanding of the political that a minority had. Having provided the resources for an Islamic justification of these guarantees, Azad was aware that this justification would not be the primary one acceptable to all the different groups within the Indian polity. However, this did not mean that it had to be silenced or undermined in shaping the Constitution, rather, an Islamic construction of the political and an Islamic justification of the Constitution had to be as relevant as a secular justification in being the evaluative criteria for the guarantees provided by the Constitution.

Azad's framework was based on a key principle: legitimacy could not lie only in representation alone, but in enabling a variety of justifications emerging from different epistemologies to be determining parts of the public reason nurturing India's constitution. While it accepted that undeserved inequalities derived from historical-social contingencies that shaped a minority must be redressed through the Constitution, it appealed to another idea strongly as well: that the shaping of the political could not proceed through a dichotomous position of representative (and separatist) Muslim nationalism versus imperial liberalism or nationalist secularism, but through an assertion that a significant minority can shape the major reasons, justifications and frameworks around which a political conception is adopted for the society as a whole.

7.15 Azad and the Esteem Conception of Pluralism

The conception of pluralism and toleration demanded by Azad, as an Islamic thinker and a leader of a significant minority in India, from the Constitution of India, did not submit to a 'permission conception' of toleration in which pluralism and toleration are understood as emerging from a relation between an authority/majority and a 'different' group/minority, where the authority gives a qualified permission (often conceived as the right to freedom of religion) to the minority to live according to their beliefs (Forst 2013). Nor was it a mere *modus vivendi* to develop institutional arrangements that would demonstrate a preference for peaceful coexistence over conflict. It even went beyond a conception of qualitative equality and respect for distinct ethical-cultural identities on the basis of which certain exceptions from existing legal structures are provided,[13] and according to which many have assessed and applauded India's accommodation of diversity. Azad's conception of pluralism, through his assertion for a right to Islamic justification in India, came close to an 'esteem conception' of pluralism and toleration (Ibid), where mutual recognition between citizens involved taking an others' perspective, in our case an Islamic justification for Constitutional essentials in India, as ethically attractive and valuable to democracy in India as a whole.[14]

---

[13]This view was questioned for its imperial roots in Part I of this paper.

[14]These approaches towards toleration are taken from Rainer Forst (2013), *Toleration in Conflict: Past and Present,* trans. Ciaran Croni, (Cambridge: Cambridge University Press). While Forst's

It is through this framework that Azad attempted to demonstrate how a Muslim ought not to give up her right to treat the whole of India as her domain too, or share in shaping its political life. The expectation from his proposal was that there would be a social bond created between the majority and the minority, with the majority reaching out to the demands of, and learning more about the justifications for these, of the minority. The minority, on the other hand, would have the assurance of shaping the good of the political community in a substantive manner on its own terms.

7.16 Why Has Azad's Argument Not Retained Its Discursive Power Over Time?

While Islamic religious belief has been protected through the fundamental right to the freedom of religion in the Constitution of India, Islam's relevance as a political doctrine has seen a trajectory where it has gone from being *irrelevant* to the political domain due to its theological framings, to being blatantly *objectionable* to majoritarian sensibilities. Nehruvian secularism, following from British liberal imperialism, gave 'positive' reasons, such as the inevitability of viewing pluralism through an epistemically secular lens, thus sidelining Islamic arguments from shaping the politics in independent India. Unfortunately, the *only* permissable political argument used to trump the 'negative' reasoning of Hindu majoritarian politics against Islamic justification of India's political conception in the public sphere[15] are these 'positive' arguments of Nehruvian secularism.

However, both these 'positive' and 'negative' reasons specify a range of limits to the toleration of religious reasons in the public sphere. Islamic reasoning in India now lies at a point on this limit where reasons for its rejection have predominantly been portrayed as stronger than reasons for its acceptance.

One can turn to academic writing on political thought in India to assess why Azad's argument did not retain its discursive power over time. Post-colonial India's writing on history, politics and constitution making, has blatantly overlooked Azad's role in shaping the background conditions to the Constitution of India, focussing more on his anti-colonialism rather than his justification of post-colonial constitutionalism. While Nehru has often been given credit for the constitutional framework outlined in Part III of this paper, Azad, with his clear formulation of a constitutional scheme for the treatment of minorities has been read as only borrowing this idea from Nehru. There is nothing to prove that Azad's formulation of a political framework for guarantees to minorities in India was actually provided by Nehru. Even if this did happen,

magnificent work details various models of toleration drawn from detailed analysis of the history of TransAtlantic political thought, this paper works with these conceptions as useful analytic models rather than historical descriptions.

[15]Such as the (politically and historically incorrect) argument that Islamic justifications now have no place in India with the creation of Pakistan.

Azad's justifications for the same varied from Nehru's politically secular vision for constitutional pluralism in India.

This academic conflation between the justificatory discourses of Azad and Nehru indicates a paucity within scholarship on Indian history and writing on constitutionalism and political thought, which has failed to acknowledge thinkers like Azad as visionaries of the plural political conception that India came to adopt at the time of independence from British rule. As the president of the Congress in the final years of colonial rule in India, Azad played a leading role in the defiance of imperial structures of rule, as well as in providing a vision for Constitution making in India.

7.17 Conclusion

Azad, a political figure who was constantly been labelled by the colonial state as a *jihādist*, a pan Islamist, as non-secular person and, therefore, fundamentalist, was deeply responsive to the impact of this colonial discourse on what he called the 'paranoia of communal Hindus'. He often called out what he called 'the fear of the majority' when claims to employ Islamic justifications were publicly perceived as an Islamic conspiracy in India (Hameed 2014).

In arguing that (i) the distinction between the political and what was considered religion did not hold, that (ii) this allowed India as a whole to reach into the realm of all that came to be recognized in the 20th century as religion to shape the political conception of the constitution as a whole, and that (iii) this religion could be that of a minority, Azad demanded from the Indian polity, and the Constitution that would provide it a collective self-expression, an acknowledgement of the deep diversity that constituted it.

This would require a self-definition of a polity which could provide an alternative universality for diverse adherents of non-liberal doctrines comprising the *demos* of independent India. The self-definition constructed by Azad using Islamic concepts, contained a particular political agency when it emerged initially, i.e. when he constructed his constitutional aspirations using the methods and conceptual frameworks of *tawhīd*, *jihād* and self-rule—a political agency that gained from employing a 'lived in' vocabulary and epistemology to shape the political principles that a people could aspire for. But there was a marked rupture between this kind of political domain that Azad emphasized in his constitutional aspiration and the political domain that eventually developed through dominant interpretations of the Indian Constitution and its public.

It is not the contingencies of Partition, however, that this paper holds responsible for the silence of this kind of argument in the discourse on Indian constitutionalism, but (i) the dominance of secular assumptions in thinking about constitutionalism and (ii) the focus on identity constructed around sociological categories alone rather than an active engagement with Islamic modes of justification in the constitutional reasoning of post-colonial India

Against the background of liberal imperialism, and the current foreground of majoritarianism in India, bringing Azad's constitutional aspirations to the fore would require acknowledging the legitimacy it has in a plural polity for providing the alternative universality that Indian constitutionalism is in pursuit of.

References

Azad, A. K. (1920). *Khilafat Aur Jaziratul-Arab,* trans. Abdul Qadir Beg, Bombay: Central Khilafat Committee of India.

Azad, A. K. (1990a). Al Hilāl: Maqāsid Aur Political Tāleem, in: India's Maulana Abul Kalam Azad. New Delhi: Vikas Publishing House.

Azad, A. K. (1990b). Al Hilāl: Al Jehad fi Sabil al Hurriyat, in S. Hameed (Ed.), India's Maulana Abul Kalam Azad. New Delhi: Indian Council for Cultural Relations.

Azad, A. K. (1985). Presidential address to the fifty-third session of the indian national congress, Ramgarh, 1940, in *Congress Presidential Addresses* (Vol. 5, pp. 1940–1985). New Delhi: Indian Institute of Applied Political Research.

Azad, A. K. (1962). *The Tarjumān al-Qur'ān*. Hyderabad: Sr. Syed Abdul Latif's Trust for Quranic & Other Cultural Studies.

Azad, A. K. (2002). Al-Jihad, Al-Jihad in Ali Ashraf (Eds.). The Dawn of Hope, New Delhi: Northern Book Centre.

Chatterjee, P. (1993). *Nationalist Thought and the Colonial World: A Derivative Discourse?*. Minneapolis: University of Minnesota Press.

Cohn, B. (1996). *Colonialism and Its Forms of Knowledge: The British in India*. Princeton, NJ: Princeton University Press.

De, R. (2015). Constitutional Antecedents. In S. Choudhary, M. Khosla, & P. B. Mehta (Eds.), *The Oxford Handbook to the Indian Constitution* (pp. 23– 46). New York: Oxford University Press.

Douglas, I. H. (1988). *Abul Kalam Azad: An Intellectual Biography*. New Delhi: Oxford University Press.

Forst, R. (2013). *Toleration in Conflict: Past and Present.* trans. Ciaron Croni, Cambridge: Cambridge University Press.

Hameed, S. (2014). Maulana Azad, Islam and the Indian National Movement. Karachi: Oxford University Press.

Jalal, A. (1994). *The Sole Spokesperson: Jinnah, the Muslim League and the demand for Pakistan*. Cambridge: Cambridge University Press.

John, M. (2019). Framing religion in constitutional politics: a view from Indian Constitutional Law. *South Asian History Culture, 10,* 124–135. https://doi.org/10.1080/19472498.2019.1609260.

Kaviraj, S. (2010). *The Imaginary Institution of India: Politics and Ideas*. New York: Columbia University Press.

Krishnaswamy, S. (2011). *Democracy and Constitutionalism in India*. New Delhi: Oxford University Press.

Mamdani, M. (2012). *Define and Rule: Native as Political Identity*. Cambridge, MA: Harvard University Press.

Mantena, K. (2010). *Alibis of Empire: Henry Maine and the ends of Liberal Imperialism*. Princeton, NJ: Princeton University Press.

Mehta, U., Choudhary, S., Khosla, M., & Mehta, P. B. (2016). Indian Constitutionalism: Crisis, Unity, and History, in: The Oxford Handbook of the Indian Constitution. New Delhi: Oxford University Press.

Minault, G. (1982). *The Khilafat Movement: Religious Symbolism and Political Mobilization in India*. New York: Columbia University Press.

Rawls, J. (1997). The idea of public reason revisited. *Univ. Chicago Law Rev., 64,* 765–807.

Waldron, J. (2012). Two-way translation: The ethics of engageing with religious contributions in public deliberation. *Mercer Law Rev., 63,* 845–868.

Shaunna Rodrigues is a Teaching Fellow and PhD candidate at the Department of Middle Eastern, South Asian and African Studies at Columbia University. She also holds a Masters and MPhil in Political Studies from Jawaharlal Nehru University. Her work focuses on ideas of empire in political theory, concerns of minorities and constitutionalism in India, and the political thought of B.R. Ambedkar and Abul Kalam Azad.

Part II
Transformative and Constitutional Morality

Chapter 8
Law and Constitutional Democracy: Meanings, Iterations and Consequences

Anushka Singh

Abstract The defence of positive law in constitutional democracies has rested minimally in its procedural correctness. The law duly enacted through constitutionally laid down procedures by the legislating authority can deviate from the original statute only through a judicial interpretation. The contemporary moment in Indian democracy in the twenty-first century, however, is witnessing a specific use of the anti-sedition law where the majority of cases registered under this law do not conform to the definition of the offence contained either in the text of the statute or its judicial interpretation. This work focuses on the working of a law in the domain of executive orders where deviating usages are preeminent. The problematic of this work is centred on the law against sedition in India where the focus is on the language of law as a mode of communication through which meanings are transmitted. The transformation brought about in law in the process of its implementation which deviates from the original text or its judicial interpretation is ordinarily dismissed as either a misreading of law or its misuse in the hands of the law enforcing officials, that is, the police persons. In this work, an attempt is made to counter the framework of the misreading/misuse of law which is often advanced to encircle the deviating usages of law as aberrations to defend the text of the law and to deny the power of mutability that law attains in its quotidian life. Through a study of the law against sedition, this work will show that this encircling of deviations and their abandonment by the state is selective and certain deviating usages find validation in the executive discourse of the state.

8.1 Introduction

The process by which any law is implemented is essentially transformative not solely in terms of the capacity of the law to alter the prevailing system but also in terms of the alteration that the meaning of the law may undergo itself. The transformation brought about in law in the process of its implementation, which deviates from the original text of the law, is ordinarily dismissed as either a misreading of the law or its misuse

A. Singh (✉)
School of Law, Governance and Citizenship, Ambedkar University Delhi, Delhi, India
e-mail: anushka@aud.ac.in

© Springer Nature Singapore Pte Ltd. 2020

A. Roy and M. Becker (eds.), *Dimensions of Constitutional Democracy*,
https://doi.org/10.1007/978-981-15-3899-5_8

in the hands of the law enforcing officials, that is, the police persons. In this work, an attempt is made to counter the framework of the misreading/misapplication/misuse of law which is often advanced to selectively encircle the deviating usages of law as aberrations to defend the text of the law and to deny the power of mutability that law attains in its quotidian life. The problem of this work is centred on the law against sedition in India. Through a study of the law, this work will show that this encircling of deviations and their abandonment by the state is selective and certain deviating usages find validation in the executive discourse of the state.

Sedition is a political offence defined as expressions made against the authority of the government and the state which have ramifications for state security and public order. Acts of political opposition not protected under the constitutional right to freedom of dissent are penalized as seditious. The contemporary moment in Indian democracy in the twenty-first century is witnessing a specific use of the anti-sedition law wherein the majority of cases registered under this law do not conform to the definition of offence contained either in the text of the statute or its judicial interpretation. The defence of positive law in constitutional democracies has minimally rested in its procedural correctness. The law duly enacted through constitutionally laid down procedures by the legislating authority can deviate from the original statute only through a judicial interpretation. The working of law in the domain of executive orders where deviating usages are preeminent, as this work will show, reveals a dilemma in relation to the framework of positive law and the selective appropriation of deviating meanings of law by the state bears a consequence on the legitimacy of law within a constitutional democracy. The dilemma is located in the hermeneutical space which unfolds in the process of law enforcement.

The language of law has conventionally resisted the possibility of polysemy as law can be universally abided by only if it represents a uniform command. The law invocation process, however, demands the iteration of a legal provision every single time it is used. In the repeated use of law, that is, its iteration, it is subjected to interpretations. Whether a particular act committed falls within the ambit of the criminality of a said offence or not, is a question that always demands interpretation of law. Interpretations, however, often run the risk of assigning meanings to the text different from the original, implying that in its iteration the meaning of a legal text can be transformed. The nature of legal iterations, however, suffer a constitutive split between the judicial and the executive iterations. While judicial iteration following the rules of interpretation supersedes the original statute,[1] the executive iteration has to work in conformity with the original statute either altered or upheld by the judiciary. Against this background, this work explores the questions around whether the iteration of law, in course of its everyday invocation, creates/is allowed to create new legal meanings; what are the sites of production of these meanings; who are the agents of production; what are the ends these meanings serve.

Employing the analytical frame of iteration this work interrogates its application within the scholarships that have used iteration as a medium to further the notion of 'subaltern legality'. The notion of subaltern legality is then juxtaposed with the

[1]For a detailed account of the various approaches to legal interpretation, see, Fallon (2015).

study of two different legal sites exhibiting the use of sedition law in India in form of two different case studies—(i) law invocation by local state executive on behalf of complaints made by private citizens in cases of alleged 'anti-national' expressions, (ii) iteration of sedition conditioned by the local caste structure.

8.2 Iteration of Law and Its Consequences for Legal Meaning

The purpose of communication is to transmit meanings and in order to do so it should be repeatable. Iteration stands for this repetition of a communication. The works of J. Derrida have advanced this notion of iteration. According to Derrida, the fact that a communication is iterable, that is, it is repeatable, makes it a legible communication, however, repetition of any form of communication is never the replication of the original but is an alteration (Derrida 1991, p. 90). To quote Derrida, '…this is the possibility on which I wish to insist: the possibility of extraction and of citational (iterational) grafting which belongs to the structure of every mark, spoken or written, and which constitutes every mark as writing even before and outside every horizon of semiolinguistic communication; as writing, that is, as a possibility of functioning cut off, at a certain point, from its "original" meaning and from its belonging to a saturable and constraining context' (Derrida 1991: 97). In the Derridian notion, the unintended contexts that an expression creates for itself, essentially lie at the heart of his idea of polysemy and how communications travel. Thus, the original meaning as intended by the author cannot limit the possibility of an alternate understanding of the communication.[2] In fact, the idea of iteration problematizes the very notion of the 'original' because if there is no such source which binds the succeeding communications, the idea of the original losses its specificity.

The nature of legal communication following the medium of writing, however, is distinctive. Writing as the most conventional form of communication assumes that meanings would be transferred in a homogenous manner where the written text represents the meaning intended by the author (Pada 2009: 69). This happens to be a typical assumption about written law seen as embodying the language of the state—its author—conveying the intended meaning to its subjects through the original statute. The foundation of modern legal order lies in the act of writing, which according to Goodrich, places the law beyond the spatial and temporal limitations of oral tradition and unwritten power, giving legal order an objectified existence (Goodrich 1986). A disaggregated notion of state also hinges upon law being the language through which it speaks where the authoritative functions of enactment, implementation and

[2]Austin in his speech-act theory refers to utterances that go beyond the intended meaning of the author, as parasitic discourse. Derrida critiques Austin for using parasitic discourse as dysfunction of language. Austin's student Searle responded to Derrida's criticism saying Austin meant that parasitic discourse signifies a relation of logical dependence and not dysfunction of language, see, Searle (1997).

adjudication of the law, are all carried out in official capacity only by the different state institutions.

Through the notion of iteration, however, emerges the impossibility of congruence of meanings between the author and the audience. Iteration in context of law, thus, is the repeated use of law every single time it is invoked, with each invocation being symptomatic of a variation or an alteration in its 'original' meaning. Here, the police station as the formal-institutional space becomes the site of iteration and the police officers invoking legal provisions while registering complaints, become the official agents of iteration. The question arises, does the 'officialness' of the site and the agents, control for the legal meanings that emerge while a law is repeatedly used? Veena Das in her work on how police persons implement rules, takes the Derridian argument further about the possibility of a written sign breaking from its context. She argues that law as a form of written communication makes itself iterable, however, with iteration there always exists a 'possibility of a gap between a rule and its performance', rendering instability to meanings (Das 2004: 227). The language of the state—the rules and the laws—are often illegible to state's own functionaries. Das discusses the ambivalence in police persons regarding their role as law enforcers who in the process of implementing law, behave like embodiments of law themselves (Das 2004: 235). The officials believing themselves to be embodying law, act as authoritative sources as they produce legal meanings in the course of enforcing law while the 'original meaning' remains illegible to them.

Das' notion of illegibility is far from an innocuous explanation regarding the prevailing legal illiteracy among police officials resulting in misapplication of law and is in fact the means through which state enters the life of its subjects and yet remain obscure as the law of the state remains misapplied. She argues, 'in the life of the state, that very iterability becomes not a sign of vulnerability but a mode of circulation through which power is produced' (Das 2004: 245). This idea of state penetrating the community through police actions that run contrary to the text of the laws providing for those actions, can be made to bear resemblance to Walter Benjamin's notion of the 'law of the police'.[3] The use of violence (read force/authority) by police appears to be a form of law-preserving violence where police intervenes to restore law and order, however, the police actions are more often than not unconnected to the positive law providing for the same. The actions of the police take form of law-making violence which is not abandoned by the state. Benjamin explains, 'the "law" of the police really marks the point at which the state, whether from impotence or because of the immanent connections within any legal system, can no longer guarantee through the legal system the empirical ends that it desires at any price to attain' (Benjamin

[3]Benjamin while writing about the relationship between law and violence (the German word *Gewalt* which signifies force, power, domination, authority and also violence) discusses two kinds of violence, that is, law-making and law-preserving. The former is the violence of power making, establishing new laws using violence as a means towards 'natural ends' while the latter is the violence embedded in state institutions where violence as a means is used towards 'legal ends' for the purpose of preservation of legally existing state. Benjamin, however, argues that the distinction between the two forms of violence gets suspended in the order of the modern state and police as the institution of modern state becomes the site where the two kinds of violence stand conflated.

1986: 287). The law-making power hence is granted to the police which works in defiance to positive law intervening 'in countless cases where no clear legal situation exists' (Benjamin 1986: 287). The 'law of the police' exists in the everydayness of a specific law while having little or sometimes no relationship with the originary moment of that law, that is, the original text. This can be read to imply that police acts in cases where no clear illegal act has been committed as per the legal definition of crimes. Similarly, this work, in looking at the cases of sedition in India, studies those iterations that have been registered as seditious by the police while not conforming to the legal understating of the offence.

In India, sedition was first defined under section 124A of the Indian Penal Code (IPC) in 1870, criminalizing acts of spreading disaffection against the government. The term disaffection is explained as possession of feelings such as hatred, contempt, enmity and disloyalty towards the government (section 124A, Chapter VI, IPC). Post-independence the Supreme Court interpreted the offence of sedition narrowly, to transcend its colonial language. In 1962, in *KedarNath Singh v. State of Bihar,* the Supreme Court (SC) interpreted disaffection as the 'tendency to incite violence or disorder' in society (*Kedar Nath Singh* 1962). Any expression against the government, however, strongly worded, short of any tendency to result in violence or disorder was not to be penalized as seditious.

The 1962 verdict serves as the authoritative antecedent for any interpretation of the offence of sedition, though the antecedent is substantially problematized by the existing definition of sedition contained in section 124A, IPC. Between the two antecedents, there is an obvious disjunction. On the one hand, IPC penalizes a speech act in its illocutionary effect without clearly laid down criteria on when a speech act is capable of producing an illocutionary impact, on the other hand, SC judgment makes a partial attempt at penalizing the perlocutionary effect of a speech act.[4] The ambit of criminality defined on the basis of IPC section penalizes the mere expression of disaffection against the government assuming that the harm has been constituted in the act of expression itself. The 1962 judgment, however, limits the ambit of criminality by allowing only those expressions to be penalized which have the tendency to incite violence and disorder by virtue of expressing disaffection against the government, assuming that the expression can result in an unlawful consequence. Though the judgment in not defining the word 'tendency', could not build a tight causal connection between a speech and its consequence.

---

[4]The speech-act theory developed by J. L. Austin is helpful in an analysis of the ambit of criminality of speech-related offences. It is premised upon the assertion that speech are also actions in narrow senses or wide, hence the distinction between speech and action is false. The speech crime jurisprudence rides on this supposition that speech is capable of producing harmful action hence should be proscribed. Austin explains speech acts as having two kinds of effects—illocutionary and perlocutionary. An illocutionary act is the performance of an act *in* saying something rather than performance of an act *of* saying something (Austin 1969, p. 99). A perlocutionary act is that which is produced as a consequence of saying something—the actual effect of the speech act whether intended or not by the utterer (Austin 1969: 101). The basic difference between the two is that in case of an illocutionary act the speech itself *constitutes* an action while in case of perlocutionary act, the act is the consequence of the speech, in other words, speech *causes* action.

While law may be treated as a form of communication, it does substantially vary from other forms of communications and has its own specificity as a form of language. The works of Peter Goodrich, D.H.J Herman, Dennis Patterson, etc. on legal hermeneutics have established that the binary between objectivity and subjectivity does not sustain the character of legal interpretations and law is understood to have been shaped by subjectivities and in turn shape subjectivities. Nevertheless, legal interpretation is believed to have an objective character to an extent that it is bound by an authoritative text as its origin (Mootz III 1988). This authoritative antecedent hence acts as a reference point for quotidian interpretations of the statutes. This reference, however, in the course of law's iteration, cannot control for the meaning that a particular iteration may give birth to, often in contravention with the text or the larger constitutional principles. The question is, when such deviating meanings are produced in the hands of state executive officially entrusted with the task of enforcing law, how does that reflect on the original meaning of the statute. In case of sedition, the contradictory antecedents of the law, even though technically the SC order prevails over section 124A of IPC, need to be viewed in context of adding to the illegibility of law for the state executive who in the process of acting as law's embodiment, is constantly taking the meaning of sedition beyond its authoritative frame and unfurling the 'law of the police'.

8.3 'Subaltern Legality' and the Birth of 'Democratic' Iteration

Every iteration has parts of the original communication—its identity, for it to be recognized as an iteration of the other. This would mean that it is neither exactly the same communication nor completely a different one—what gets transformed through iterative practices is the meaning.[5] The notion of iteration in the field of legal research has been explored to show how law is transformed through iterative processes in a manner that the agents of iteration belonging to the margins have been able to benefit from it. Most of these works have looked at law's journey as perceived by its subaltern subjects. They have argued that between the implementation of a law and the ways in which the ground actors receive it, legal meaning transforms in a way that facilitates the struggle for rights. This work refers to such scholarships as furthering a notion of 'subaltern legality'.[6]

---

[5]In Derrida's own words, 'Every sign, linguistic or nonlinguistic, spoken or written (in the usual sense of this opposition), as a small or large unity, can be cited, put between quotation marks; thereby it can break with every given context, and engender infinitely new contexts in an absolutely nonsaturable fashion. This does not suppose that the mark is valid outside its context, but on the contrary that there are only contexts without any center of absolute anchoring', see Derrida (1991: 97).

[6]The notion of 'Subaltern legality' is adopted from the work of Santos and Rodriguez-Garavito who argue that there is a growing resistance to the hegemonic account of the top-down process of globalization in context of global legal transformations, by forms of alternate legal frameworks

These scholarships engage with the question of the 'meaning' *in* and *of* law. The often-quoted work of Robert Cover in such scholarships, unfolds the problematic concerning the interpretations of law. The question regarding the iterability of law emanates from the fact that legal language can also be reproduced and altered as law is also shaped by its habitus. Cover stresses on law as a social construct and production of legal meanings as a cultural process. He argues that we live in a 'normative universe, the *nomos*', created and maintained by a world of rights and wrongs (Cover 1983: 4). The legal institutions and the principles of justice are also part of the same normative universe and their meanings are produced through social and cultural interactions that take place within the universe. He argues that the process of jurisgenesis, that is, the creation of legal meanings is not the prerogative of the state alone, in fact, it is a 'social and a collective process' (Cover 1983: 11). What emerges from Cover's understanding is that the process of jurisgenesis renders law subjective and varying. The fact that legal meanings are produced within and amidst interactions taking place in the social milieu, law can neither claim an objective character nor a single source. Cover's claim is that the legal meanings cannot be confined to conformity with authoritative antecedents of law. The intention of the author of the law cannot determine its interpretation by its recipients.

A similar line of argument appears in the work of Seyla Benhabib in context of the rights of the 'others'—immigrants, refugees, aliens—globally. Benhabib borrows Derrida's idea of iteration and examines how it plays out in the discourse on citizenship and human rights. She suggests, '…between the norms of international law and the actions of individual democratic legislatures, multiple "iterations" are possible and desirable' (Benhabib 2004: 176). The process of iteration in Benhabib's scheme of things gives birth to a 'jurisgenerative politics' which refers to the act of people re-appropriating and reinterpreting norms and principles governing them, and in the process becoming 'authors of the laws' from mere subjects (Benhabib 2004: 181). She shows through contemporary cases how the process of democratic iteration unfolding within institutional spaces of the state, has led to a rupture in the existing legal norms and transformed them to an extent.[7]

---

being created by populations harmed by globalization. They adopt what they call a 'subaltern cosmopolitan legality' approach to explain the plurality of resistance to global legal norms, emerging from the ground; an approach which reimagines legal institutions from below, see, Santos and Rodríguez-Garavito (2005).

[7]In one of the illustrations, she discusses a case brought before German Constitutional Court in 2003 in which a woman German school teacher of Afgani origin was disqualified from the public position she held because she requested to teach in class with her scarf worn around conducting her duties as a civil servant of a secular state. When the woman moved court, the court referred the case to the legislature, however, in doing so, the court made a rather pertinent political move. Before referring the case to the legislature, the court stated that the fundamental rights of citizens in Germany allowed equal access to public offices and freedom of conscience. On both accounts, the disqualification of the woman from the school does not seem justified. The court said, '…legislature is nevertheless free to create the legal basis by determining anew within the framework set by the constitution the extent of religious articles to be permitted in the schools… In this process, it must take into consideration the freedom of conscience of the teacher as well as of the students involved, and also the right to educate their children on the part of parents as well as the obligation of the state

The unfolding of the hermeneutical space while the law travels is not always a result of a conscious mobilization or struggle for rights as is the case in the works of Santos and Benhabib. It often takes the form of inadvertent political acts in which the political actors themselves are not conscious law interpreters. Julia Eckert's work on the rumour of rights, embodies such an unfolding. Eckert in context of her anthropological sites in India shows how certain rumours about laws which are far from their positivist reality, give strength to political actors to wage struggles for their own rights and take recourse to legal institutions. She argues, this is how legal norms are altered through iterations and the iterated notions are not necessarily misnomers but are part of jurisgenesis (Eckert 2012: 166). Eckert, however, concedes that the extent to which these transformed meanings can make political difference, remains contingent.

Despite a number of departure points within the range of scholarships discussed above, a common line of argument in these works shows that the iteration of law works to the advantage of the subjects of law. Hence if legal communication is iterable, it would result in the process of jurisgenesis—creation of legal meanings—relating to specific experiences of people on ground. In the scholarships discussed above, iteration becomes the site of the construction of subaltern legality. In the Derridean framework, however, the process of iteration is not necessarily always a part of emancipatory politics. For instance when Benhabib says that 'iteration enriches meaning', she moves away from the Derridean notion of iterability by adding normativity to the process. Benhabib consciously makes the distinction between iteration of any other form of communication with that of iteration of law. Her argument is that law as a medium of communication, retains a claim to an original source, which is an authoritative source. All interpretations that occur in the process of iteration hence have a referent point, in her case, she makes constitutional principles, the referent point. Lasse Thomassen has argued that by doing so, Benhabib limits the effects of iteration to the normative content of the constitution thereby now allowing iteration to have a subversive effect on the meaning of law (Thomassen 2011: 138). Hence, it is a particular kind of appropriation of the notion of iteration that emerges in the works of Eckert or Benhabib where the presumed passive subjects of law become the agents of iteration who consciously or unconsciously, interpret law towards a democratic possibility.

A study of the quotidian life of the law, as emerges in this work, however, suggests that the efficacy of an iteration in causing an alteration in legal meanings depends on the agent of iteration and its place within the formal-institutional spaces. Police persons acting in capacity of the state executives, retain the power to sanction any variation from the authoritative antecedents of law while being equally capacitated

to retain neutrality in matters of worldview and religion' (p. 199). Benhabib says that in doing this, the court may have failed to give a constitutional defence of pluralism but it did carve out a space to reinterpret the clash between citizenship rights and cultural identity of minorities. In a similar fashion, the mobilization to recognize the second and third generation children of immigrants had led to a new German citizenship law in January 2000. The urge of the court to the legislature to reflect upon the changing realities of the population has led to a change in the citizenship law, see, Benhabib (2004: 198–211).

to undermine alternate iterations emerging from the subjects of law on whom it is invoked. This is how the 'law of the police', as in the Benjaminian framework, unfolds marking the presence of law in the absence of legal situations. The following two sections elaborate the argument through case studies on the use of the sedition law in India.

8.4 'Anti-national' Expressions and Their Legal Reception

The meanings of sedition in the registration of cases under section 124A IPC have varied from cheering for a rival cricket team to the extreme cases of acts of waging war and terrorism, in contemporary India. In most cases, either the police of its own volition has registered a case of sedition or has acted on a complaint. In both instances, however, it is the police that decides upon the laws to be invoked. The first case study focuses on the use of the law against alleged anti-national expressions where the iterated notions of sedition registered under section 124A of IPC by the local state executives, have deviated substantially from both the authoritative antecedents of law. Most such cases do not reach fruition in terms of conviction and the executive interpretations have been dubbed as misuse or misapplication in the judicial discourse, however, these iterations have defined the executive practices in relation to the law of sedition. These iterations also, by virtue of taking shape within the formal police complaints, find way into the institutional space of the state becoming part of its official discourse.

The focus of this section is on those alleged anti-national expressions in which the police acted on behalf of complaints made by individuals/political groups. Some of the cases discussed below follow a common pattern where questions on Kashmir particularly raised by minority community have become seditious. The point of debate is not whether the acts in question would constitute offences but whether they fit the ambit of criminality of the offence of sedition. In 2010, following the reports of a fake encounter in Machchil by the armed forces, Kashmir witnessed widespread protests against security forces. People took to streets throwing stones at the troops to show their discontentment. The forces in retaliation used tear gas, air firing and also live ammunitions injuring and killing the protesters at many occasions (The Hindu 2010). Alongside, Noor Muhammed Bhat, a lecturer in Gandhi Memorial College, Kashmir University framed a question for students taking exams in English literature course—whether stone pelters were the real heroes? Subsequently, he was arrested in December 2010 and charged for sedition, was released from police custody after 20 days of imprisonment after the Jammu and Kashmir High Court granted interim bail on a surety bond of 25,000 Rupees (University World News 2011). Citing reason that he had set an 'anti-establishment' paper, the University suspended him even after his release and barred him from setting exam question papers for five years (Tehelka 2011). In another case in March 2014, 67 Kashmiri Muslim students of Swami Vivekanand Subharti University in Meerut, Uttar Pradesh, who were found celebrating the victory of the Pakistani cricket team in a match against

India, were charged for sedition. The case was filed after the local leaders of *Bharatiya Janata Party* (BJP) complained and demanded 'stern actions' against the students for engaging in 'anti-national' activity (Hindustan Times 2014). State government later dropped the charges of sedition after much criticism in national media and the intervention of the Jammu and Kashmir Chief Minister.

In July 2016, in Madhya Pradesh, the management of Green Wales School in Shahdol district was charged for sedition for allegedly marking Jammu and Kashmir incorrectly on India's map in the school diary. Its director Mohammad Sharif Niyazi, principal Govind Chand Das and publisher of school diary Arun Kumar Agrawal were arrested and sent in judicial custody by local court for 14 days after a private complaint against them was made (First Post 2016). In August 2016 again, in Chhattisgarh, Tauseef Ahmad Bhat, a Kashmiri youth who worked with a mobile phone company in Bhilai, Madhya Pradesh, was arrested for sedition for "liking, sharing and forwarding anti-India posts" on Facebook. One Facebook post represented India as a mouse, while another showed China recognizing Kashmir as disputed. The post asked for freedom for Kashmiris and had the flags of Pakistan and China (The Indian Express, August 2016a). Police acted after a group of people from the right wing parties *Vishva Hindu Parishad* and the *Bajrang Dal* filed a complaint against them.

The ambit of 'anti-national' activities in such cases has also included acts of causing insult to 'national symbols'. For instance, in August 2014, in Kerala, Mohammad Salman, a 25-year old student was arrested on the charge of sedition after he refused to stand up for the National Anthem at a movie theatre in Thiruvananthapuram, Kerala. A few people present in the theatre later lodged a complaint and Salman was picked up from his home at midnight (Change.org 2014). Sessions Court refused bail on the grounds that his act was 'anti-national' and a more serious crime than murder (The Indian Express 2014). In another instance, Kamal C Chavara, a writer and theatre activist in Kerala, had published a novel in which he narrated a story of a school where the students were withheld by the teacher from using the loo during school hours. At the end of the day, the students would sing the National Anthem and rush to the loo after. In narrating the story he had written, for those children singing National Anthem meant they could now use the toilet (The Indian Express, December 2016b). In December 2016, Chavara had shared this excerpt from his novel on his Facebook page following which he was charged for sedition for allegedly insulting the National Anthem, after a youth wing of BJP, *Bhartiya Yuva Morcha* complained to the police. After public criticism and flanks from opposition parties, the police withdrew the sedition charge.

In another case in Uttar Pradesh's Badaun district in August 2017, Babloo alias Raza Khan was arrested under sedition after right wing organization *Bajrang Dal* complained at local police station that Khan had posted on Facebook with a tagline 'I support Pakistan' (The New Indian Express 2017). In 2019, in February, 14 students of Aligarh Muslim University were again charged for sedition for alleged anti-India slogans. The students had supposedly chanted 'Azadi' (freedom) slogans within the campus premises when *Bharatiya Janta Yuva Morcha* members complained against them (The Indian Express 2019).

Such cases denote an iterated understanding of sedition constituted in what are popularly construed as 'anti-national' speech acts. In local parlance, it finds translation in the word 'deshdroh'/'rashtradroh' (acts against the nation) as opposed to the literal translation of sedition as 'rajdroh' (an offence against the state). The iterated notions of sedition emerging in the above cases condition two arguments. Firstly, the dominant discourse of nation constructed by the state reduces acts of 'irreverence' to symbols of the nation to anti-national acts. Secondly, such acts become significations of sedition in the process of law execution by state executive. Both arguments demand explication.

The transformed understating of sedition as deshdroh is conditioned by the dominant discourse of nation in which the state is rendered supreme. It is structured by that form of nationalism in which state creates nation.[8] The process is marked by cultural unification, standardization and homogenization (Baruah 1999: 4). In this state created official nationalism, contours of the discourse are built upon the visible symbols of the state—the flag, the anthem, the parliament, territorial boundaries, etc. What is striking in case of a post-colonial society like India, is the fact that the sudden conjunction between the two separate entities of nation and state was informed by the political moment of independence from colonial rule. As Sudipta Kaviraj points out that Gelner's conception of nationalism in which the state creates the nation through a process of cultural standardization, holds true of the kind of nationalism India witnessed after independence, but not for its origins pre-independence (Kaviraj 2010). All through the anti-colonial struggle, the Indian independence movement made claims about Indians—the subjects of the colonial state—as a distinct community of people ruled by aliens. The propagation of the idea of Indians as a nation did not address the heterogeneities that exited within, neither challenged it; it in fact subsumed the differences for a national identity to emerge with a lone objective of independence from colonial rule. The act of sedition during colonial times was believed to have borne out of the feeling of nationalism as it challenged the colonial state and a seditionist was regarded to be a nationalist. With increasing number of nationalists being charged under the law of sedition for having committed sedition against the colonial government, the relation between sedition and nationalism became starker.

With independence, the making of a democratic state theoretically dissolved the tension that existed between nation as the community of people and state as the institution of rule and governance. This was the rise of state nationalism in which

[8]The juxtaposition of Anderson's and Gelner's work on nation helps enumerate the above argument. Anderson's conception of nation as an imagined community of people where the members never meet or hear of each other yet 'in the minds of each lives the image of their communion' (Anderson 1983, p. 6), refers to how the process of 'imagining' creates a community of people with a feeling of belongingness. Ernest Gellner, writing before Anderson, differed on how the nation as a community was 'created'. Challenging the common social science thinking which says that nations precede the creation of states he argued that nations were created through a uniform process of cultural production of individuals by preexisting modern states. States were not a result of the demands put forth by specific nations, in fact they created nations through a feeling of nationalism. Gellner wrote 'nationalism… invents nations where they do not exist' (Anderson 1983, p. 7).

state alone had the right to award the 'national' and penalize the 'anti-national'. Kaviraj discusses that the constant reiteration of the central tenets of state nationalism ensured that no challenges were raised and nationalism and national interest justified all state actions. This form of nationalism makes state central to public life, as Ashis Nandy writes, 'nationalism is partly a response to the awareness that the world is dominated by and organized around nation state, a degree of statism is an unavoidable adjunct to nationalism' (Nandy 2006: 3503). The epithets of the institution of state became the epithets of the nation, the oneness and sanctity of which could not be questioned.

The dominant discourse of nation does explicate that certain forms of conduct including speech acts of the kind discussed in this section, attain offensive stature in majoritarian culture, a consequence of which is the ghettoization of people belonging to specific identities as offenders. This explains why popular demands are made for prosecution of these 'anti-national' activities but the registration of cases of sedition to criminalize such activities is not a direct corollary of such demands.

This brings us to the second argument about law implementation process. In cases discussed above, the identity of the complainant is significant. It's a common assumption that when people seek criminal prosecution and take recourse to law, it is usually a consequence of a violation or injustice. When individuals approach police for registration of cases against alleged anti-national acts, they are only working with the notion of the criminality of such acts. Which particular category of offence do they fall into is the prerogative of the state executive. In registering these complaints under the offence of sedition, it is the state that effects the iteration of sedition as deshdroh. The registration of such cases further validates an understanding of sedition as anti-national and has a cascading effect on more such complaints. This also conditions the popular discourse of sedition as acts of assumed sense of harm to the tangible symbols of nation. In the process, the state or its visible representation—the government, against which the offence of sedition was originally defined, identifies itself with the nation bringing about an equivalence between state and nation.

The fabric of the cases discussed vary in terms of the identity of the alleged seditionist, the geography of the cases registered where security sensitive locations such as Kashmir become comparable with mainland such as Uttar Pradesh, and the signification of the harm differing in each case ranging between defeat in a cricket match to disrespect to the National Anthem. The use of the law flattens out the variations and each kind of expression while retaining its specific character within its individuated context, emerges as an iteration of sedition brought into life through police practices. While iterations, following the Derridian framework, always signify the possibility of a 'cut off from the "original meaning"', the nature of the iterative practices followed by the state executive suggests that not each kind of iteration is allowed to alter the original meaning. The differing iterations when viewed from the individuated contexts of each case may symbolize a dissonance in the meaning of sedition within the executive practices as well but the selective registration of the cases of sedition unfurls the 'law of the police'. In choosing to use the specific IPC section pertaining to sedition in cases of private complaints brought to the police stations by members of the rights wing establishment, only certain kinds of acts are iterated as seditious in the police registers. In doing so, the law of the police constructs legal situations in which the alleged anti-national expressions become illegal acts as well as seditious iterations. This section has discussed how deviating iterations of the law become legally efficacious and a part of the state discourse when the complainant's version converges with state executive. The second case study shows how other deviations fail to become legally efficacious.

8.5 Sedition as a Challenge to Local Caste Structures

While the law is interpreted routinely by ground actors in course of its iteration, not every altered understanding finds acceptance in the institutional legal discourse. This section discusses those cases in which the ground actors have insisted on application of the law of sedition in consonance with its positivist explanation while the state executives have chosen to rely on iterated notions of sedition emerging out of localized contexts, much in contradiction with the version in IPC or the Supreme Court verdict. Through these cases, sedition emerges as a caste-ridden concept in the state of Haryana.[9]

In 2012, in a village called Bhagana in the Hisar district of the state of Haryana, news reports of a mass exodus of Dalit (Scheduled castes) families from the village, surfaced. Around 75 Dalit families had fled from the village and sat on a dharna in front of the secretariat in Hisar to protest against a social boycott imposed on them by members of the dominant caste, the Jats. Simultaneously, media also reported that charges of sedition had been levelled against some Dalits in relation to the same incident. On the ground, however, a distinct understanding of sedition had taken shape enmeshed in social cleavages. The bone of contention between the Jat and the Dalit communities in Bhagana became the village common lands which the Haryana government, under a particular scheme had acquired for distribution among the poor households (SCs, few backward castes and BPL families) as free residential plots. However, in Bhagana, as was the case in most parts of Haryana, this scheme was being used to distribute lands also to the Jats to ensure their lawful occupation over common lands. The redistribution was in the hands of a committee which had an overwhelming presence of the Jats. Additionally, money was collected from Dalit families in lieu of allotting plots in spite of which the process had been stalled once the term of the Dalit sarpanch in the village ended. Despite protests from the Dalit families asking the administration to intervene, nothing had come of it for

[9]Details about these incidents were gathered through filed work in Haryana in the months of August and September 2014 through conversations with locals as well as interviews with some of the accused. The Dalit activists who have questioned the caste hierarchy and the supremacy of the Jat community have suffered legal repression under all political regimes. Each political party has ensured electoral victory with the support of the Jat community. It was only in 2014 that for the first time in nearly two decades that Haryana was given a non-Jat chief minister in the BJP ruled state government. Though the pressure mounted by the community on political authorities is still significant. For details on the case, see, Singh (2018: 236–242).

more than a year. In the meanwhile, a dispute arose over a triangular piece of land in the village which was called the 'Chamar Chowk' which conjoined three Dalit households. The Dalits wanted to rename the place after Ambedkar. The Jats took it as an act of Dalit assertion that challenged their position and collectively imposed a social boycott on the Dalit families of the village. A six feet wall blocking any entry into the Dalit area was constructed followed by banning the Dalit presence from common areas such as water pumps, etc. and disallowing them to work in fields owned by Jats. With administrative apathy, the families were compelled to flee and they sat on the district headquarter as a mark of protest. Consequently, in the district headquarter, Hisar, villagers led by some Dalit activists including members of the political party *Bahujan Samajwadi Party* (BSP), had organized a protest in which an effigy of the Chief Minister was burnt. Following the incident, an FIR under sedition was registered by the police and six Dalit activists were arrested. Effigy burning in a democracy is not a crime. This was conceded by higher officials of the police (Qureshi 2014) as well as the union minister,[10] following which the charge of sedition was withdrawn. A charge that was withdrawn in less than 30 days, however, offers an insight into the law enforcement process creating that hermeneutical space which results in multiplicity of legal meanings.

The activists charged under sedition opined that law of sedition penalizes those who act against the country while they were fighting caste discrimination. The popular translation of sedition as deshdroh found resonance in their thoughts as well but their understanding of deshdroh differed. For them, their resistance and defiance of the caste order upheld the constitutional values of equality and justice. Sitaram Daboria, a Dalit activist charged under sedition believed that 'they (activists) were the only "real citizens" of the country fighting against the social evils' (Daboria 2014). In using laws such as sedition against them, they believed that the government shielded the caste order. Sanjay Chauhan, one of the accused worked under the banner of *Bahujan Azad Morcha* taking up Dalit issues in Haryana. He ran a *Sanatan Dharma* Trust which supported inter-caste marriages and believed that his anti-status quoist activities were the reason why he was charged for deshdroh (Chauhan 2014). Balraj, another accused in the sedition case affirmed that the charges of deshdroh had gone up in the wake of Dalit activism" (Balraj 2014). It was one of the ways in which the government colluded with the dominant caste to counter the emerging Dalit consciousness. For him, the use of sedition was selective—against the Dalits in favour of the Jats.

In the assertions of those charged under sedition, its offensive connotation remained intact, the criminality of which could be traced back to how the law was originally defined. Their thoughts hinged upon how the localized state—the police administration, ruling political clout and the dominant caste—in the repeated invocation of sedition law had moved towards making sedition an offence against the local system characterized by the caste hierarchy.

---

[10]It came through in the interaction with the villagers at the secretariat that the then Union minister Kumari Shailja, had met the District Commissioner after the incident and reprimanded him for making it a case of sedition.

There are multiple incidents of sedition law being invoked against Dalit activists in Haryana. Members of three rights organizations, namely, *Jagrook Chhatra Morcha*, *Krantikari Mazdoor Kisan Union* and *Shivalik Jan Sangharsh Manch,* have been repeatedly charged under the law, 2003 onwards. The charges have been levelled in relation to acts such as organizing a cycle rally to demanding a withdrawal of university bill which made education unaffordable for Dalit students, for protesting in front of the chief minister's convey against police firing on peasants, for resisting the practice of men of the dominant caste forcibly claiming Dalit women (Singh 2018: 242–254). A close reading of these cases reveal that the basis of the charge of sedition lies either in acts that have challenged caste discriminatory practices or have protested against political authority favouring the dominant castes.

The frequent registration of these cases by state executives under political influence in a climate where the dominant caste decides upon the nature of political incumbency, is telling of an altered notion of sedition. In the caste-ridden society of Haryana, the iterated notion of sedition is an act that challenges caste hierarchy. The understanding of sedition on the ground among those who were at the radar of the law did not affect legally valid iterations. For instance, the Dalit community in Bhagana, Haryana had retorted, 'when the Jats—the dominant caste in Haryana—had burnt the police chowki and damaged rail tracks while protesting against the state government for being unable to ensure the inclusion of Jat community under Other Backward Classes (OBC), they were not charged for sedition, but when we burnt an effigy, we were'.[11] Similarly, those charged under section 124A in the Bhagana movement believed that sedition understood in the local parlance as deshdroh, was being committed by those who went against the constitutional ethos, those who violated the right to equality and betrayed the people. Such an iterated notion of sedition, however, didn't find acceptance within the institutional legal space. These instances suggest that while the ground actors' understanding of the law may also deviate from the original while the law is being implemented, the variation in the meaning, unlike the first case study, however, fails to construct a legal situation where the police/law can intervene.

The two case studies when juxtaposed, point out that effectively the police persons remain the agents of iterations and the site for production of the iterations of law remains the police station. Unlike the claims of subaltern legality where deviating legal meanings as perceived by the ground actors have taken the form of legal iterations that have furthered the struggle for rights of those on the margins, the effects of the iterations of the law of sedition remain confined to the institutional response towards them. In case of a convergence between the understanding of the law of the ground actors and the local state executives, a deviating iteration gets registered under the law of sedition. Contrarily, in case of a divergence in the understanding between the two parties, the deviating iteration becomes inconsequential. The explanation for the two contrarian effects lies in the specific nature of the laws related to

[11]A group of villagers sitting on protest at the Secretariat had spoken to the author about the discriminatory use of law in the state, one among them had made the quote in Hindi. Conversations with villagers of Bhagana at Hisar Secretariat on 22 August 2014, at Hisar, Haryana, India.

political offences such as sedition. The next section explicates this argument while locating it within the debate on the question of subjectivity in and the politics of, legal interpretations.

8.5.1 *Deviating from the 'Original': Law and Language*

The hermeneutical approach to study law has substantially problematized the notion of objectivity in law. This approach studying the interpretation and meaning of written law has exposed the subjectivities inherent in the process of interpretation and their consequences for legal meanings. The different variants within legal hermeneutics converge on the claim that legal meanings can't be determined to be fixed at any point suggesting that interpretations offer the possibility of multiple meanings. While polysemy in law emerges as a consequence of the hermeneutical approach, an extreme position concerning the indeterminacy of legal meanings comes from the idea of reductive legal nihilism.[12] Owing to the specificity of legal language where law takes form of universal command, even those who advocate a hermeneutical approach to law, warn against an uncritical application of hermeneutics while interpreting the text of law (such as Goodrich 1986; Sherman 1988). Their caution is against the most reductive idea of legal nihilism, adherence to which is counterproductive to legal interpretations. Works such as those of Goodrich advance a more refined understanding of legal nihilism and defend its nuanced version in which nihilism does not mean that 'all meanings are possible'.[13]

The internal variations within the tradition notwithstanding, the tradition of legal hermeneutics even in its minimalist form poses a challenge to the claims of objectivity in law. The challenge is exhibited in the supposition that polysemy is possible through interpretative processes even though there are differences within the hermeneutical tradition on the methodology of interpretation. Iteration then becomes one of the ways in which polysemy in law takes shape. In the repeated use of law, deviations in meaning occur conditioned by the interactions taking place within the habitus of law. Polysemy destabilizes the notion of law as being the language of state alone and the prerogative of state to define offences, as the subjects of law through iterative practices reassign meanings to the legal language. It further incapacitates the state to produce sovereign speech acts. Judith Butler in her work on Hate Speech had famously quoted, 'the state produces hate speech' (Butler 1997, p. 77) implying that when a speech crosses the line to become an offence is decided by the state which claims to give precise meanings to acts through the language of law. Butler calls it

[12] O. M. Fiss defines and critiques legal nihilism as emerging from the proposition that for any legal text including the constitution, there can be any number of possible meanings and interpretation is a selection of one of the many meanings, see, Fiss (1982).

[13] Goodrich says this to oppose the reductive idea of nihilism which O.M. Fiss defines and critiques. Goodrich's idea of legal nihilism is that it 'speaks to the possibility of a public language of legal modernity and of open debate as to the values contained in and resulting from the practice of the law' see, Goodrich (1986).

the sovereign speech act, one that claims illocutionary power, i.e. to constitute action in expression and not as a consequence.

For its destabilizing effects on the powers of the state, polysemy in law is resisted. While interpretive processes are accepted to be an intrinsic part of the law adjudication process, limits are imposed on the possibilities of interpretation while granting the authoritative space only to courts where interpretations take shape within the formal-institutional space. The presence of hermeneutical tradition in law thus is predominantly felt in the judicial discourse. The extension of the hermeneutical space outside, poses a challenge of acute legal nihilism. The interpretations of law taking shape outside the formal institutions of state, run a risk of an absolute dilution of the original legal meanings. It emerges hence as an obvious explanation that non-institutional iterations deviating from the 'original', are debunked in judicial discourse as misapplication or misuse of law. The interpretation of law in the executive domain then appears to be a contingent space theoretically at the mercy of judicial validation.

When viewed in context of how laws are routinely interpreted on ground by local executives and the kind of legal validation these iterated notions of law receive, the framework of judicial iteration superseding the executives' begin to fall flat. The politics of interpretation thus unfold. A study of the implementation of the law of sedition as emerging through the empirical cases examined in this work reveal the following patterns.

All criminal offences are indirectly offences against the state as law, order and security are state's responsibilities. Hence state is an implied victim in all criminal offences. The particular nature of political offences such as sedition, however, reduces state to victimhood in terms of being the intended target of the harm caused by the offence. In context of the first set of cases of the use of sedition against 'anti-national' expressions, the FIR is registered at the behest of private complaints. The private complainants in choosing to approach the police are interpreting forms of speech acts as 'anti-national' which are appropriated by the state as acts intending to cause disaffection against the government, by registering them as sedition. The consequence of registering these cases as sedition is that in these episodes the status of the state as the victim, is recognized not by the state but by those individuals that file complaint against assumed 'seditious' acts. The state executive in registering these cases emerges as the passive victim as well as the prosecutor, who has been driven to take recourse to the law of sedition to avenge a sense of personal harm not recognized by itself but brought to cognisance by non-state actors. Thus, the state identifies itself with the personal sense of harm that members feel by virtue of an assumed insult to the dominant discourse of nation and extends the meaning of sedition to mean anti-nation or deshdroh. Eventually, interpretations deviating from the authoritative antecedent of law of sedition, become part of the institutional space in capacity of legal iterations sanctioned by at least the local state executive.

In context of the second set of cases in Haryana, the victimhood of the state is contingent upon the local power structure conditioned by caste. Here the cases were registered not on the basis of complaints but by police of their own volition nevertheless on behalf of the dominant local caste. In prime-facie episodes of Dalit challenge to caste domination, sedition was used against Dalit activists. The implication of such use of law enmeshed in social cleavages is that political authority is constituted not just by the representatives in government but a ruling coalition of which the dominant caste is a part. The iteration of sedition as an offence against such an authority, yet again formed part of the official discourse of state despite its negation by higher executive officials and judiciary, by virtue of a repeated pattern of use of sedition against Dalit activism.

Each set of cases creates its own exclusionary space where certain deviations from the original meaning are given space while others are dismissed. A possible explanation to why only certain kinds of deviations become legally efficacious emerges in the specific conceptualization of political offences, i.e. offences against the political authority in which the state is both the victim and the prosecutor. In other criminal offences, while the victim of the crime maybe a private citizen, the state by virtue of being the implied victim becomes the prosecutor against the accused. The distinction between the victim and the complainant or prosecutor is crucial for the conception of the offence in question. Laura Nader in her work has argued that it is the plaintiff (complainant) that largely decides the direction and the purpose to which the law would be used (Nader 2002). This work borrows her argument to show that the purpose for which the law of sedition is used is predominantly decided by the state executive that chooses to use the law. This work, however, stretches the argument further to hinge upon the possibility of an alternate conception of the offence at the instance of a contradiction related to the definition of a crime between the victim and the prosecutor. In such a situation, an iteration may unfold challenging the dominant vocabulary of state in which offences and laws penalizing them, are defined. The specific nature of political offences of which sedition is a kind, where the distinction between the victim and the prosecutor is dissolved, may limit the possibility of an alternate iteration. The role of state as a prosecutor against the seditionist is conditioned upon the reduction of state as a victim of sedition. In the registration of a case of sedition, state can only act as a prosecutor once it assumes victimhood by presenting the seditionist as a threat or harm. There is a contiguity of meaning of sedition in the event of the conflation of the victim and the prosecutor. In the absence of a contradiction, a possibility of a legally efficacious iteration of sedition external to the existence of the state as victim, is not possible. In other words, a case of sedition will only be registered when state is willing to claim victimhood.

The usurpation of the language of victimhood by the state, however, transposes it from a victim to an aggressor which takes recourse to the penal provision, in this case the law of sedition, to retaliate against the attacker—the seditionist. The inversion of the victim–aggressor relationship is unique to political offences where the state is the target of the offence hence the victim. The moment the state claims victimhood, the subject of the law is transposed into an attacker against whom the victim that is the state, acts as an aggressor to vanquish him/her in the process making him/her a victim of legal repression.[14]

[14]Ujjwal Kumar Singh has argued that state crimes (or political offences) construct an anachronism between the state and the rebel. The moment the rebel is successful, he/she escapes legal punishment

The state's claim to victimhood giving way to the acceptance of only specific kinds of iterations within formal-institutional space needs to be argued separately on two accounts—first, the authority of the interpreter and second, the content of the interpretation in relation to the 'original' meaning. It is amply clear from the cases revisited that the state executive has registered cases under sedition that are far removed from its authoritative antecedents. It implies that polysemy is inherent in the process of law enforcement. Does it have a liberatory potential even if argued in context of a law like sedition which evidently works to protect those in power?

The discourse of authoritative iterations deviating from the original, questions the fundamentals of law's normativity. The pattern of law invocation in cases of sedition implies that the normativity of law is derived not from its content but the authority of the interpreter. If the interpreter is a state official, the deviation from the original becomes authoritative law in its everydayness. As most cases depict, they even find validation from lower judiciary much enmeshed itself in the local power dynamics. If authoritative deviations from the original unfolding in the domain of executive orders are given space, do they create futures for transformation in legal meanings? If the answer is in negation, it would imply that the provisional meanings of sedition adopted by local state executives would continue to prosecute expressions that fall outside the ambit of sedition till judiciary debunks the cases as misapplications of law. It would also mean that the meanings that law acquires in its quotidian life, have no significance. This debunking of executive interpretations through judicial verdicts would allow state the liberty of distance from deviating iterations. While the extra-legal would be allowed to unfold in the executive domain and become the local norm, the language of positive law would remain intact. The 'law of police' thus as Benjamin wrote, would allow the fulfilment of empirical ends that state desires but cannot secure lawfully such as maintaining the statuesque defined by caste or privileging the majoritarian discourse on nationalism.

If the answer is in affirmative, it would imply that if deviating iterations by state officials find acceptance then rules of legality would have to find a way to give space to iterations coming from non-state actors also, purely for the merit that deviation from the 'original' can also have legal meaning. The intention of this work is not to succumb to the variant of reductive legal nihilism discussed above, instead to locate interpretations which amount to nothingness of meanings when compared to the source of 'authoritative' law, within the discourse of the state. The location of such interpretations in the domain of executive order and the legal and social consequences they have on the system of justice, this work argues, serves as an internal critique to the language of state which selectively dismisses alternate iterations coming from people while constantly breeds other deviations in the executive domain, challenging law's claims to objectivity. The framework of iteration giving way to polysemy in law, thus becomes a potential challenge to the notion of sovereign speech of the state.

---

as the state has already been subverted. This allows the state to justify stronger legal measures against political offences, see, Singh 2008. Singh's framework can be used to understand how the usurpation of victimhood allows greater powers to state to act as an aggressor.

References

Anderson, B. (1983). *Imagined communities: Reflections on the origin and spread of nationalism*. London: Verso.

Austin, J. L. (1969). *How to do things with words*. Great Britain: Oxford University Press.

Balraj. (2014). *Interview conducted on 22 August 2014, at Ambedkar Phool Market*. Hisar, Haryana, India: Nagori Gate.

Baruah, S. (1999). *India against itself, Assam and the politics of nationality*. New Delhi: Oxford University Press.

Benhabib, S. (2004). *The rights of others aliens, residents, and citizens*. Cambridge University Press

Benjamin, W. (1986). Critique of violence. In P. Demetz (Ed.), *Walter Benjamin- reflections: Essays, aphorisms, autobiographical writings* (pp. 277–300). New York: Schoken Books.

Butler, J. (1997). *Excitable speech, a politics of the performative*. United Kingdom: Routledge.

Change.org. (2014). Petition for scraping false charge against Salman. Retrieved December 20, 2014, from https://www.change.org/p/chief-minister-of-kerala-kerala-cm-scrap-false-sedition-charges-against-salman-and-ensure-his-immediate-release.

Chauhan, S. (2014). *Interview conducted on 22 August at Ambedkar Phool Market*. Hisar, Haryana, India: Nagori Gate.

Cover, R. (1983). *The Supreme Court, 1982 Term—Foreword: Nomos and Narrative*, Yale Law School Legal Scholarship Repository, Faculty Scholarship Series. Paper 2705, Retrieved January 7, 2018, from http://digitalcommons.law.yale.edu/fss_papers/2705.

Daboria, S. (2014). *Interview conducted on 25 August at the District Court, near Court room 8*. Haryana, India: Hisar.

Das, V. (2004). The signature of the state: The paradox of illegibility. In V. Das & D. Poole (Eds.), *Anthropology in the margins of state* (pp. 225–252). New Delhi: Oxford University Press.

Derrida, J. (1991). Signature, event, context. In P. Kamuf (Ed.), *A Derrida reader between the blinds* (pp. 80–111). New York: Columbia University Press.

Eckert, J. (2012). Rumours of law. In J. Eckert at al. (eds.), *Law against the state* (pp. 147–170). Cambridge: Cambridge University Press.

Fallon, R.H. Jr. (2015). The meaning of legal "meaning" and its implications for theories of legal interpretation. *The University of Chicago Law Review*, *82*(3).

First Post. (2016), Retrieved July 27, 2016, from http://www.firstpost.com/india/school-authorities-booked-in-sedition-case-for-using-wrong-map-of-kashmir-in-diary-2901010.html.

Fiss, O. M. (1982). Objectivity and Interpretation, Yale Law School Faculty Scholarship Series, 1217. Retrieved February 13, 2018, from http://digitalcommons.law.yale.edu/fss_papers/1217.

Goodrich, P. (1986). Law and modernity. *The Modern Law Review, 49*(5), 554–555.

Hindustan Times (2014). Retrieved April 6, 2014, from http://www.hindustantimes.com/india-news/police-file-case-of-sedition-against-kashmiri-students-for-celebrating-pak-win/article1-1191549.aspx.

Kaviraj, S. (2010). Nationalism. In N. Jayal & P. B. Mehta (Eds.), *The oxford companion to politics in India* (pp. 317–333). New Delhi: Oxford University Press.

Kedar Nath Singh v. State of Bihar on 20 January, 1962 AIR 955, 1962 SCR Supl. (2) 769, Retrieved June 3, 2019, from https://indiankanoon.org/doc/111867/.

Mootz III, F. J. (1988). *The ontological basis of legal hermeneutics: A proposed model of inquiry based on the work of Gadamer, Habermas and Ricoeur*, Scholarly Works. Paper 49. Retrieved January 2, 2018, from http://scholars.law.unlv.edu/facpub/49.

Nader, L. (2002). *The life of the law, anthropological projects*. London: University of California Press.

Nandy, A. (2006). Nationalism, genuine and spurious: mourning two early post- nationalist strains. *Economic and Political Weekly, 41*(32), 3500–3504.

Pada, R. T. S. (2009). Iterability and différance: Re-tracing the context of the text. *Kritike, 3*(2), 68–89.

Qureshi, H. (2014). *Interview conducted with Inspector General of Police on 25 August at Police Headquarters, Haryana, India: Hisar.*
Santos, B. S., & Rodríguez-Garavito, C. A. (2005). Law, politics and the subaltern in the counter-hegemonic globalization. In B. S. Santos & C. A. Rodríguez-Garavito (Eds.), *Law and globalization from below: Towards a cosmopolitan legality* (pp. 1–26). United Kingdom: Cambridge University Press.
Searle, J. (1997). Reiterating the differences: A reply to Derrida. *Glyph, 1*, 198–208.
Sherman, B. (1988). Hermeneutics in law. *The Modern Law Review, 51*(3), 386–402.
Singh, A. (2018). *Sedition in liberal democracies*. New Delhi: Oxford University Press.
Singh, U. K. (2008). Penal strategies and political resistance in colonial and independent India. In K. Kannabiran & R. Singh (Eds.), *Challenging the rule(s) of law, colonialism, criminology and human rights in India* (pp. 227–256). New Delhi: Sage.
Tehelka. (2011). Retrieved November 2, 2014, from http://archive.tehelka.com/story_main48.asp?filename=Ws070111KASHMIRII.asp.
The Hindu. (2010). Retrieved June 12, 2012, from http://www.thehindu.com/opinion/lead/understanding-kashmirs-stone-pelters/article550058.ece.
The Indian Express. (2014). Retrieved September 8, 2014, from http://indianexpress.com/article/india/india-others/kerala-court-denies-bail-to-youth-who-didnt-stand-up-during-national-anthem/.
The Indian Express. (2016a). Retrieved August 8, 2016, from http://indianexpress.com/article/india/india-news-india/kashmiri-held-for-sedition-chhattisgarh-cops-probe-who-made-anti-india-fb-post-2956483/.
The Indian Express. (2016b). Retrieved December 19, 2016, from http://indianexpress.com/article/india/malayalam-writer-arrested-national-anthem-insult-kamal-c-chavara-4434372/.
The Indian Express. (2019). Retrieved April 12, 2019, from https://indianexpress.com/article/india/amu-jnu-sedition-case-anti-india-slogans-what-is-sedition-what-isnt-5583392/.
The New Indian Express. (2017). Retrieved May 13, 2018, from http://www.newindianexpress.com/nation/2017/aug/08/badaun-man-booked-for-sedition-held-for-i-support-pakistan-facebook-post-1640279.html.
Thomassen, L. (2011). The politics of iterability: Benhabib, the Hijab, and democratic iterations. *Polity, 43*(1), 128–149.
University World News. (2011). Kashmir: 'Seditious' Literature Lecturer Freed. Retrieved May 16, 2012, from http://www.universityworldnews.com/article.php?story=20110107100943147.

Anushka Singh teaches at the School of Law, Governance and Citizenship, Ambedkar University Delhi and is the author of Sedition in Liberal Democracies (Oxford University Press, 2018). She is trained as a political scientist and has previously taught at the University of Delhi. She was awarded her PhD from the Department of Political Science, University of Delhi in 2016. She has also been the recipient of a visiting fellowship for doctoral research at Tagore Centre for Global Thought, King's College, University of London, in 2014. Her research interests are in political theory, intersection of law and politics, free speech and the question of harm, and nature of state.

Chapter 9
Paramount State and the 'Princely Subject': Privy Purses Abolition and Its Aftermath

Garima Dhabhai

Abstract This paper proposes to examine the transition of sovereignty from 'princely' to a 'popular' form in the erstwhile princely domains of India after independence, and a corresponding transition of princes into citizens, especially after the abolition of privy purses by the Indian government in 1971 through the 26th amendment act. The debate around the abolition of princely titles and legal privileges in 1971 marks an important entry point, among many others, into the nature of Indian state and the paradigm of *paramountcy* as a form of power in the domain of popular sovereignty. The judgment in the Privy Purses case raises some important questions pertaining to legality of state action and the distinction between 'political' and 'legal' acts. The insertion of *paramountcy* as a way to assert state's power has implications for a theory of sovereignty in postcolonial India as well as the ramifications for Indian citizens in their rights against the state. The institution of rulership and its definition in the constitution along with its subsequent abolition gives an insight into a distinct imagination of Indian democracy as such.

9.1 Introduction

> When India became a Dominion every vestige of sovereignty was abandoned, equally so, by the States. They all surrendered to the peoples of the land who through their representatives in the Constituent Assembly hammered out for themselves a new Constitution in which all were citizens, in a new order having but one tie, and owing but one allegiance, devotion, loyalty, fidelity to the Sovereign, Democratic Republic that is India... (AIR 1993)[1]

[1] Shri Raghunathrao Ganpatrao versus Union of India. AIR 1993 SC 1267.

This paper is a revised version of the one presented at a conference on 'Constitutional Democracy in a Comparative Perspective' held in JNU, New Delhi on 15–16 March 2018. I thank the editors and participants in the conference for their comments on the paper.

G. Dhabhai (✉)
Presidency University, Kolkata, India
e-mail: garima.polsc@presiuniv.ac.in

© Springer Nature Singapore Pte Ltd. 2020

A. Roy and M. Becker (eds.), *Dimensions of Constitutional Democracy*,
https://doi.org/10.1007/978-981-15-3899-5_9

India became an independent nation-state in 1947, declaring itself as democratic-co-constituting 'people' as the basis of its power. Older molds of power and sovereignty seemingly made way to herald a new regime based on the Constitution. This paper will examine an episode from the political history of postcolonial state in India that marked the transition of former princes into citizens owing to the abolition of Privy Purses by the Government of India in 1971. Through the narrative of this transition, the paper aims to analyze the nature of constitutional democracy in postcolonial India that is replete with crevices indicating apparently anachronistic forms of power. When the former princes challenged the abolition of privy purses in 1971 in the Supreme Court of India, the Indian state responded by invoking the idea of 'paramountcy' against the petition.

Paramountcy, which in this case was a postcolonial invocation, had colonial antecedents in India, when it generated a complex legal and political terrain in the princely states over the nineteenth and twentieth centuries. In a letter from the Viceroy to the Nizam dated 26th March, 1926, the principle of paramountcy is asserted:

> Crown's supremacy was not based only on treaties, but existed independently of them.[2]

Paramountcy entailed the usage of discretionary powers by the British Crown in case of situations of contingency for common protection of all (Sever 1985). In this sense, it was perceived to be beyond treaties and agreements by the British officials. Paramountcy thus involved prerogative, usage and custom. It was a pillar of 'indirect rule' (Fisher 1984) in the princely states, yet it remained perpetually undefined. As Karen Leonard puts it, '...indirect rule was fuelled by elites within the states, especially the ones who were trained in the mores of the British- the 'western educated Indians from colonial India...men who have seen themselves as analogues of the British' (Leonard 2003). Henry Maine, the well-known British legal philosopher, had distinguished paramountcy from sovereignty by calling the former a 'de-facto' exercise of power, implicating it as excess to the legal attributes of de-jure or sovereign power.[3] The ambiguous nature of the term 'paramountcy' is reflected in these words of the Butler Committee Report '*Paramountcy must remain paramount*'.[4] It was a historical relation that was tantamount to lapse after the Crown ceases to be in power. Conceptually, its definition is self-generated, and is contingent upon political situations, demanding political acts, later on to be discussed in reference to the 'act of state'. It is free of law, based on a vulnerable moment of contingency, filling its emptiness with referents. This paper explores the concept of paramountcy as invoked in the postcolonial context. The debate on the abolition of privy purses marks an important entry point among others, into understanding the nature of Indian State

[2]House of Commons, Accounts and Papers, vol. 22 (1926). Further Correspondence Regarding the Claim of the Nizam of Hyderabad to the Restoration of the Province of Berar (Sever 1985: 460–62).

[3]For more discussion on the philosophical and legal traditions of British imperialism in the Indian context, see Mantena (2010), Copland (1997), Legg (2014), Benton (2006).

[4]The committee was formed in the late 1920s in response to the demand made by the Chamber of Princes to define paramountcy. Report of the Indian States (Butler) Committee. February 14, 1929 (Sever 1985).

and the paradigm of power at a time shortly before the declaration of National Emergency (1975–1977).

The paper is divided into three parts, charting the shift in the relationship between the Indian State and the princes through the 1950s to the 1970s. The optimism surrounding the merger had faded away by the 1970s and the invocation of paramountcy by the Indian State then raises some important questions pertaining to legality of state action seen as 'political act' that overrode the juridical and the constitutional limits to authority.

In the first section titled 'Princely Integration and Privy Purses', we would delineate the optimism among the framers of the Constitution around the merger of princely territories in the late 1940s and then proceed to understand the discourses that informed the reversal of the State's policy towards princely figures in the 1970s in the next two sections. The major instance that would form the crux of the argument in the second section titled 'Privy Purses Abolition: Political Power over the Princes' is the abolition of privy purses with the ensuing judicial discourse around it. Through this the paper seeks to argue that the modalities of power in postcolonial India with respect to the erstwhile princely states reproduced an ambiguous legality from the colonial period that was beyond the constitutional law, presuming the princes as lesser sovereigns in a formally democratic context. The paramount power that the Indian State claimed against the former princes in the wake of privy purses abolition in 1971 was not only a reproduction of the configuration of sovereignty that was in place during the colonial period but also had structural resemblance to the extraordinary laws that ironically base the assertion of democracy by the State on the disavowal of citizens' rights.[5] In the case of privy purses' abolition, such an assertion was made by the State against a class of citizens, whose historical power was blunted and redefined in the new nation-state. The assertion of paramountcy by the Indian State formally endowed these princely figures with a form of sovereignty that had no valence while suspending them from the body politic at the juncture of declaration of paramountcy. It is to these concerns that the paper would return subsequently. In the third section called 'Property, Wealth and Regulating the "Princely" Subject' we would extend the argument further by focusing on the debates over princely property arising out of varied interpretations of the covenants signed by the princes during the merger with the Indian State in the late 1940s. The discourse on property had also come into sharp relief in the period of 1970s, with the 42nd Amendment enacted during the Emergency that retracted the much debated Right to Property from the section on Fundamental Rights. The aim of this section is to understand the political and economic logic of the assertion of paramountcy made by the State in the 1970s—delving into the practices of governance with regard to the princely subject.

[5]For more discussion on the structure of extraordinary laws and the aporia of democracy in India, see Singh (2003).

9.2 Princely Integration and Privy Purses

During the merger process, one of the things promised to the princes was 'Privy Purses'. What were privy purses and what was their significance at the inception of nation building? To answer this question, one needs to delve into the speech by Sardar Vallabhbhai Patel, the Minister of States in the late 1940s and early 50s. This speech given on 12th October 1949 in the Constituent Assembly brings out the 'political and moral' justification of Privy Purse settlement with the princes. He had said, 'these guarantees form a part of the historic settlements which enshrine them in the consummation of the great ideal of political, geographical and economic unification of India'.[6] It was but a 'small price for the bloodless revolution, which affected the destinies of millions of our people'.[7] In the same session of the Assembly, in response to the comments of Jai Narain Vyas, a Congress leader and Praja Mandalist from Jodhpur, which sought to eliminate feudalism and deny the rights of citizenship to the princes, another votary of integration and princely guarantees, K. M. Munshi[8] had said, '…those (feudal) elements which have survived this (bloodless) revolution are as much citizens of the Republic as anybody else and it must be the duty of all other people, and especially the administration to enforce the rule of law in such a manner that all vestiges of feudalism disappear' (CAD Vol. X 1949). He added, '…every person born in India is a citizen of India. In making what Sardar called the 'bloodless revolution', we did not propose to produce outlaws' (ibid). Thus, an annual fixed amount of privy purses were promised to the rulers of the States on the consultation of the Indian States' Finances Enquiry Committee, calling these 'political' in nature in lieu of the 'economic benefits' of integration of the princely states. The covenants that the rulers entered into with the Indian state on signing the Instrument of Accession, also guaranteed them 'full ownership, use and enjoyment of all private property (as distinct from state property) belonging to him on the date of his making over administration of that State to the Rajpramukh'.[9] The 'private properties' of the rulers were agreed on mutually between them and the Government of India. Rulers had furnished an inventory of their moveable and immoveable properties in accordance with the Covenant. As far as the state of Jaipur was concerned, the Maharaja was also given exclusive shooting rights in certain preserves. The immoveable property comprised of 'family property' of the ruler and property where he had full rights of disposal.[10]

---

[6] Constituent Assembly Debates, Volume X, October 12, 1949.

[7] Ibid.

[8] Manu Bhagavan discusses the role of K. M. Munshi as the more moderate voice of the Hindu Mahasabha, who made its ideas 'palatable' to the new democratic public. Munshi was also instrumental in the foundation of Swatantra Party later on with a stronghold among the former princes. See Bhagavan (2008). Francine Frankel mentions the 'vertical networks controlled by princes and zamindars' as the pillar of support for the Swatantra Party. See Frankel (2005: 359).

[9] Article XII of the Covenant, File No. 10/3/72, Pol III, Ministry of Home Affairs, National Archives of India, New Delhi (hereafter, NAI).

[10] As per the Estate Duty Bill passed in 1954, rulers could also dispose off their dynastic and hitherto inalienable property, provided they were not seen as 'official residence' of the royal family. Ibid.

If this was the position of Indian State in the 1950s, it took a dramatic turn within the next two decades, renegotiating the power of the centre over the states[11] and of the so-called *people* over the princely figures. The following pages will offer a narrative of the transformation of the position of former princes, especially after the abolition of privy purses by the Indian government in 1971 through the 26th Amendment Act.

9.3 Privy Purse Abolition: Political Power over the Princes

A petition by the princes led by the Maharaja of Gwalior was sought against the order issued by the President of India, following the advice of the Council of Ministers on 6th September 1970.[12] The order came in the wake of the failure in the passage of Constitution (Twenty Fourth Amendment Bill), 1970 in the Rajya Sabha. The bill had sought to abolish articles 291, 362 and 366(22) of the Indian Constitution, thus derecognizing all the 'rulers' of the Indian States. Articles 291 and 362 had guaranteed the privy purses as per the covenants signed between the Dominion of India and heads of former princely states.[13] The ordinance also inserted Article 363A in the Constitution to formalize the abolition, by placing the treaties and agreements signed with the princes before the enactment of the Constitution outside of the judicial purview. By default then, matters arising as such were to be dealt with directly by the State's executive branch, in spirit of exceptional laws. The State had claimed the presidential order abolishing the privy purses as an 'act of state', which implied a sovereign political act unquestionable in the court of law. It was first defined in 1966 Fletcher-Moulton L. J. Salman versus the Secretary of State for India as ' a sovereign act which is neither grounded in law nor does it pretend to be so...it is a catastrophic change constituting a new departure' (AIR 1971).

---

[11]The Congress government, which ruled over the Centre at the time, had a tenuous relationship with several erstwhile princes who had entered the democratic fray in opposition to the Congress belonging to the Jan Sangh or Swatantra Party. For more on the political career of princely families, see Richter (1971).

[12]Presidential Order of 6th September, 1970: 'In exercise of power vested in him under Article 366(22) of the constitution, the President hereby directs that with effect from the date of this order, (name of the Prince with title) ceases to be recognized as a ruler/Bhagdar of (name of the State). By order and in the name of the President' in The Times of India. September 8, 1970. Delhi.

[13]Article 291, 'where under any covenant or agreement entered into by the Ruler of any Indian State before the commencement of this Constitution, the payment of any sums, free of tax, has been guaranteed or assured by the Government of the Dominion of India to any Ruler of such State as privy purse-a. Such sums shall be charged on and paid out of the Consolidated Fund of India; and b. the sums so paid to any ruler shall be exempt from all taxes on income'. Article 362, 'in the exercise of the power of the Parliament or of the Legislature of a State to make laws or in exercise of the executive power of the Union or of a State, due regard shall be had to guarantee of assurance given under any such covenant or agreement as is referred to in Article 291 with respect to personal rights, privileges and dignities of the Ruler of an Indian State'. Shukla (1963). *The Constitution of* India, 4th edition. Delhi. cf. Frankel (2005: 442).

The final judgment in this case (AIR 1971) upheld the petition and declared the Presidential order as ultra vires.[14] This judgment also came at a time when the relations between the judiciary and the executive were rife with tensions on the interpretation of the 'basic structure' of the Constitution. Previously in 1967, the Supreme Court had defended the landowners' fundamental right to property citing fundamental rights as part of the basic structure, which may not be altered by the legislative or executive process (Frankel 2005: 442–443). The 1971 judgment on the privy purses too could be seen as a part of this practice of judicial review, dubbing the privy purses as constitutional guarantees. However, the Union of India, as a respondent in the case, defended its action in issuing the abolition order as a *'political act'* as recreated in Article 363A, arising out of the merger agreements and covenants, and thus, as beyond the jurisdiction of the courts. The dominant interpretation of Article 363 of Indian Constitution placed merger and the covenants resulting out of it beyond the purview of the judiciary, and making any properties as presumably 'gifts' from the State to the rulers.[15] Several property disputes between the government of India and the princely states treaded this slippery terrain laid down by Article 363 and remained suspended due to ambiguity of jurisdiction, a discussion on which warrants another paper (NAI 10/3/72). An instance may briefly highlight this uncertainty. In 1972, just after the 26th amendment act was passed, the Government of Rajasthan sought a clarification from the Home Ministry, Government of India, regarding a sale of Rambagh Palace, which was declared as the ruler's private property, which could be maintained by the Maharaja. Eventually the palace was sold to Oberoi Limited (NAI 10/3/72).[16] The rulers had shown disconcert on the possible harassment they may have to face from the local officials 'on account of the position being nor clear'.[17] The disputes on covenants, owing to their ambiguous constitutional position, were the reflection of a powerful Executive vis-à-vis the ruler-citizen. It also recreated the power of the Central government over the states.

Meanwhile, in the 1971 case, the Union of India in its response against the petition filed by Maharaja of Gwalior asserted the principle of 'paramountcy' implied within this political act as recreated by this very Article 363. 'Rulership' was seen as a '*gift from the President*' rather than a right which could be claimed. In its response supporting the abolition of Privy Purses, the government representative contended that the executive has inherited the concept of Paramountcy from the British Crown.

> The source of the right to receive the Privy Purse and to be accorded the privileges claimed was a political agreement and the privy purses was in the nature of *political pension*; that in recognizing or derecognizing a ruler the President exercised a political power which was a sovereign power and that the rights and obligations were liable to be varied or repudiated in accordance with the 'State policy'; that the jurisdiction of the courts to enforce rights and obligations arising out of the covenant were excluded, because, the rights and obligations

[14]The privy purses were finally abolished in 1971 through the 26th Constitutional Amendment Act and this abolition was upheld in the judgment given by the Supreme Court in Shri Raghunathrao Ganpat Rao versus the Union of India case on 4th January, 1993.

[15]10/3/72, NAI.

[16]Also see File no. 22(5) GA-A/70, NAI.

[17]File no. 21/3/72, Pol III, M/o Home Affairs, NAI.

> arose out of the act of state; that the concept of paramountcy of the British Crown was inherited by the Union of India and therefore, the recognition of Rulership was a 'gift of the President'; and further that the petitioners stood excluded by Article 363, for they were seeking either to enforce the covenants and agreements *or were seeking to enforce the provisions of the Constitution 'relating to' such covenants"* (emphasis mine). (AIR 1971: 3)

According to the opinion of the Attorney General of India, Article 363 of the Constitution recreates 'paramountcy' for the executive by barring the order from judicial review as it emanates from an *act of state*, an agreement signed between two parties in international arena. However, the petitioners' advocates claimed that:

> an action authorized by law against the citizens of the Union cannot be supported under the shelter of paramountcy. After the withdrawal of British power and the extinction of paramountcy of the British the Dominion Government of India did not and could not exercise any paramountcy over the States. The functions of the President stems from the Constitution, not from a 'concept of the British Crown' identified or unidentified. (AIR 1971: 6)

In such a scenario, what did the retention of '*paramountcy*' as a practice of defining the state vis-à-vis the erstwhile princes entail and presume? At this juncture, one may pause to return to the colonial period and the complex structure of sovereignty that the British government had devised vis-à-vis the presumably feudal and primitive enclaves interspersing the British Indian territory. Princely states not only posed a challenge to the territorial sovereignty of the British but were also heterogeneous in terms of governance practices. As a result, they were put under the charge of Foreign Office, treated at par with neighbouring British imperial possessions such as Afghanistan, Persian Gulf states and Burma (Benton 2006: 11–12). Charles Lewis Tupper, an official in the British administration in Punjab, was responsible in putting forth a general theory of British rule in native states in his four-volume manual in 1895. It delineated the relations between the British government and their Indian feudatories while formalizing the legal policy of the former (Benton 2006: 13). Tupper devised the idea of 'political law', based on principles of stratified sovereignty and usage. This treatment of the princely states was similar to the strategy followed in other politically volatile areas such as the hill tracts and frontier regions of the Empire. The princely states' based their sovereignty as per British accounts on status rather than territoriality and hence, were seen as detrimental to a contiguous national community. The British, therefore, in the name of good governance, assumed a sovereign power superior in scale to that of the princes- namely, paramountcy. This reverberated Henry Maine's minutes of 1864 on the legal status of princely states, justifying British intervention to maintain peace and order there. He had said, 'the mode and degree in which sovereignty is distributed between the British government and any given native state is always a question of fact, which has to be separately decided in each case'. (cf. Benton 2006: 21–22).

Coming back to the case of 1971, the response of the Indian State on the Privy Purses issue raised some important questions pertaining to the legality of state action and the distinction between a political *act of state* and 'legal' acts. The invocation of *paramountcy* as a way to assert state's power presumed the extra-constitutional status of princes and had implications for a theory of sovereignty in postcolonial

India as well as the ramifications for Indian citizens in their rights against the state especially when citizens are qualified and disqualified through political practice. As the petition of 1971 put it, 'paramountcy as claimed by the British rulers was one of the manifestations of imperialism…it is a power exercised by a superior sovereign over subordinate sovereigns' (AIR 1971: 105). The judgment interpreted the 'rulers' as a legal category, bestowed by the Constitution to fix their claim to privy purses. The rulers, therefore, were not sovereign in this case, but legal citizens, whose power emanated from the Constitution rather than any pre-constitutional arrangements. Moreover, what becomes significant here is the overlap between their status as 'rulers' as defined in the Constitution and their status as citizens. Their citizenship came to be historically imbricated and qualified for special provisions such as the privy purses within the constitutional structure itself. The court saw the state's claim as paramount over these princes as a 'deliberate defiance of the Constitution by the willful repudiation of contractual obligations against a class of citizens' (AIR 1971: 123). The response of the Indian State sought to justify the abolition by dubbing it as an act suitable in a democratic context, emplacing it very well within the populist rhetoric of the day, whose other cornerstone was bank nationalization undertaken by the Indira Gandhi regime.

As the Union of India put it, 'The respondent in its counter affidavit has taken the stand that the people of this country having become conscious of their social and economic rights would not tolerate any longer the concept of rulership or the Privy Purses or any of the privileges incorporated in the covenants and the merger agreements. Therefore it is the duty of the government to give effect to the *will of the people* (AIR 1971: 100)'. (emphasis mine)

In this sense, the state while acting as the representative of the 'people' and invoking popular sovereignty as the basis of this assertion resorted to a colonial idea of power, i.e. paramountcy. The notion of popular sovereignty invoked by the State was operationalized through the will of the representative, which constructed the 'people' at the same time while claiming to represent them, albeit as a paramount power. The popular sovereignty in India in the 1970s then was far away from democratic tropes of its representation; rather it relied on a relic of power that situated the democratic assertions in a time warp, taking one back to a historical moment, whose knots had apparently been resolved by the promise of privy purses to the princes by the Constituent Assembly.

In its bid for democracy the Indian State articulates paramount power in a tenuous relationship with popular sovereignty, which it seeks to represent, by excluding the dyadic ruler-citizen from its fold. The assumption of unprecedented political power by the State therefore, suspended any 'legal' resolution on the question of merger and princely past.

9.4 Property, Wealth and Regulating the 'Princely' Subject

A few years after the abolition of privy purses, in a report in 1978, the Ministry of Finance under the Government of India deliberated on the ways in which 'huge amount of precious gems and jewellery' possessed by the princes may be brought under the gamut of a museum display and public domain. The anxiety of the state was 'illegal' sale of such precious gems abroad for earning foreign exchange in violation of Foreign Exchange Regulation Act. Since 1950s there were notifications by the Government of India regarding tightening of customs regulations for the princes, especially when it comes to taking jewellery abroad.[18] There were deliberations, way back in 1948 about asking rulers to attach a list of jewellery with their passports. Interestingly the correspondence then had presumed that the rulers may give a wrong list and hence, it was to be emphasized that customs may, on suspicion, 'be reluctantly compelled to search the person of the Prince and his party'.[19] In a 'secret and personal' exchange between the rulers and the Ministry of States dates 19th August, 1949 rulers were urged to 'limit foreign travel to occasions of health and business' to save remittances abroad and correct the Balance of Payments situation in the country. It was deemed as 'essential for national interest'. The customs immunity, which hitherto was given as a privilege to the rulers was also to be withdrawn in the wake of reports of rulers taking jewellery abroad to sale.[20]

Locating the precious gems and jewellery for the museum also became a mode for marking them out in the larger apparatus of postcolonial governance as the 'princely subject' with a feudal past. The State even deliberated upon giving fiscal exemptions to incentivize declarations of treasure by erstwhile royalty, by designating their family heirlooms as 'works of art'.[21] After the merger of the princely states, the Government of India recognized any 'jewellery in existence before the 13th day of April 1950 as part of his own (ruler's) insignia' as heirloom and allowed it to be retained by the ruler for use on ceremonial occasions. However by 1971, post the abolition of privy purses, it was presumed that 'there appears to be no need for the display of regalia' and hence those items of regalia, which is State property and maintained by it may be returned back. The 1972 Antiquities and Art Treasures Act also provided for 'compulsory acquisition of pieces of antiquity and art treasure for being placed in the museum'.[22] Jewellery in such a context was reinterpreted as 'national wealth' and art and was to be preserved through creation of national trusts, in form of museums. The rulers were not able to monetize their own properties, now arrested through the idea of 'heritage'. For instance, the City Palace of Jaipur remained the private property of the ruler on the condition that 'the buildings housing the Art treasures, such as carpets, manuscripts, armory and historical records that are to be converted

[18] Ministry of States, File No. 298-P/50, 1950, Political Branch, NAI.

[19] Ministry of Finance, Correspondence on Jewellery Museum, F.2 (25) Ex F III/48, GOI, NAI.

[20] Ibid.

[21] File No. 23/1/78, Pol. III, NAI.

[22] File No. 21/11/71, Pol III, M/o Home Affairs, Correspondence regarding impact of 26th Amendment Act, 1971 on the private properties of the rulers, NAI.

into a National Trust, to be continued to be used for the said purpose and to be maintained by the Trust or by the new government'.[23] A discussion ensued among the Government of India in 1972 when the Trust formed by the Maharaja in 1959 was called 'His Highness the Maharaja of Jaipur Museum Trust',[24] which was housed in a portion of the City palace and was open to public. That it was an ordinary rather than a National Trust created confusion on the status of City Palace as the ruler's private property. The condition of a National Trust was important for its recognition as 'private property' as per the covenant since it housed 'art treasures'. It is only after a legal advice came from the Law Ministry in June 1972 interpreting the Trust as 'public' and declaring the covenants as outside the jurisdiction of courts and hence, non-justiciable that the matter found a closure (NAI 10/3/72).

Antiquity and Art Treasures Act that was devised in 1972 sought to regulate the wealth and treasures of princely states, especially pieces of jewellery categorized as 'antiquity'. In fact the museum of 'gems and jewellery' was envisaged under the jurisdiction of the Department of Revenue, Ministry of Finance. This stirred a debate among the government departments, some questioning its legal validity given the covenants guaranteeing these moveable properties to the rulers. The covenants entered into by the rulers and the Indian State at the time of signing the Instrument of Accession had categorized their possessions in terms of state properties (to be transferred to the new Indian State), private properties and personal properties, out of which the first was seen as inalienable while the last one was absolutely disposable by the person of the ruler. However, the second category presented a legal and definitional conundrum for the Indian state and in as late as in 1972, its fresh interpretations were sought and supplied by legal bodies, most prominently by the state Law Departments, Advocate General and Attorney General of India (NAI 10/3/72). A trail of correspondences left behind by the Ministry of States, General Administration Departments of erstwhile princely regions and legal experts points to the reappraisal of economies of integration of princely states, in the aftermath of privy purses abolition. Qualified as 'act of state', the covenants and inventories were seen as non-justiciable in courts of law, and were seen as stemming out of treaties. The bid for the museum therefore generated anxiety among the princely owners of moveable property, who suspected a larger design of acquisition of this by the state by claiming it as 'State Property' after abolition of rulership.[25]

Coming back to the instance of Jaipur princely state in Rajasthan, between 11th Feb and 13th June, 1975, a search was conducted by the Income Tax Department in various premises of Jaipur royal family, including Jaigarh Fort, Rambagh palace, Rajmahal Palace and Moti Doongri palace as per newspaper reports from the period.[26] Rumour mills were rife with reports of considerable amounts of gold in form of coins,

[23]File No. 10/3/72 Pol. III, 3rd May 1972, Ministry of Home Affairs, National Archives of India, New Delhi.

[24]It is now called Maharaja Sawai Man Singh II Museum and is a centre of many 'heritage' related activities.

[25]File No. 23/1/78, Political III, Ministry of Finance, Department of Revenue, NAI, New Delhi.

[26]April 5, 1975. Rajgharane ke seel band kamron ki jaanch sheegrh shuru hogi.*Rajasthan Patrika.*

bars, ornaments and gold biscuits with foreign markings were taken in truck loads to Delhi. Action was taken against the royal family members, who incidentally belonged to the opposition Swantantra Party, and they were asked to pay a fine of the order of Rs. 1.50 crores in lieu of the confiscation and to register gold articles of ancient origin and historical interest under Antiquities and Treasures Act, 1972. The family petitioned against the Collector's order and invoked the covenant signed in 1949, which accounted for the gold under the possession of royal family. However, later on Gayatri Devi was arrested on charges of under the FERA.[27] One of the reasons for the withdrawal of Congress support for the princes may be the internal party politics, which led to its divisions. New political parties were formed by leaders who defected from the Congress in the period before 1970s, primary among them being Swatantra Party formed by C. Rajagopalachari and K M Munshi. If one remembers the CA debates, it was leaders like Munshi who had supported the grant of special status to the princes. Several princes had joined the Swatantra Party and were successful electorally in the regions of their rule (Richter 1971; Bhagavan 2008). Sudipta Kaviraj places privy purses abolition as a strategy used by Indira Gandhi to realign the ruling coalition and adopt a populist tenor of 'progress' and 'socialism' (Kaviraj 1986).[28]

9.5 Conclusion

The 1970s in India's political history is seen as a period marked by populism and creation of a discourse of 'internal threats' to the Indian state, which legitimized the imposition of Emergency. Regime of suspicion and insecurity was let loose and any opposition to the Executive, which was now free to rule through Presidential Ordinances was dealt with a heavy hand. Even research on certain aspects of Emergency is not possible owing to the missing archives and documentation of the period in the public realm (Tarlo 2003). However, a few snippets are available to understand the mode of governance in that period. Especially its political economic and populist angles have been analyzed to bring home the rhetoric of development and nationalization (Frankel 2005). This period also becomes important in the political history of postcolonial Indian State due to the undermining of constitutionalism and emergence of 'political power' over and above legal sovereignty, as it were, in the name of people. In this paper, we have tried to understand the structure of this power in terms of 'paramountcy' through a deliberation on the instance of privy purses abolition and its implication for the ruler-citizen.

During the same period as privy purses' abolition, renewed anxieties about princely properties and paraphernalia as delineated in the third section bring out the question of settlement of princely states that loomed large on the horizon of new

[27] *Rajasthan Patrika*, April 30, 1975. This was based on a Rajya Sabha speech by Pranab Mukherjee on this issue.

[28] Kaviraj (1986). Indira Gandhi and Indian Politics. *Economic and Political Weekly*. 21(38/39), 1697–1708.

Indian democracy from the early years of independence, and may be read in the light of a long processes of integration and subsequent creation of a national public. Regulation of princely property was also deemed as management of their former status in the cities of their rule. The regimes of property acquisitions and transfer in princely states are still laden with these historically textured regimes, where lines are difficult to ascertain between 'private' and 'public' property, princely infrastructure and state offices and between erstwhile royal subjects and *democratic public*.

By the way of conclusion, we may delineate the three-part argument of this paper:

a. *Princely to popular sovereignty*: The merger of princely states into the Indian Union was accompanied by the transformation of princes into citizens circumscribed within the Constitution and guaranteed privy purses owing to their contribution to the nation building process. The linear narrative of the nation inching towards modernity was scripted with the merger.
b. *Princes as legal subjects*: In 1971, the abolition of privy purses was challenged by the princes on grounds of their status as citizens, albeit historically marked ones. They lodged a judicial battle to retain themselves as legal subjects in the postcolonial context.
c. Popular sovereignty as paramountcy; princes as extra-legal sovereigns—The Union of India, in its response in the 1971 case folds princes back into the realm of independent sovereignty, back to the moment of pre-constitutional original agreements; re-inscribing them as 'feudal' and seeking to wipe out the anachronistic princely privileges from the memory of the Republic. The princes are brought back to the juncture of negotiation with the postcolonial state as subordinate sovereigns rather than as right-bearing citizens. The resolution of the 'princely question' as done in the 1950s was undone and reopened for negotiation. The logic of populism and political economy imbricated in the postcolonial Indian state defied the logic of the original contract with the princes, at the time of founding the nation. This was one moment of populism from the 1970s when the Executive headed by Indira Gandhi sought to redefine popular sovereignty by first hollowing it out of the history of transition and then by redefining it in terms of 'people's will', represented through the enunciation of paramountcy.

Perhaps the structure of paramountcy as the reflection of popular sovereignty continues in the contemporary Indian context too, which is in grip of a constitutional and institutional crisis along with a hyper-visible populist politics. But that question is for the posterity to settle.

References

Benton, L. (2006). The Geography of Quasi-Sovereignty: Westlake, Maine and the Legal Politics of Colonial Enclaves. *History and Theory of International Law Series*, Working Paper 2006/5.

Bhagavan, M. (2008). Princely states and the Hindu imaginary: Exploring the cartography of Hindu nationalism in colonial India. *The Journal of Asian Studies, 67*(3), 881–915.

Copland, I. (1997). *Princes at the Endgame of Empire*. Cambridge: Cambridge University Press.

Fisher, M. (1984). Indirect Rule in the British Empire: The Foundation of Residency System in India (1764-1858). *Modern Asian Studies, 18*(3), 393–428.
Frankel, F. (2005). *India's Political Economy: The Gradual Revolution 1947–2000* (II ed.). Delhi: Oxford University Press.
HH Maharajadhiraja Madhav Rao Jiwaji Rao Scindia Bahadur vs. Union of India, 1971 AIR SC 530.
Kaviraj, S. (1986). Indira Gandhi and Indian Politics. *Economic and Political Weekly., 21*(38/39), 1697–1708.
Legg, S. (2014). An International Anomaly: Sovereignty, the League of Nations and India's Princely Geographies. *Journal of Historical Geography, 43,* 96–110.
Leonard, K. (2003). Reassessing Indirect Rule in Hyderabad: Rule, Ruler, or Sons-in-Law of the State? *Modern Asian Studies, 37*(2), 363–379.
Mantena, K. (2010). *Alibis of Empire: Henry Maine and the Ends of Liberal Imperialism.* New Jersey: Princeton University Press.
Richter, W. (1971). Princes in Indian Politics. *Economic and Political Weekly, 6*(9), 535–542.
Sever, A (ed.) (1985). Documents and Speeches on the Indian Princley States, Vol. II (pp. 460–462). BR Publishing Corporation.
Singh, U. (2003). Democratic Dilemmas. *Economic and Political Weekly,* 38(5).
Tarlo, E. (2003). *Unsettling Memories: Narratives of Emergency in Delhi.* Berkeley: University of California Press.

Garima Dhabhai teaches in the Department of Political Science at Presidency University and has submitted her doctoral thesis on tropes of memory and its representation through heritage in urban space of contemporary Jaipur in Jawaharlal Nehru University in 2018. She had been awarded the Fox Fellowship to Yale University in 2015-16 and has published parts of her research in journals and edited volumes. Garima is interested in questions of political economy, princely states, urban heritage, conservation practices and political spectacles in postcolonial India.

Chapter 10
Indigenous Peoples Rights to Land in India and Europe

Radhika Chitkara

Abstract The evolution of human rights norms relating to indigenous peoples (IPs) land rights coincides with the ascendence of land-intensive development paradigms across the globe, throwing historical conflicts between States and IPs over land and resource sovereignty into sharp relief. As States assert their overall sovereignty over territorial resources to determine their allocation for developmental priorities, they do so through the nullification of indigenous governance and ownership of land, and the transformation of the underlying ethos of their use. As domestic constitutional arrangements have come under increasing strain, IPs have turned towards international human rights not only to regulate State conduct but also to challenge its monopoly over determination of developmental priorities, particularly through the right to self-determination. A comparative reading of different human rights systems enables progressive articulations of the form and content of IP land rights and the extent of State obligation in light of the adoption of the UNDRIP in 2007. This paper turns to a comparative analysis of rights recognition and State obligation in Europe and India, as two regional human rights systems that emerged contemporaneously, governing sovereign States with IPs within their territories, and based on liberal democratic constitutional frameworks with a commitment to human rights. The first section identifies a framework within which the European and Indian human rights systems may be compared. The second and third sections analyse the form and content of rights recognition and State obligation in Europe and India, through textual guarantees and case studies of the ECtHR decision in *Handolsdalen Sami village and others* v. Sweden, and the Supreme Court of India in the *Niyamgiri* decision. The concluding section serves to identify opportunities for normative borrowing for a fuller recognition of IP land rights in both Europe and India, and the manner in which State and IP relations on land and resource sovereignty may be reconfigured.

R. Chitkara (✉)
Jindal Global Law School, Delhi, India
e-mail: rchitkara@llm17.law.harvard.edu

© Springer Nature Singapore Pte Ltd. 2020

A. Roy and M. Becker (eds.), *Dimensions of Constitutional Democracy*,
https://doi.org/10.1007/978-981-15-3899-5_10

10.1 Introduction

The evolution of human rights norms relating to indigenous peoples (IP) land rights coincides with the ascendence of land-intensive industrial development paradigms across the globe, which has thrown historical conflicts between States and IPs over land and resource sovereignty into sharp relief. As States assert their overall authority and control over territorial resources to determine their allocation for developmental priorities, they do so through the nullification of indigenous governance and ownership of land, and the transformation of the underlying ethos of their use. IPs have increasingly turned towards international human rights as domestic constitutional arrangements have come under increasing strain, not only to regulate State conduct but also to challenge its monopoly over allocation and determination of developmental priorities.

The adoption of the United Nations Declaration against Indigenous Peoples (UNDRIP) in 2007, recognizing collective self-determination and land rights, has thus been hailed as a 'jurisgenerative moment' in human rights law (Carpenter and Riley 2014). Its foundational reliance on the right to self-determination reveals its roots in processes of decolonization inaugurated by the creation of postcolonial States (Gilbert 2006; Kingsbury 1992). Although non-binding as an instrument, the UNDRIP is widely considered to encode existing international law, regional human rights norms and domestic constitutional arrangements into universally applicable human rights guarantees (Davis 2012; Barnabas 2017).

Human rights generally (re)define the relationship between States and people as one of rights and obligations, defining limitations on sovereign powers of the State under international law (Alston and Goodman 2013). The elevation of IP land rights to the *supra*-State level serves to reconfigure the constitutive relationship between States and IPs within their territories through the same medium of rights and obligations. This establishes independent standards of determining the content of IP land rights beyond those recognized domestically by the States themselves. In turn, how does the instrument of State obligation transform sovereign rights over land, territory and resources in relation to IPs?

For the purposes of this paper, the term 'land rights' is understood expansively, as including any kind of interest in land deriving from its use and occupation, which may encompass management rights as territorial control on one end, to *simpliciter* rights to herding, fishing and occupation on the other.

A comparative reading of different human rights systems enables progressive articulations of the form and content of IP land rights and the extent of State obligation. This paper turns to a comparative analysis of IP land rights recognition and State obligation in Europe and India, as two regional human rights systems that emerged contemporaneously. The Constitution of India was adopted in 1950, while the European Convention on Human Rights (ECHR) was adopted in 1953, both of which govern sovereign States with IPs within their territories, and are based on liberal democratic constitutional frameworks with a commitment to human rights. Although the content of rights recognition under the ECHR and the Constitution of India differ, as a reflection of their specific colonial histories, IPs therein face common marginalizations from their lands. While the European rights framework reflects norms that established State sovereignty in the formulation of the model of the modern State, the Constitution of India reflects negotiations of constitutional rights of IPs at the moment when the Indian State came into being. Nevertheless, in the contemporary period, common threats to IPs in both regions include the expansion of sovereign State authorities over their lands, settler societies and corporations.

The first section delineates existing standards relating to IP land rights recognition and the content of State obligation, to identify a framework within which the European and Indian human rights systems may be compared. This is achieved through a comparative reading of norms under the international and regional human rights systems. The second and third sections identify the form of rights recognition and content of State obligation in Europe and India, through an analysis of textual guarantees and jurisprudence of their respective highest adjudicatory forums. In Europe, the decision of the European Court of Human Rights ('ECtHR') in *Handolsdalen Sami village and others* v. *Sweden* serves as a case study.[1] The decision of the Supreme Court of India in *Orissa Mining Corporation Limited* v. *Ministry of Environment and Forests* serves as its counterpart.[2] The concluding section juxtaposes the form and content of IP land rights and State obligation in Europe and India, and the role played by comparative methods in each of the systems. This section finally serves to identify opportunities for normative borrowing for a fuller recognition of IP land rights in both Europe and India.

10.2 IP Land Rights: Towards a Framework

IP human rights norms emerge from the recognition that the existing regime does not adequately represent their claims and interests, and may even be complicit in undermining them (Anaya 2004; Thornberry 2002). The prolonged negotiations on recognizing self-determination, autonomy and collective rights as human rights in the drafting of UNDRIP reflect some of these contestations (Xanthaki 2007; Gilbert 2007; Corntassel 2007). These contestations were successful in revealing the specificity of the 'inherent' and 'universal' human rights, by bringing to the fore forms of violations produced by processes of colonization, racial and ethnic discrimination, and industrialized forms of development on them.

The historical contexts of these processes of dispossession vary across space and time, as colonial States established sovereignty over indigenous territories over the seventeenth century and onwards (Keal 2007; Anaya 2004). Co-terminus with the creation of territorially bound sovereign nation States in Europe and its worldwide colonies, colonial societies appropriated indigenous land and resources, imposed

[1] Application no. 39013/04, 17 February 2009.
[2] (2013) 6 SCC 476.

alien legal and property regimes, and extinguished customary rights and institutions through the use of Law (Anaya, Indigenous Peoples in International Law 2004; Espiel 1990). Under international law, the extension of sovereign authority of States was facilitated by the doctrine of *terra nullius*, under which the occupation and control of lands by IPs was nullified (Thornberry 2002; Xanthaki 2007; Shaw 2008). Politically negotiated arrangements between States and indigenous peoples as distinct sovereigns were gradually domesticated as internal constitutional rights of indigenous peoples within State boundaries (Shaw 2008; Gussen 2017; Aguilar et al. 2010). This subjected indigenous peoples and their lands to the hegemonizing authority of the colonial States, with limited or no rights to constitutional autonomy and self-governance over their territories.

By further overwriting customary forms of collective resource use and management, States established alien property regimes, often private property, to govern land relations between private actors. Meant to ensure easy transferability and alienation of resources, the precedence accorded to these formal property relations was instrumental in the fragmentation, alienation and occupation of indigenous lands by dominant groups and industry (Anaya 2004). The resulting demographic changes compounded dispossession and exacerbated the loss of traditional ways of life and cultural identity of indigenous peoples.

Postcolonial States in the Global South continued these dispossessions, or established new settler projects, in their own processes of modern State formation through the twentieth century (Xanthaki 2007; Carpenter and Riley 2014). Today, the same sovereign powers of eminent domain and the right to dispose of natural resources in general interest permits both colonial and postcolonial States alike to expropriate indigenous lands for industrial development and mining at a large scale.

These historical and continuing processes of dispossession have found expression in both universal and particular human rights norms. Universal norms, such as those contained in the Universal Declaration of Human Rights (UDHR), ICCPR and ICESCR, include rights inherent to all persons by virtue of being human, and have general applicability across regions and contexts. Although some rights in all these instruments also apply to peoples and minority groups, universal rights classically belong to individuals. As subjects of international law, States are the primary duty-bearers to respect, protect and fulfil the human rights of those individuals and minority groups found within their territories. They are binding on all States that sign and ratify those instruments, and owing to their wide acceptance have attained the flavour of customary international law as well (Schutter 2014; D'Amato 2010).

Particular human rights include those that address discrimination against specific vulnerable groups such as the Convention on Elimination of Racial Discrimination (CERD), Convention for the Elimination of all forms of Discrimination Against Women (CEDAW), International Conventions on the Rights of the Child (ICRC), etc., which are interrelated, interdependent and mutually reinforce universal human rights. While addressing specific forms of violations for these vulnerable groups, many of these particular rights retain the architecture of universal norms for being individual-centric (with some exceptions for people and minority groups) for rightsholders, and State-centric for duty-bearers.

Rights of indigenous peoples have also earlier been derived from CERD (Gilbert 2017) and CEDAW in the case of indigenous women (Kambel 2012). The UNDRIP most specifically relates to the rights of indigenous peoples *qua* indigenous peoples. The UNDRIP is an outcome of an intensive drafting and negotiation process and is widely considered to reflect the consensus between States and indigenous peoples (Xanthaki 2007). It is anchored in the foundational right of peoples to self-determination, that is, their right to freely determine their political status, dispose of natural wealth and freely pursue their economic, social and cultural development.

Human rights are also particularized through their application to specific regions, such as the Americas, Europe, Africa, among others, to reflect shared values, histories of marginalization and constitutional aspirations. Regional instruments indicate greater diversity in the subjects of human rights, including peoples, families, minority religious and ethnic groups.

This section surveys expressions of IP rights to land under universal and particular human rights norms at the universal and regional levels. Such a survey serves to identify an emergent framework on the form, content, and corresponding State obligations of the right to land, within which a comparative analysis of the European and Indian systems may be undertaken.

10.2.1 Qua Universal Human Rights

There is no express right to land under the universal human right framework (Gilbert 2013). Indigenous rights to land find expression in universal norms either through express guarantees to property, or those derived from cultural right of minorities to practice and propagate their culture.

Article 17 of the UDHR contains guarantees of property ownership, individually as well as in association with others. The two foundational human rights instruments, the ICCPR and ICESCR, do not guarantee a right to property per se, but the right has been read into the instruments in conjunction with existing rights, such as the right to housing for indigenous peoples in the content of the right to self-determination (United Nations Housing Rights Programme 2005).

The ILO Convention 107 (Indigenous and Tribal Populations Convention 1957) also recognizes individual and collective rights to property, but is embedded in an overall framework of individual rights with an emphasis on the assimilation of indigenous peoples into mainstream society (Xanthaki 2007; Anaya 2004). ILO Convention 169 (Indigenous and Tribal Peoples Convention) contains stronger land rights protections for indigenous peoples (Tomei and Swepston 1996). Regional human rights instruments recognize property rights widely, including the ECHR under Article 1 of Protocol 1, American Convention on Human Rights under Article 2.1, and the Banjul Charter on Human Rights and Peoples Rights under Article 14.

Admittedly, instruments recognizing property rights expressly include property in its collective dimensions. Such a right casts corresponding obligations on States to refrain from arbitrary dispossession of rightsholders, formally recognize property rights of IP over their land, and exercise due diligence in protecting the right from violations by both private and State actors.

Existing legal frameworks may recognize collective property forms, but may not treat the prior and historical use and occupation of land by indigenous peoples as property rights per se. The doctrine of *terra nullius* under international law, by which States acquired the right to establish control over previously 'unoccupied' lands was premised on precisely this erasure of the existing governance, occupation and use by indigenous peoples. Even if recognized as 'property', States may impose onerous evidentiary requirements for indigenous peoples to establish their prior ownership or use, effectively negating the right itself.

By framing IP rights within formal property regimes, States retain their authority as the source of rights. IP land rights are thus, derived from the State, and are equally subject to its sovereign powers of eminent domain and expropriation. On their own, recognition as property rights may also not displace the precedence of domestic law over customary property relations, which has been framed in colonial logics of fragmentation, alienation and appropriation.

Where property rights are not expressly recognized, collective rights have also been derived through cultural rights. The Committee on Economic, Social and Cultural Rights has invoked Article 27 of the ICCPR, that is, the cultural rights of minorities, to recognize indigenous peoples' unique cultural relationship with their lands and resources. Article 27 protects individual right to culture, but acknowledges that this is necessarily enjoyed in common with others. Members of indigenous communities are protected from dispossession from their traditional lands as a dimension of the right of minority groups to practice and propagate their culture. Derived from this right, the Committee has, at least on one occasion, recognized indigenous peoples' self-determined collective arrangements of resource use, through recognition of customary norms, practices and property regimes. It also recognizes some form of right to resource governance through the right to protect and preserve the resource base from destruction (McGee 2009; Peterson 2013).

Critics of this approach argue that it propagates essentialist readings of indigenous cultures, stymies its organic evolution, and empowers States to constrain rights with a change in cultural practices and traditional livelihoods (Xanthaki 2007).

Against a challenge to the imposition of alien political authorities and legal systems, the universal human rights framework preserves the exclusive political authority of States over indigenous peoples and territories. Institutions of colonial States retain the monopoly to determine and implement applicable laws, to normatively adjudge the form, content and exceptions to individual human rights, and to identify developmental priorities in public interest. Sovereign rights preserved through exceptions to human rights or other international law principles, such as eminent domain, are evidence of how the universal framework reproduces the historic dispossession of indigenous peoples.

10.2.2 *Qua Particular Rights*

Riding on churnings within human rights norms at the international and regional levels the previous decades, the UNDRIP makes radical departures from the axioms of the first generation human rights, as universal rights of undifferentiated individuals with the obligation upon States to respect, protect and fulfil. UNDRIP recognizes collective rights of indigenous peoples (IP) *qua* peoples with particular histories and contexts of marginalization. It contains extensive guarantees to the right to land and territories, especially under Articles 25–32. These are specific enumerations of the overall right to self-determination by which they have the right to 'freely determine their political status, and freely pursue their economic, social and cultural development'.[3]

Prior to the UNDRIP, common Art.1 of the ICCPR and ICESCR expressly recognize the right of all people to freely dispose of their natural wealth and resources for their own ends, and the right to not be deprived of their means of subsistence. In both Conventions, this right is a part of the provision guaranteeing economic, political and cultural self-determination to peoples.

However, this comprehensive right of self-determination was not extended to indigenous peoples within State territories, as States contested whether they are included within 'peoples' (Anaya 2004; Mccorquodale 1994; Kingsbury 1992). During UNDRIP negotiations, States argued that 'peoples' refers to 'whole peoples', and not to subgroups within a territory. This view is anchored in the need to retain the territorial integrity of States, as recognizing indigenous peoples as 'peoples' entitled to self-determination could lead to secession. However, separate from the right to secession under international law, the UNDRIP articulates a human right to self-determination of peoples within State territories, as an inherent right to determine their political status and course of human development (Keal 2007; Gilbert 2007; Anaya 2004).

Anchored in self-determination, the bundle of land rights under UNDRIP recognize the right of IPs to their lands and territories based on traditional forms of occupation and use (tenure rights); to own, use, develop and manage them; to due recognition of their laws, customs and tenure systems; the right to conserve and protect the environment, knowledge and cultural heritage in relation to the land (Anaya 2005).

Under Articles 25–32, the UNDRIP also recognizes the right to develop lands as per self-determined priorities of IPs, and the right to participate in decision-making affecting their land, including through free, prior and informed consent, and to fair and equitable compensation in case of expropriation. Such an articulation casts wider corresponding obligations on States with a strong political rights orientation. States are obligated to extend due cooperation to indigenous peoples and their institutions in ensuring that their rights are respected and protected, to take no decisions affecting their lands without their participation in decision-making, and to fairly adjudicate

[3] Article 3, UNDRIP 2007.

through impartial and independent tribunals established in consultation with indigenous peoples. Radically, the UNDRIP also includes a right against militarization of indigenous territories to ensure that their rights of decision-making over land may be freely exercised.

Although the UNDRIP is not binding on its own, it codifies existing international and domestic law arrangements of over autonomy between States and indigenous peoples, and carries immense persuasive value in the interpretation of binding human rights obligations under other instruments. Even prior to the adoption of the UNDRIP, but especially since 2007, universal norms at the international and regional levels have been interpreted with a self-determination content in their application to indigenous peoples' land rights. This includes the right to housing (United Nations Housing Rights Programme 2005), protection of human rights defenders (Special Rapporteur on the Rights of Indigenous Peoples 2018), access to justice (Institute for the Study of Human Rights 2014), among others.

In 2001, the Inter-American Court of Human Rights (IACtHR) delivered its opinion in the *Mayagna (Sumo) Awas Tingni Community* v. *Nicaragua* case, holding that the failure of the State to demarcate communal lands of the indigenous AwasTingni community, based on customary law, practices and their historical occupation, constituted a violation of the right to property under Article 21 of the ACHR. The notion of property under the ACHR was autonomous of its meaning under domestic law, but even so, communal rights of the AwasTingni community based on customary tenure was already protected under the domestic Constitution. The grant of concessions to third parties on the same undemarcated communal lands was also a violation of Article 21.[4]

The Committee on Economic, Social and Cultural Rights in 2002 noted that the loss of traditional lands to timber and mining companies without consent of indigenous communities was a violation of their cultural rights as minorities, and cast an obligation on States to ensure their participation peoples in decision-making affecting their lands and cultural identity (McGee 2009). In 2010, the African Commission on Human and Peoples' Rights held in the *Endorois*case that the expropriation of indigenous land by the State was a violation of the right to property under the African Charter on Human and Peoples' Rights. Kenya was obligated to recognize communal property rights of the Endorois community through appropriate domestic legal mechanisms.[5]

The evolution of indigenous land rights as self-determination at the international and regional levels reflects a high degree of constitutional borrowing and transfusion of norms across instruments and institutions. The IACtHR cited Nicaragua's own constitutional arrangements relating to indigenous autonomy and land rights in the

[4] *The Mayagna (Sumo) Awas Tingni Community* v. *Nicaragua*, 31 August 2001, Inter-Am. Ct. H.R., (Ser. C) No. 79 (2001).

[5] *Centre for Minority Rights Development (Kenya) and Minority Rights Group International on behalf of Endorois Welfare Council* v. *Kenya* (Merits, Provisional Measures), Communication No. 276/2003, African Commission on Human and Peoples' Rights, 4 February 2010.

Mayagna (Sumo) AwasTingni Community decision to justify its obligation to recognize, demarcate and refrain from interference in traditional communal lands. On its own, the decision has been widely influential in international and regional human rights jurisprudence. It has expanded recognition of indigenous property rights over communal lands based on their historic use and possession, autonomous of definitions under domestic law.

Negotiations in the drafting of the UNDRIP also reflect this transfusion of constitutional norms into human rights. As some States feared threats to territorial integrity in recognizing the right to self-determination, representatives of indigenous peoples referred to existing arrangements of autonomy in domestic constitutional arrangements across the world, to argue for codification of this practice as a human right (Carpenter and Riley 2014). Article 46 was added to clarify that the Declaration does not imply rights impairing the '*territorial integrity or political unity of sovereign and independent States*' contrary to the Charter of the United Nations. As indicated above, self-determination rights of IPs have also percolated widely in the interpretation of universal rights to housing, protection of human rights defenders, etc.

10.2.3 A Framework

The foregoing survey identifies some articulations of the human right to land for indigenous peoples. The following tentative framework identifies a matrix of forms of rights recognition and contents of State obligations, against which the succeeding comparison between European and Indian norms will be undertaken.

- **What form of recognition?** Land rights may either be recognized under universal norms relating to property or cultural rights or under particular norms relating to IPs.
- **Who are the rightsholders?** Rights may belong to individuals, members of groups, and to communities as a whole. Indigenous rights are often collective under customary arrangements.
- **What is the source of rights?** Human rights norms may either rely on domestic law as the source of land rights, or set independent standards based on customary usage.
- **What is the content of the right?** Rights recognized may be of ownership, use and occupation (tenure rights); of management, conservation and protection; of recognition of customary laws and land tenure. They may also relate to political rights of participation in decision-making relating to the use of lands; of free, prior and informed consent in expropriation of their lands; and of adequate compensation. The content of rights dots a continuum along which the right to self-determination in relation to lands is recognized.
- **What are the rights and obligations of States with respect to indigenous lands?** Norms may expressly protect the sovereign right of States to expropriate lands in general interest, and also lay down conditions and limitations on its

exercise. Indirectly, the content of State obligations relating to indigenous rights to land may act as further limitations.

10.3 The European Human Rights System

The ECHR does not expressly recognize indigenous peoples or distinctly protect their right to land. Unlike the universal human rights instruments, it also does not recognize people's right to self-determination to freely pursue their political status and pursue their economic, social and cultural development. One of the early regional instruments on human rights, the ECHR primarily recognizes individual rights, with group rights such as those to language and culture recognized as rights of individual members of groups, to be enjoyed in common with others.

In the absence of express recognition, IPs in Europe have invoked minority rights protections, notably Article 8 relating to the right to family and private life and Article 14 guaranteeing the right to equality and non-discrimination. Indigenous peoples have also invoked the right to peaceful enjoyment of possessions under Article 1 of Protocol 1 to the ECHR. Commonly, these complaints are accompanied by claims regarding violations of procedural rights affecting effective access to remedies before domestic forums, including under Article 6 (right to fair trial) and Article 13 (right to effective remedy) (Koivurova 2011; Gismondi 2016).

Notably, the European Commission (Commission) and the European Court of Human Rights (ECtHR) have decided few of these complaints on their merits, with a large number having been dismissed at the stage of admissibility itself (Koivurova 2011; Kovacs 2016). Common reasons for rejection of complaint at the stage of admissibility include lack of standing by applicants under Article 34, failure to exhaust domestic remedies under Article 35(1), or being manifestly ill-founded under Article 35(3).

This section surveys the treatment of indigenous land rights claims before the Commission and ECtHR to determine the extent of rights protection, and content of State obligation. It describes strategies for rights protection under the minority rights framework and the right to property, with the ECtHR case of *Handolsdalen Sami Villages* v. *Sweden* ("*Handolsdalen*" case)[6] as a case study.

10.3.1 Minority Rights Protections: Article 8 and Article 14

Article 8 ECHR recognizes the right to respect for family and private life, home and correspondence. It also recognizes the power of the State to interfere with this right by law necessary in a democratic society in the interest of, *inter alia,* public safety

[6] *Supra* note 1.

and economic well-being of the country. Indigenous peoples invoking this provision challenge State action on the basis that interfering with their use of territories harms their cultural identity and traditional way of life (Kugelmann 2007; Research Division, European Court of Human Rights 2018).

Article 14 guarantees enjoyment of rights without discrimination on the basis of, *inter alia*, race, national or social origin, national minority, property, etc. Notably, the protection of Article 14 against discrimination does not have general application but is limited to the enjoyment of rights expressly recognized in the ECHR. Article 14 claims, therefore, scarcely stand on their own legs, and are commonly appended to complaints alleging violations of Article 8 etc. (Kugelmann 2007).

In terms of respect for cultural identity, non-discrimination and group rights, there is significant overlap between claims of IPs and national and ethnic minorities within a State. However, rights to self-determination and those over land and territories set apart claims of IP from those of minorities. Under the ECHR, the task is to locate a distinct right to land and territories through a framework for minority protection, which is illustrated in the standard-setting case of *G and E* v. *Norway.*[7] Here, the Lapp community in Norway under threat of submergence by the Alta dam alleged violations of, *inter alia*, Articles 8 and 14, on the basis that their use of the same territories for grazing, hunting and fishing constituted a part of their traditional way of life. The Commission found that Article 8 mandates respect for a particular lifestyle of a minority group as part of their private, home and family life, and in principle, the construction of the Alta dam constituted interference with this right. However, the Commission still held the application to be inadmissible as per the proportionality standard under Article 8(1), to find that the spread of the area lost to them due to the dam is insignificant relative to the whole territory that remains available to pursue herding. The Commission further justified this interference under Article 8(2), on the basis that it is in accordance with law, and necessary in a democratic society for the economic well-being of the country. The remedy for justifiable interference with this right lies in possible claims for compensation, but there cannot be said to be any violation of State obligation (Koivurova 2011).

Article 8(2) preserves the overarching sovereign right of the State to define, constrain or abrogate (with adequate compensation) rights to land and territories in general interest.[8] States may account for the traditional way of life of minorities in decision-making,[9] but there is no decision-making right of IPs per se. On its own, Article 8 does not cast an obligation on the State to recognize land rights of indigenous peoples and is unable to constrain the inscription of overall State authority on indigenous territories. On the contrary, as the bearer of State obligation enjoying a wide margin of appreciation, Article 8 reinforces, instead of delimiting, sovereign State powers over indigenous territories.

[7] *G. & E.* v. *Norway*, Application No. 9278/81, 3 October 1983.

[8] *Buckley* v. *United Kingdom*, Application No. 20348/92, 25 September 1996.

[9] *Chapman* v. *United Kingdom,* Application No. 27238/95, 18 January 2001.

10.3.2 Right to Possessions: Article 1 of Protocol 1

The Commission and the ECtHR have received multiple complaints challenging legislative, administrative and judicial actions of States for violating indigenous peoples' exclusive or nested rights to their territories (Gismondi 2016; Kovacs 2016). Almost none of these articulate claims encompassing overall collective rights to land and territories, and are limited to violations of individuals' fishing, grazing or hunting rights (as in the case of the Nordic Sami people) (Koivurova 2011; Torp 2013).

Article 1 of Protocol 1 recognizes the right of natural or legal persons to peaceful enjoyment of his possessions. The provision comprises three distinct rules. The first is the right to peaceful enjoyment of possessions; the second is the right against deprivation of possessions, subject to public interest, conditions prescribed by law, and general principles of international law. The third rule relates to the overarching right of States to control the use of property for general interest, payment of taxes, etc. Any determination under this provision must first ascertain whether the claim constitutes 'possessions' within the meaning of the first rule, whether there has been any interference with the possession, and if yes, which of the three rules best describe the nature of interference. While covering a wide range of economic interests, 'possessions' includes only existing rights, and those based on legitimate expectations. In case there has been interference, the Court may still find that no violation of the right has taken place, if the State is able to justify the interference with a legitimate aim of securing public interest ('legitimate aim'), that a balance has been struck between the interests of the general public and the individual right ('proportionality'), and that the interference is lawful and legally certain ('legal certainty') (Carrs-Frisk 2003; Research Division, European Court of Human Rights 2019).

Individuals and organizations from Sami villages in Finland, Sweden and Norway have brought multiple complaints before the Commission and ECtHR claiming that the ECHR protects their property rights to reindeer herding, fishing and grazing on traditional territories to the exclusion of interference by the State and non-Sami settlers (Gismondi 2016; Kovacs 2016; Otis and Laurent 2013). The *Handolsdalen* decision of the ECtHR case best demonstrates possibilities and continuing limitations of the ECHR in this respect, although this too was eventually dismissed as inadmissible. In the *Handolsdalen* case, Sami villages raised the following issues: *first*, whether the right of Sami villages to winter grazing constitutes 'possessions'; *second*, whether property rights of indigenous peoples exist independent of State recognition; and *third*, whether States, through domestic law, have the authority to change or restrict existing property rights of indigenous peoples.

Domestic tribunals in Sweden had upheld the primacy of property rights of private landowners over the winter grazing rights of five Sami villages lying within their traditional homelands. Private landowners had sought a declaratory judgment from domestic courts that the Sami villages had no rights of winter grazing on their private lands in the absence of a contract between the landowner and the village.

The Sami villages challenged this determination before the ECtHR, alleging violations of, *inter alia*, Article 1 of Protocol 1. Sami villages claimed that the right to winter grazing over the disputed area constituted 'possessions', as it had been recognized as a property right under domestic law, and that in the alternative, there was a legitimate expectation of obtaining a property right. The dispute with private landowners arose due to the failure of the legislature to clearly demarcate the estates of private landholders and territories for winter grazing. They submitted that domestic Parliamentary Committees had recognized the pre-existing and inalienable rights of Samis to that territory, which had not been changed through subsequent legislation. The Samis further alleged that the legislature of the State had no authority to change existing rights, or to impose restrictions on their exercise.

In its response, Sweden accepted that Sami winter grazing rights generally constituted 'possessions' under domestic law, but argued that there was no existing right, or legitimate expectation, of winter grazing on the disputed estates of the private landowners in the absence of express conferment by domestic tribunals. As domestic courts did not act arbitrarily or in a manifestly wrong manner in deciding these claims, there could be said to be no interference with Article 1 rights of the Sami villages.

Thus, whether grazing rights per se constituted 'possessions' was not in issue between the parties, but whether the right also existed on the estates of private landowners located within the Sami homeland, who derived their title from domestic law. While domestic courts treated the dispute as one relating to competing proprietary claims of private actors, at the regional level, the Sami villages challenged the precedence accorded to formal property regimes of the State over the pre-existing rights of the Samis to their homeland. By challenging both, domestic law as the exclusive source of property rights as well as the authority of States to change pre-existing rights, the Samis lay claim to independent sources under international law permitting articulations of self-determination through an exercise of property rights. If affirmed, such an interpretation of Article 1 of Protocol 1 elevates indigenous property regimes and sources of law to the status of a human right, such that non-recognition of the same by the State would constitute a violation of the ECHR.

Earlier jurisprudence of the ECtHR supports the unmooring of the human right to property from domestic recognition to some extent. The ECtHR has consistently held that the term 'possessions' has an 'autonomous meaning', independent of its formal classification under domestic law (Carrs-Frisk 2003), such that a right which is not specifically recognized as a property right under State law may still count as 'possessions' within the meaning of the ECHR. However, in determining whether a legitimate expectation exists to create a proprietary interest, Article 1 of Protocol 1 continues to rely heavily on determination by domestic courts and legislatures (Research Division, European Court of Human Rights 2019; Otis and Laurent 2013).

In this case, the ECtHR severed the estates of private landowners from the overall territorial homeland of Samis over which they had recognized rights under domestic law, and held that winter grazing on these private estates did not count as 'possession' within the meaning of Article 1 of Protocol 1. As the demarcation of territories under domestic law is to be made judicially based on available evidence, it varies from case to case and is not an existing possession. On whether there was a legitimate expectation of winter grazing, the ECtHR held that the existence of legitimate expectation is also dependent entirely on domestic law, either through legislation or through judicial determination. The ECtHR has only limited powers to enter into mistakes of fact or law by national courts in the absence of arbitrariness, and in this case, domestic courts went through reams of evidence rigorously over years and came to their conclusions.

Notably, the ECtHR affirmed that Article 1 of Protocol 1, in principle, recognizes some forms of indigenous land rights as possessions. However, it re-ascribed the dispute as one between private parties akin to the Swedish domestic tribunals, limiting the question of State obligation to ensuring judicial redress by an independent and impartial domestic tribunal. The ECtHR did not address whether the Samis had proprietary rights independent of State recognition and whether the State had the authority to abrogate or change the same. Despite earlier jurisprudence holding that 'possessions' has an autonomous meaning, by deferring to domestic law the ECtHR reiterated the monopoly of States to determine the legal regime governing property.

Already, under the second rule, States have the right to restrict property rights under specified exemptions, and also enjoy the right to acquire property under the third rule. Within the exceptions laid down in the second rule, States enjoy a high degree of margin of appreciation in determining the existence of a legitimate aim, proportionality and legal certainty.[10]

Some forms of land rights of indigenous peoples may be protected as property under the ECHR, but the right is empty of its self-determination content. Under all three rules encompassed by Article 1 of Protocol 1, the ECHR defers to the authority of States in determining property regimes within their territories, the exceptions under which property rights may be interfered with, and also retains the right to abrogate or impose conditions on the exercise of the same.

Overall, a textual analysis of the ECHR and jurisprudence of the Commission/ECtHR reveal limited recognitions of IP land rights as human rights (Otis and Laurent 2013). Absent express recognition, they are derived from universally applicable individual rights, most notably through the right to home and private life and the right to possessions. Both rights in principle recognize limited rights of use, occupation and ownership, but cave under the overall authority of States for resource allocation in general interest. They are also empty of any self-determination content, as no rights of management or decision-making are recognized, domestic law remains an exclusive source of rights, and States enjoy a wide margin of appreciation in determining rights and exceptions.

Pertinently, ECHR's limited recognition of IP land rights reflects scarce reliance on comparative jurisprudential developments at the international and regional levels. Judge Ziemele's partial dissent on the issue of Article 6 violation in *Handolsdalen* reveals opportunities for expansion of IP rights recognition with support from norms at the universal level. While the ECtHR did not find that the burden of proof imposed by domestic tribunals for establishing indigenous title over traditional homelands was onerous, and therefore a violation of the right to fair trial, Judge Ziemele differed by placing reliance on the ILO Conventions and UNDRIP. The partial dissent notes that

[10] *Sporrong and Lönnroth* v. *Sweden*, Application no. 7151/75, 23 September 2982.

IPs are by definition disadvantaged before domestic tribunals as the entire legal system presumes rights in favour of private landowners, such that the burden of proving Sami rights rests exclusively on them. It noted the wide influence of international and regional human rights norms relating to IPs in interpreting State obligations at the domestic levels through special measures to overcome discrimination and achieve equal rights (Koivurova 2011).

10.4 The Indian Human Rights System

India is a signatory to all the major human rights conventions, including the ICCPR, ICESCR, CEDAW, CERD among others, and also voted in favour of the UNDRIP at the General Assembly. In addition to the generally applicable universal norms, there is no regional human rights system in Asia/South Asia. Instead, the Constitution of India has functioned as the primary legal document recognizing human rights and binding State obligations. Specifically, Part III of the Constitution relating to fundamental rights contains extensive civil, political and cultural rights, whose breadth has been further expanded through a collaborative reading with the non-binding Part IV on Directive Principles of State Policy (DPSP), which contains guiding principles on State action. Universal human rights norms and the DPSP have had wide influence in the interpretation of fundamental rights, leading to the recognition of a range of social, economic and developmental rights, particularly within the rubric of the right to life and personal liberty under Article 21 (Khosla 2010; Thiruvengadam 2007).

Functionally, the Supreme Court of India acts as the counterpoint to the Commission and ECtHR as the highest adjudicatory body on human rights, with extensive powers of judicial review. Supreme Court decisions rely heavily on universal human rights norms and comparative jurisprudence in interpreting fundamental rights, adjudicating violations, and crafting remedies relating to State obligation (Khosla 2011). The Supreme Court has the normative power to determine the content of rights. It also the authority to strike down unconstitutional laws and State action, issue directions for fulfilment of rights, and also make recommendations for legislative action.

India does not recognize 'indigenous peoples' within its territories. Article 342 of the Constitution identifies the category of 'Scheduled Tribes' (STs), based on cultural factors, geographical isolation and backwardness (Advisory Committee 1965). STs expressly enjoy universal rights under the fundamental rights chapter, including individual and collective rights to equality under Article 14, non-discrimination under Article 15, and the protection and propagation of their religion under Article 25. The category of STs does not fully capture the kinds of IPs present within Indian territory and rights for IPs under the Constitution and domestic law are not limited to STs either. This section refers to STs while addressing specific rights applicable only to them, and to IPs in relation to rights applicable to both STs and non-STs.

The Constitution recognizes differentiated and special arrangements of autonomy with STs and other IPs under Articles 244, 275 and the Fifth and Sixth Schedules. The Fifth Schedule applies over geographically demarcated 'scheduled areas' and other areas with a high concentration of ST populations, and the Sixth Schedule applies to IPs in four specific states in demarcated 'tribal areas'.

IPs' right to land has been recognized under both universal fundamental rights, as well as special arrangements of autonomy under the Fifth and Sixth Schedules. For a comparative analysis of indigenous land rights recognition between Europe and India, this section elucidates the contours of the right through a description of universal and specific rights guarantees under the Constitution, with the Supreme Court decision in *Orissa Mining Corporation Limited v. Ministry of Environment and Forests* ['*Niyamgiri* case'] as case study.

10.4.1 Universal Rights to Equality, Life and Religion: Articles 14, 15, 21 and 25

Articles 14 and 15 recognize the right to substantive equality, with negative obligations upon the State to refrain from discrimination based on race and ethnicity, and the positive obligation to secure equality for socially and economically marginalized groups including STs. Article 25 protects the freedom of all persons to profess, practice and propagate their religion. Article 26 specifically protects the right of religious denominations and sections thereof to manage its own religious affairs. Limitations to both these sets of rights contained within the provisions exempt State interference for regulation of secular functions of religious denominations, and to overcome intra-community discrimination. As both sets of rights belong to individuals and groups, and expressly recognize STs and other marginalized groups as subjects of rights, the issue is whether these have been recognized as the sources of land rights. In this matrix, Article 21 guaranteeing the right to life and personal liberty is also of relevance, as the Supreme Court has interpreted the right widely as a life with dignity, encompassing a right to livelihood,[11] rights to tradition and cultural heritage,[12] and a right to environment, preservation of natural resources, clean water and air for all.[13]

On their own, Articles 14 and 15 have not been recognized as the source of land rights. However, the guarantee of substantive equality has been frequently cited in Supreme Court decisions on laws relating to indigenous rights generally,[14] and Fifth Schedule specifically.[15] In *Union of India* v. *Rakesh Kumar*, decided in 2010, the Supreme Court upheld the validity of a statute providing for 100% reservations in favour of STs for the post of Chairperson of local units of self-governance in scheduled areas. Long-standing Supreme Court jurisprudence under Articles 14 and 15 had stipulated a ceiling of 50% in reservations for marginalized groups.[16] The

---

[11] *Olga Tellis* v. *Bombay Municipal Corporation*, (1985) 3 SCC 545.

[12] *CERC* v. *Union of India*, (1995) 3 SCC 42.

[13] *MC Mehta* v. *Union of India*, AIR 1987 SC 1086.

[14] *Samatha* v. *State of Andhra Pradesh*, AIR 1997 SC 3297; *supra* note 2.

[15] *Union of India* v. *Rakesh Kumar*, (2010) 4 SCC 50.

[16] *Indra Sawhney* v. *Union of India*, (1992) Supp. (3) SCC 217.

Supreme Court upheld a differential standard in scheduled areas, as the object of the Fifth Schedule is to protect autonomy, rights, culture and resources of STs, distinct from the general mandate of substantive equality under the fundamental rights chapter. The rights and special protection granted to STs under the scheduled areas cannot be less than that which is guaranteed under the general law applicable.[17]

The right to life under Article 21, and to religion under Articles 25 and 26, on the other hand, have been expressly recognized as the source of some forms of land rights, most notably in the 1997 decision of the Supreme Court in *Samatha* v. *State of Andhra Pradesh*,[18] and the *Niyamgiri* case. While elaborating the scheme and object of the Fifth Schedule, the decision recognized the essential relationship of the right to life with traditional lands.[19]

The *Niyamgiri* decision of 2013 invoked religious rights of indigenous peoples as the source of some land rights. As it was based on generally applicable domestic laws relating to forests, environment and rights, it applies to IPs and customary lands across the country, and unlike *Samatha,* is not limited to scheduled areas.

The *Niyamgiri* case related to the Indian government's cancellation of approvals for the transfer of forests for an alumina refinery. As per the government, the refinery had violated the terms of its environmental clearance, in which it had misrepresented its dependence on a bauxite mine, which was separately pending permission for transfer of forests over an adjoining area. This adjoining area were the *Niyamgiri* hills, comprising biodiversity-rich forest lands within the traditional homeland of particularly vulnerable *DongriaKondhs*. The refinery challenged the cancellation of approval.

The Indian government argued that approval could not be granted as the hills were essential to the religious customs and practices of the *DongriaKondhs*, which are protected under Articles 25 and 26 of the Constitution, and over which extend collective ownership and management rights under domestic law. As processes for the demarcation of property rights over individual and customary lands had already been completed, but which did not extend to the hills as religious sites, at issue was whether the *DongriaKondhs* nevertheless had any rights to determine the use and development of the hills.

The Supreme Court turned to constitutional rights and protections in the Fifth Schedule and international human rights instruments to determine the scope of religious and cultural rights protections of indigenous peoples. It found that the object of the Fifth Schedule is to secure the autonomy, culture and overall social and political justice of STs over their traditional homelands. By virtue of this constitutional right to autonomy, lands in scheduled areas are governed by customary law and are subject to the decision-making authority of customary institutions of STs. The Supreme Court also relied on the ILO Conventions and the UNDRIP to support the right of the *DongriaKondhs* to maintain their '*distinctive spiritual relationship with their traditionally owned or otherwise occupied or used lands*'.

[17] *Supra* note 15.

[18] *Samatha* v. *State of Andhra Pradesh, supra* note 14.

[19] *Supra* note 2.

The Supreme Court concluded that domestic law incorporated indigenous peoples human rights to religion and culture by recognizing their individual and collective rights of ownership and use to customary lands and vesting powers in their customary institutions to protect and preserve them. It held that the customary institutions of the *DongriaKondhs* as recognized under domestic law had the right to decide the impact of the refinery on their religious rights, and to ensure the preservation and protection of the hills. The State has an obligation to protect tribal autonomy and their religious and cultural rights, and it is thus obligated to institute independent processes by which customary institutions can participate in decision-making over their lands. It directed the government to place these issues before the relevant customary institutions, and also issued directions to ensure that the process is conducted freely. In the aftermath, all *DongriaKondh* customary institutions determined that the refinery will adversely affect their rights, and refused to permit mining in the hills. The Indian government thus also maintained the cancellation of approvals.

The decision upheld extensive rights of preservation and decision-making over indigenous lands as a dimension of the right to religion. Beyond domestically recognized property rights, the decision upheld the political component of indigenous right to land, of determining its use and development, and relied wholly on existing domestic law in defining its scope. However, by reading domestic law as an extension of constitutional and human rights, the decision indicated that these rights also have an existence autonomous of domestic law.

Further, the extent of sovereign rights of the State over indigenous lands was not in issue per se, as the case was a dispute primarily between the State and private corporate entities, where the State was acting in furtherance of its obligation to protect indigenous rights. The Constitution does not recognize the sovereign right of eminent domain over land and resources on its own, unlike the ECHR. Instead, it is recognized as an exception to the constitutional right to property under Article 300A, which states that persons may not be deprived of their property except as per law. Beyond international law, this is recognized in India through colonial legislations and expanded through Supreme Court jurisprudence to encompass not only the right to expropriate but the ultimate ownership of all resources within its territory (Ramanathan 2010; Ministry of Tribal Affairs 2014). Under the Sixth Schedule, this sovereign right is expressly preserved. Thus, while rights to property, preservation and decision-making of indigenous peoples have been recognized, the State continues to have the authority of control and overall allocation of resources for general developmental needs. *Niyamgiri* does not address whether decisions of indigenous customary institutions over land use are binding on States when both differ on their developmental priorities.

10.4.2 Particular Rights to Land and Resources: Fifth and Sixth Schedules

Particular rights to land and resources of STs and IPs are contained in the Fifth and Sixth Schedules of the Constitution through the right to autonomy (Samaddar 2005).

The Fifth Schedule provides a framework for the administration of scheduled areas with high ST population and historical relations with their land, by which the Governor is empowered to modify or annul laws made by the legislatures, and pass special regulations to regulate allotment and prohibit alienation of land to noon-STs. The power to declare scheduled areas and determine its boundaries, however, remains with the President of India, who is a functionary of the State (Savyasaachi 1998; Sharma 1977).

The Fifth Schedule has been further elaborated through the Panchayats (Extension to Scheduled Areas) Act 1996 ('PESA Act'), as a charter of rights and governance mechanisms in scheduled areas. The Fifth Schedule and PESA do not take effect on their own but require legislation to operationalize the rights and principles contained therein.

PESA recognizes customary rights of STs in scheduled areas to their lands, forests and resources (Ministry of Tribal Affairs). Under section 4, PESA also upholds the primacy of customary law, traditional management of resources, and the right of customary institutions to be consulted in decisions relating to the development and use of their lands and resources (Bijoy et al. 2010; Singh 2015). The *Samatha* judgement of the Supreme Court testifies to the strength of Fifth Schedule and PESA protections of indigenous right to land. At issue was the validity of mining leases granted by the State to private corporations over forests lying within scheduled areas, when domestic law prohibited the alienation of land in scheduled areas to non-STs. The Supreme Court struck down the mining lease on the basis that the prohibition on alienation of land also extended to the expropriatory power of the State in scheduled areas. In the decision, the Court noted the object and purpose of the Fifth Schedule to protect rights and autonomy of STs over their land, which constituted their most important economic, social and spiritual resource anchoring their right to life.[20]

The Sixth Schedule demarcates 'tribal areas' into autonomous districts and councils, where representative indigenous institutions enjoy wide powers of legislation, administration, and adjudication. These representative institutions can pass laws to recognize customary law, determine use and allocation of land, management of resources, among others (Bijoy et al. 2010; Singh 2015). The right to use and allocation of land is constrained by an express limitation preserving the right of the State to expropriate land for public purposes.

In summary, the human rights system in India, gleaned from the Constitution and jurisprudence of the Supreme Court of India, recognizes IP rights to land both through universal and particular norms. Universally, collective rights of management, use and decision-making over lands are recognized through the right to religious freedom

[20] *Samatha* v. *State of Andhra Pradesh*, *supra* note 14.

and the right to life. While reflecting deference to domestic law on the extent of rights protection, the reliance on international human rights norms to interpret State obligation under the fundamental rights chapter reveals that the rights may have an autonomous existence as well. It also recognized particular rights to land for IPs living in specified scheduled or tribal areas through the right to autonomy, in respect for the right to self-determination. Under these particular rights, customary laws and regimes of management and use are recognized, with decision-making rights vesting in customary indigenous institutions. The overall power of delineating of such areas lies with State functionaries. Further, both universal and particular rights are constrained by a wide and expansive reading of the sovereign right of eminent domain contained in colonial laws and constitutional jurisprudence of the Supreme Court.

10.5 Conclusion

Despite their contemporaneous adoption, human rights in Europe and India have followed widely different trajectories in the protection of indigenous land rights. Europe does not expressly recognize IPs as the subject of rights, which is limited to individuals largely unmarked by social and political identities. The task then, is to locate specific histories and contexts of marginalization within a universal human rights framework.

In Europe, rights to non-discrimination, culture and property have served this role to a limited extent. The ECtHR has recognized that traditional livelihoods of members of indigenous communities constitute a part of their cultural rights, but has upheld wide sovereign powers of expropriation in overall general interest. Minimizing collective right violations to those of individual rights presumably stacks the odds against IPs when weighed against overall public interest under a proportionality test, as was in evidence in *G and E* v. *Norway*. *Handolsdalen* demonstrated that some forms of collective land rights have found better recognition under the human right to possessions, but only if recognized as proprietary interests under domestic law. While property rights of IPs on their lands have been recognized in principle under Article 1 of Protocol 1, deference to domestic law empties the right of its self-determination content. Again, States expressly enjoy sovereign rights of expropriation and a wide margin of appreciation.

In India, IPs are protected by both universal and particular rights guarantees. In common with Europe, India also views land rights in context of religious rights, and in addition, shows nascent recognition of its relationship with the right to life. Particular rights recognize differentiated arrangements of autonomy over scheduled and tribal areas, customary law, and rights of decision-making, management, ownership and use of lands. Land rights manifest primarily as self-determination rights, with property rights components. Universal rights here play a different role than in Europe, as expanding the scope and content of particular rights guarantees, illustrated by the *Niyamgiri* decision.

Simultaneously, eminent domain and sovereign rights of expropriation have also expanded judicially. Overall State control and authority over lands is maintained through colonial administrative powers, without certainty on whether decisions of indigenous customary institutions are binding on them.

Pertinently, the Supreme Court has extensively read domestic constitutional rights guarantees in light of India's obligations under international human rights, where interpretations of domestic law have drawn from universal human rights norms. On the other hand, the failure of the European system to draw from jurisprudential developments in the international and regional systems is often cited as a factor in its limited scope of recognition.

What, then, are the opportunities for constitutional borrowing between Europe and India? While sharing the form of territorially bound sovereign States and their powers over land, to some extent both reside in differentiated rights universes. Where one primarily recognizes individuals as subjects, the other recognizes individuals and collectives generally, and indigenous peoples particularly.

The European system may choose to politically negotiate with States the recognition of particular rights for IPs, with an emphasis on self-determination and collective rights to land. Pending the adoption of such a negotiated document that would radically alter the foundations of the European system, certainly, the common recognition of universal human rights norms offers one opportunity for interpretational exchange. The European system may borrow from the expansion of IP rights through cultural rights and the right to life under the Constitution of India, such that collective tenure and management rights may be recognized in recognition of historical relationships, customary management and dependence on land.

On the other hand, the application of the same universal and particular rights have been constrained in India due to the ever-expanding scope of sovereign rights of eminent domain and expropriation. The Constitution of India and its interpretation by judicial bodies may benefit from the scope and limitations of the sovereign right expressly laid down in the European system.

In the absence of such comparative borrowings, the human rights frameworks in both Europe and India remain limited in their possibilities to reconfigure relations between States and IPs on the issue of self-determination and control over indigenous lands and territories.

References

Committee, Advisory. (1965). *Report on the revision of the lists of Scheduled Castes and Scheduled Tribes*. New Delhi: Government of India.

Aguilar, G., LaFosse, S., Rojas, H., & Steward, R. (2010). The constitutional recognition of Indigenous peoples in Latin America. *Pace International Law Review Online Companion*, 44–96.

Alston, P., & Goodman, R. (2013). *International hman rights: Texts and materials*. Oxford: Oxford University Press.

Anaya, S. (2004). *Indigenous peoples in international law*. New York: Oxford University Press.

Anaya, S. (2005). Indigenous peoples' participatory rights in relation to decisions about natural resource extraction: The more fundamental issue of what rights indigenous peoples have in lands and resources. *Arizona Journal of International and Comparative Law, 22,* 7–18.

Barnabas, S. (2017). The legal status of the United Nations declaration on the rights of Indigenous peoples. *International Human Rights Law Review, 6,* 242–261.

Bijoy, C., Gopalakrishnan, S., & Khanna, S. (2010). *India and the rights of Indigenous peoples: Constitutional, legislative and administrative provisions concerning Indigenous and Tribal peoples in India and their relation to International law on Indigenous peoples.* Chiang Mai: Asia Indigenous Peoples Pact Foundation.

Carpenter, K. A., & Riley, A. R. (2014). Indigenous peoples and the Jurisgenerative moment in human rights. *California Law Review, 102*(1), 173–234.

Carrs-Frisk, M. (2003). *The right to property: A guide to the implementation of Article 1 of Protocol No. 1 to the European Convention on Human Rights.* Strasbourg: Council of Europe.

Corntassel, J. (2007). Partnership in action? Indigenous political mobilization and co-optation during the first Indigenous decade (1995-2004). *Human Rights Quarterly, 29*(1), 137–166.

D'Amato, A. (2010). *Human rights as part of customary international law: A plea for change of paradigms.* Retrieved December 12, 2019, from Faculty Working Papers, Northwestern University School of Law: https://scholarlycommons.law.northwestern.edu/cgi/viewcontent.cgi?article=1087&context=facultyworkingpapers.

Davis, M. (2012). To bind or not to bind: The United Nations Declaration on the Rights of Indigenous Peoples five years on. *Australian International Law Journal, 19,* 17–48.

Espiel, G. (1990). *Study on the implementation of UN resolutions relating to the Right of Peoples under Colonial or Alien domination to self-determination.* United Nations.

Gilbert, J. (2017). CERD's contribution to the development of the Rights of Indigenous Peoples under International Law. In D. Keane & A. Waughray (Eds.), *Fifty years of the international convention on the elimination of all forms of racial discrimination: A living instrument* (pp. 91–105). Manchester: Manchester University Press.

Gilbert, J. (2006). *Indigenous Peoples' and Rights under International Law: From victims to actors.* New York: Transnational Publishers.

Gilbert, J. (2007). Indigenous rights in the making: The United Nations declaration on the rights of Indigenous Peoples. *International Journal on Minority and Group Rights, 14,* 207–230.

Gilbert, J. (2013). Land rights as human rights: The case for a specific right to land. *International Journal on Human Rights, 10*(18), 115–136.

Gismondi, G. (2016). Denial of justice: The latest Indigenous land disputes before the European Court of human rights and the need for an expansive interpretation of Protocol 1. *Yale Human Rights and Development Law Journal, 18*(1), 1–58.

Gussen, B. F. (2017). A comparative analysis of constitutional recognition of aboriginal peoples. *Melbourne University Law Review, 40,* 867–904.

Institute for the Study of Human Rights. (2014). *Indigenous Peoples' access to justice, including truth and reconciliation processes.* New York: Columbia University.

Kambel, E.-R. (2012). *A guide to Indigenous Women's Rights under the International Convention on the elimination of all forms of discrimination against women.* UK: Forest Peoples Programme.

Keal, P. (2007). Indigenous self-determination and the Legitimacy of Sovereign States. *International Politics, 44,* 287–305.

Khosla, M. (2011). Inclusive constitutional comparison: Reflections on India's Sodomy decision. *The American Journal of Comparative Law, 59*(4), 909–934.

Khosla, M. (2010). Making social rights conditional: Lessons from India. *International Journal of Constitutional Law, 8*(4), 739–765.

Kingsbury, B. (1992). Self-determination and Indigenous Peoples. *American Society of International Law Processess, 86,* 383–393.

Koivurova, T. (2011). Jurisprudence of the European Court of Human Rights regarding Indigenous Peoples: Retrospect and prospects. *International Journal on Minority and Group Rights, 18,* 1–37.

Kovacs, P. (2016). Indigenous issues under the European Convention of Human Rights, reflected in an Inter-American mirror. *George Washington International Law Review, 48*, 781–806.

Kugelmann, D. (2007). The protection of minorities and Indigenous Peoples respecting cultural diversity. In A. Bogdandy, & R. Wolfrum (Eds.), *Max Planck yearbook of United Nations Law* (Vol. 11, pp. 233–263). The Netherlands: Max Planck Institute.

Mccorquodale, R. (1994). Self-determination: A human rights approach. *International and Comparative Law Quarterly, 43*, 857–885.

McGee, B. (2009). The community referendum: Participatory democracy and the right to free, prior and informed consent to development. *Berkeley Journal of International Law, 27*(2), 570–635.

Ministry of Tribal Affairs. *Land and governance under the Fifth Schedule: An overview of the law*. New Delhi: Government of India and United Nations Development Programme.

Ministry of Tribal Affairs. (2014). *Report of high level committee on socioeconomic, health and educational status of Tribal Communities of India*. New Delhi: Government of India.

Otis, G., & Laurent, A. (2013). Indigenous land claims in Europe: The European Court of Human Rights and the decolonization of property. *Arctic Review on Law and Politics, 4*(2), 156–180.

Peterson, K. (2013). Free, prior and informed consent: ILO 169 and UNDRIP. *Free, Prior and Informed Consent: Pathways for a New Millenium*, 1–2.

Ramanathan, U. (2010). *On eminent domain and sovereignty*. Retrieved December 20, 2019, from Seminar: http://www.india-seminar.com/2010/613/613_usha_ramanathan.htm.

Research Division, European Court of Human Rights. (2018). *Guide on Article 8 of the European Convention on Human Rights: Right to respect for private and family life, home and correspondence*. European Court of Human Rights. Strasbourg: Council of Europe.

Research Division, European Court of Human Rights. (2019). *Guide on Article of Protocol No. 1 to the European Convention on Human Rights: Protection of property*. Strasbourg: Council of Europe.

Samaddar, R. (2005). *Politics of autonomy: Indian experiences*. Delhi: Sage.

Savyasaachi. (1998). *Tribal Forest-Dwellers and self-rule: The Constituent Assembly debates on the Fifth and Sixth Schedules*. Delhi: Indian Social Institute.

Schutter, O. D. (2014). *International human rights: Cases, materials, commentary* (2nd ed.). Cambridge: Cambridge University Press.

Sharma, B. (1977). Administration for Tribal development. *Indian Journal of Public Administration, 23*(3), 515–539.

Shaw, K. (2008). *Indigeneity and political theory*. New York: Routledge.

Singh, A. K. (2015). Constitutional semantics and autonomy within Indian federalism. In F. Palermo & E. Alber (Eds.), *Federalism as decision-making: Changes in structures, procedures and policy-making* (pp. 120–147). Netherlands: Koniklijke Brill.

Special Rapporteur on the Rights of Indigenous Peoples. (2018). *Report of the Special Rapporteur on the rights of indigenous peoples*. Human Rights Council.

Thiruvengadam, K. A. (2007). The social rights Jurisprudence of the Supreme Court of India from a comparative perspective. In Human Rights (Ed.), *Criminal justice and constitutional empowerment* (pp. 264–309). Oxford: Oxford University Press.

Thornberry, P. (2002). *Indigenous peoples and human rights*. Manchester: Manchester University Press.

Tomei, M., & Swepston, L. (1996). *Indigenous and Tribal Peoples: A guide To ILO Convention No. 169*. Geneva: International Labour Organization.

Torp, E. (2013). The legal basis of Sami reindeer herding rights in Sweden. *Arctic Review on Law and Politics*, 43–61.

United Nations Housing Rights Programme. (2005). *Indigenous peoples' right to adequate housing: A global overview*. Nairobi: UN-HABITAT.

Xanthaki, A. (2007). *Indigenous rights and United Nations standards: Self-determination, culture and land*. Cambridge: Cambridge University Press.

Radhika Chitkara is an Assistant Professor of Law Practice at the Jindal Global Law School in India. She is a researcher and clinical practitioner in the areas of indigenous peoples rights, women's rights and conflict, with an overall interest in critical methods for human rights lawyering. She is also associated with the Delhi chapter of the Legal Resource Centre, a collective of lawyers, academics and activists working on indigenous peoples rights, where she works closely with lawyers, autonomous movements, civil society organizations and victims of rights violations to provide legal aid, research and advisory support. She has obtained her LL.M. with a Concentration in International Human Rights from Harvard Law School (2017), and B.A., LL.B.(Hons.) from the National Law School of India University (2013).

Chapter 11
The (Un)Resolved Land Question: Comparing Indian and German Cases

Aditya Pandey

Abstract This paper attempts to understand, expound and analyse the emerging land question in India and Germany. Situated in the political-geographical space of global south and north, India and Germany are significant cases to understand the land question. The aim of resolving the land question was prominent during the formative moment of constitutional democracy in India as well as in the political considerations of the state formations in divided Germany. Both witnessed a dramatic shift in revived interest in land from the last decade of the twentieth century beginning symbolically with the reunification of Germany and liberalization of Indian economy, and the adoption of commercialization of land as the global model or path to resolve the land question. Despite their distinctive characteristics, viz., percentage of population dependent upon land in agriculture, landholdings, share of agriculture in economy, etc., both show a qualitative similarity in the way the land question in both is getting shaped by structural path of commodification of land and its continuous transformation as a site of improvement. The post-1990s' developments remarkably reveal that land question is developing in India and Germany along similar grounds and is posing concrete constitutional and normative questions for India and Germany.

11.1 Introduction

Acknowledging, understanding and resolving the land question remains an important aspect in substantive development and progress of a constitutional democracy towards egalitarian foundations. As land is a resource unlike any other that yields both cultural and economic goods of material as well as symbolic and psychological importance, enquiring into the way land relations are developing, the kind of agrarian structure that is emerging out of such land relations remains significant. Moreover, with heavy dependence of human as a species on land for food, daily livelihood

A. Pandey (✉)
Centre for Political Studies, Jawaharlal Nehru University, New Delhi, India
e-mail: aditya.du.politics@gmail.com

© Springer Nature Singapore Pte Ltd. 2020
A. Roy and M. Becker (eds.), *Dimensions of Constitutional Democracy*,
https://doi.org/10.1007/978-981-15-3899-5_11

and meaningful existence,[1] the way this question is changing and emerging raises political, economic and normative concerns.

Despite the universal concerns that are attached with the land question, it is considered an issue limited to the global south, especially in countries of Latin America, Africa, and South Asia. This perception is based on fact-based, logical and causal argument. It is stated that the land question is more prominent in global south and limited to it due to heavy dependence of a large number of people on land, accelerating land deals and presence of heterogeneous social movements for attaining different kinds of rights in land (Moyo and Yeros 2005, p. 1–7). It is assumed, therefore, that the land question is not a major or politically important issue in a region like Europe where the above-mentioned factors are not present in the same manner as they are in the global south. Hence, the land question is considered comparatively settled in the global north. Nevertheless, the land question seems to have come back in the global north amidst factors like rise in food prices, increased investment in land, benefits in multipurpose cropping, shift to bioenergy based economy, etc., that has led to major changes in land relations (Franco and Junior 2013; Ward et al. 2012; Heubuch 2016). It is in this context that this paper attempts to understand the (un)resolved land question by comparing the Indian and the German cases.

This paper aims to enquire (a) into the way land question is taking shape in Germany and India and (b) what questions this issue is putting forward for the future of democracy in the two countries. This paper is divided into four sections. The first is a theoretical exploration of the land question. Land question as a concept is contentious and this section attempts to bring out its major components as an interconnected web—components that often have differentiated importance as per different contexts which nevertheless converge. This section also lays down how the land question has been understood in this paper and how it is connected with the question of a democratic future. The second section focuses on the historical trajectory of the land question in Germany and India in the second half of the twentieth century. This section provides a brief insight into the attempts made to resolve the land question from mid-50s to early 90s of the twentieth century and how the issue of permeating irreconcilability between the aim of improvement and farmers' interests has remained a tough task for both countries. The third section looks at contemporary developments in the land question after reunification of Germany and liberalization of the Indian economy. This section explores the way the land question is developing in India and Germany by focusing on the emerging land system, developing land relations and agrarian structure, commercialization of land and the shifts in state policy towards land. The fourth section attempts to briefly put forward the questions which this development holds out for constitutional democracy in India and Germany.

[1] Human is used here in general sense to points towards the shared importance of land for humans as a species at large. The author is aware of the structures of power operating in society and generalizing tendencies of the word human that hides the differentiated importance of land for some groups, classes, castes, tribes, ethnicity and other marginalities, identities.

11.2 Exploring the Land Question[2]

What is the land question and what do we mean by it? Is the land question dependent upon a specific idea of land? Alternatively, to what extent does the meaning attributed to land envisages or constructs the land question? Do we need to understand land to understand the land question? Is the land question limited to redistribution, compensation and acquisition or extends beyond them? Why is resolving the land question important for a constitutional democracy? Is there *a* land question or are there land questions? If there are several land questions, can they be brought together? To put it differently, is there a common thread that can bring together land questions amidst the possibility that they may appear distinct from each other at the level of existence but they may be similar at the level of essence. These are some of the fundamental concerns that I begin with while thinking about the land question.

I would argue that land and land question are different but interrelated concepts. Generally the difference between the two is based on the premise that land is a resource whereas land question emerges when issues of public importance accumulate around it.[3] But it is in this difference that the interrelatedness between land and land question can be traced. To put it differently, the manner in which land is conceptualized as a resource determines to some extent the possibilities through which the land question is or will be perceived. Similarly, the framing of the land question reflects how land has been thought about. Hence, looking into the minute details of land becomes important for a comprehensive understanding and uncovering of the land question.

11.2.1 What is Land?

Land in the tradition of political economy remains a debated concept. Many have spoken about it as unique and unlike any other concept. Firstly, writing in the context of global land grab,[4] Derek Hall provides insight into the physicality aspect of land

[2]This section is reproduced from my unpublished M.Phil. Dissertation titled 'The Politics of Land Reform: A Case Study of Bihar.' Pandey (2018): 22–27, 41–44.

[3]C Wright Mills innovatively differentiated between 'issue' and 'trouble' while formulating the concept of sociological imagination and explained how the latter transforms into the former. Further, Mills notes that issue as a conceptual category has to do with matters that 'transcend both the local environment and the inner life of the individual'. The matters that are considered as an 'issue' are public matters or matters of utmost public importance which are concerned with moral values, or, the ways or manners in which different aspects of a person's social environment overlap and interpenetrate with other person's social environment 'to form the larger structure of social and historical life'. For Mills, the task of sociological imagination is to understand that it is not a person's trouble but an issue at hand. For more refer to, Mills (1959: 8).

[4]Briefly, land grab refers to the global and national processes of large-scale acquisition of land through various ways like direct acquisition of land without providing adequate compensation, acquisition through subtle changes in policy decision or law, etc., by the state and handing it over to

which is expressed through its usage, especially in the term 'landness' (Hall 2013, p. 7). Hall notes that despite its effective materiality or economic usage like other assets and resources, land cannot be visualized in the same way. It stands as a distinctive resource as it cannot be moved unlike its constituent components like the soil, rock or vegetation 'which can be carted away without diminishing land's landness' (Ibid., 8.). Hall remarks that because of this ever permanence the problematic of how to deal with land will remain.

Secondly, Mason Gaffney articulates the difference and the relationship between land, capital and labour by pointing that land is the space on which capital and labour are deployed for a desired result.[5] In other words, humans can only act over land which may lead to the improvement and development of capacities already inherent in land. In addition to this, while other factors like labour and capital can be produced and reproduced and may diminish or depreciate due to time lag or competition, land is permanent and recyclable whose value is only going to increase with the ongoing demographic trend and its limited, useful nature for survival of humans (Ibid., 43–45.). Further, land is a free gift of nature and a common element that has passed over generations since initial outbreaks of human civilization. This nature of land as a shared common heritage points to some extent towards the intuitive imaginations that are attached with land which principles of markets often ignore.[6] Further, Gaffney notes that land can exist and has been in existence without capital and labour, but the same is not true for capital and labour. Land while existing without labour and capital can support nature in the form of wilderness or forest but labour and capital need some land, as it is space, for existing.[7]

Thirdly, in the functional sense, land's importance as a resource base for social action makes its control inevitable. Its importance as a productivity unit, critically significant for living a meaningful life with free will and without any bondage for a multitude of people has been expressed many times (Sharma and Jha 2016, p. 2; Mishra 2011, p. 159–167). The significance increases in case of agrarian societies like India where ownership and tenurial relations in land 'acts as a source of prestige

---

private capital. This process has led to mass ejection and dispossession of people around the world. The peasants, tribals and multiple minorities have been the major victims of this process. For more refer to Nigam and Menon (2007: 61–82), Hall (2013: 17).

[5]This idea and analytical explanation has been lucidly put forward by Mason Gaffney, see, Gaffney (1994: 43).

[6]I am thankful to Pratyush Kumar for suggesting the words intuitive imagination to me. Land is enmeshed in cultural practices of usage that transcend the narrow numerical economic criteria. It may appear as a thought limited to countries where huge population is involved in agriculture. However, it came out in conversation with Kaya Thomas that in Germany, the idea of land with basis of small family farming as a cultural model and heritage is paramount. Moreover, in the generic sense, much of the issue is related to the fact that the dominant perception of capitalism only strengthens individuated and alienable private property right in land that has little elbow room or space for different ways of interacting with land.

[7]This view comes close to Karl Polanyi's description of land's difference from capital and labour. Polanyi considered land as part of nature that can never be turned into a true commodity in market. Though legally enforced and professed as a commodity it remains fictitious in nature, see, Polyani (1957: 75).

and an organizing principle for socio—economic relationships' (Hubacek and Bergh 2002, p. 1) within and outside the household as well as in other hierarchical spaces. This aspect of land can be understood by moving further down in the rung of hierarchy of interest in land. Landlessness, the situation of not owning or having any land or being effectively landless has spillover effects (Basole and Basu 2011, p. 42). It leads to a life of dependence and deference. It impacts the security of food and subsistence and makes the landless or marginally landed dependent either on market or non-market coercive relations for basic necessities of life. Being landless increases the degrees of disposableness, or to borrow a concept used by Aime Cesaire, leads to thingification.[8] Access to land in this context via legal means of tenurial rights or through owning a small parcel of land 'goes far beyond the economic significance as a means of livelihood or a habitat. It is a "quantum leap" in self-esteem, self-worth and entrepreneurship' (Ekta Parishad 2009, p. iii) or provides one with *samman bodh*.[9]

While what holds true for a transitional economy with heavy dependence in agrarian sector is equally significant for transitioned economies like Germany that is comparatively not as agrarian as India as far as the involvement of labour force in agriculture or dependence of people on land is concerned. It is significant as tenurial relation in land in these contexts has ramifications over livelihoods and production of other goods, agrarian structure or to put forward in academic vocabulary, for the larger political economy of food and agricultural system. Together, these can be seen as the distinct aspects of land which give it a comprehensive meaning and generate associated concerns. These often come in conflict with another idea of land that is intimately connected with the development of capitalism which governs the contemporary dealings with land.[10] The next subsection explains it.

---

[8]Conceptualizing power relations under colonialism, Aime Cesaire constructed thingification as a category to elucidate the relation of 'domination and submission between coloniser and colonised that is devoid of any human touch'. Thingification in the Indian context can be understood as the relation of non-human touch between landed property owner and landless dependent person who is not able to live a dignified and humane life, or exercise their will freely outside the parameters set by the landed, see, Cesaire (1955: 42).

[9]*Samman Bodh* is the expression used in Hindi to refer to a sense of self-worth, dignity and respect. It clearly explains what happens when a landless or effectively landless becomes effectively landed. This word is used by many land rights activist and landless farmers in West Champaran in the state of Bihar in India.

[10]Writing on how to do political economy, Karl Marx in Grundrisse argued that to understand society (for our purpose the land question), understanding the historical process is important as it provides the insight into the way the present period, or contemporary 'epoch' has come about. Moreover, emphasizing on the production process, Marx further pointed that the question of production has to be understood in both its particularity and universality. In his opinion, the common or universal to all production across epoch has been the relation between Mankind (Man as the subject) and Nature (land, earth, other natural things as the object). However, what form the relation between mankind and nature takes shape is different, uncommon, particular, distinct or unique to a particular period. To put it differently, it is known that production involves the relation between subject and object/mankind and nature/human and land, but the way this relation is organized, the purposes of production, and the desire or ways to achieve a particular form of relation and aim are diverse, unique and political. This insight of Marx has importance as far as understanding the land question is concerned, see, Marx (1996: 129).

11.2.2 Land and the Idea of Improvement

The meaning of land as a space for achieving higher income/revenue or productivity by changing land relations, usage of new techniques for more output, and market-oriented farming emerged and developed later around the seventeenth century in the context of the development of capitalist agriculture in England. This idea of land emerged simultaneously with the establishment of new property relations in land in seventeenth-century England. In comparison to other countries in Europe, England was the first nation in Europe whose passage to capitalist industrialization is traced in the changes in the agrarian structure that preceded industrialization.[11] Unlike the conventional explanation that focused on the removal of outer fetters[12] for development of capitalism, works on transition to capitalism have brought forward the way changes in property relations in land with simultaneous propagation of new meaning of land strengthened the process of transition. It was as a result of these changes in the conception of land and social relations in land that provided the initial basis for large-scale capitalist farming in England, leading to the development of surplus for industrialization and a domestic market that needed cheap products for survival and self-reproduction (Wood 2002, p. 133). The potential to invigorate the rise of capitalism was present in the word that later developed into an all-pervasive ethic—the idea of improvement (Ibid., 105–108).

Improvement in seventeenth-century England did not mean making better in an ordinary sense. It implied minimally three things. Firstly, at the level of conception, as Raymond Williams has noted, 'land was to be a place of investment' for productive cultivation or other things to earn profit (Williams 1973, p. 60–61). It meant cultivating land and engaging in production process for monetary profit. This intrinsically implied transformation of land from its natural state into a marketable productive resource. Secondly, at the level of activity, land was to be made more productive by engaging in efficient farming. It meant enhancing the land's productivity by using various means including the usage of technical innovations as well as consolidation of land in the form of large farms.[13] Thirdly, at the level of relation, land was to be regarded as a private property and a commodity. This implied transformation of

[11]Though there are debates on this the argument holds.

[12]The issue with this mode of explanation of the rise of capitalism is that it is ahistorical and claims that only removal of fetters was required for the transition of society towards capitalism. On the other hand, research done by historians and scholars on the question of transition from feudalism to capitalism explain that transformation of property relations in land played an important role. This involved removal of age-old customary rights of labourer attached with land under feudalism and elision of the right of labourer and peasant on common lands. This was outlined by Karl Marx in his historical essay titled 'The so called Primitive Accumulation'. For a qualitative summary of major scholars on the removal of fetter and land relation theme, refer to Wood (2002: 11–21), Brenner (2005: 25–29).

[13]Technical innovation in sixteenth and seventeenth century were usually organic. However, the idea of changing land's productivity by usage of appropriate technique received its primary potential in the idea of improvement. In addition to this form of action upon land, improvement also meant a new form of property relations that were concerned with improved farming. Wood (2002: 105–115).

land as a common, shared, intuitively imagined and attached space into private property that could be owned, disowned, alienated and traded like any other commodity. Further, transformation of land into a place of improvement implied that it can be easily bought and sold, leased in or leased out to whomsoever who could make land more productive. Immanent in the idea of improvement was a reliance on a specific form of production that rendered land's exchange value better (Ibid.). Production on land for survival and other needs has remained a prime concern for human beings since ages, but the logic of improvement did not consider this form of production as an improvement. The emphasis was laid instead on producing for market by using efficient or improved farming methods. This idea and meaning of land as a place of improvement marks the essence of capitalism's relation to land or place of land under capitalism. In other words, this forms the important thread or commonality to understand the nature and extent of the land question in the contemporary period across different contexts like India and Germany.

11.2.3 What Is then the Land Question?

When looked from the perspective of land and its transformation into a place of improvement, land question does not remain confined to the conflicts arising in case of redistribution, restitution or compensation and its legal addressal (though these remain an important part of it). Rather, in addition to these it includes multiple concerns that are attached or intrinsically related to each other like (a) the way land is being conceptualized, that is, in its totality covering its diverse aspects and comprehensive nature as a shared, intuitively imagined good, source of livelihood, etc., or just as a place of improvement, and the tensions between these; (b) the kind of structural changes happening with respect to land relations or in agrarian structure and the kind of land system developing—equitable or unequal and concentrated; and (c) following from this, the relations in land that exist and their changing dynamics viz., who works and who has been working on the land, who owns and controls it, is the owner and the controller same, who accrues benefits or surplus out of the land, and in what manner, through working or other ways (Bernstein 2010, p. 22), and (d) what are the implications of such developments or what ought to be. To summarize, in words of Roman Herre:

> …the land question concerns the system and structure of ownership of land (with a focus on land concentration) linked to the welfare of whole society, as well as, deals with question like what kind of land ownership structure is desirable and socially sound and how can land-poor and landless peasants obtain access to land. (Herre 2013, p. 69)

With this theoretical and conceptual backdrop, Sect. 11.3 would attempt to look at the historical contexts in which the land question has emerged in India and Germany.

11.3 The Land Question in India and Germany: Concerns, Aims and Methods

Resolution of the land question was on the development agenda of many newly independent and transformed states like India and Germany in mid-twentieth century (Byres 2004, p. 2). Many interrelated social, economic and political reasons were responsible for the pervasiveness of this zeal to resolve the land question.

The long and varied historical processes had led to the development of different kinds of land systems in India and Germany.[14] For example, the land system developed with marked differences in Federal Republic of Germany and German Democratic Republic because of their distinctive experiences during feudalism[15] and through later development of different inheritance patterns. As a result of this, land system consisting of small farms developed in the Federal Republic of Germany with further regional differences growing out of diverse inheritance systems. The northern and eastern part of Federal Republic of Germany had impartible inheritance (Anerbenrecht) system that differed from the system of partible or divided inheritance (Realteilung) in south and south-western regions. This led to further fragmentation of landholdings in southern and south-western part of Federal Republic of Germany than north and north-eastern parts where holdings of more or less the same size passed across generations. In comparison to the predominance of the land system with small farms with regional variations that continue till today, the situation was drastically different in Germany under Soviet occupation or German Democratic Republic. This part comprised of large landed estates or big farms[16] which formed a major share of total landholdings whose legacy can be traced back to Prussian feudalism and continuation of large estates thereafter (Access to Land 2018). Similarly,

[14]Germany has remained a unique social formation in European history. When large parts of Europe were under the grip of feudalism with heavily burdened peasantry during the middle age, Germany had a comparatively free peasantry under a feudal social formation. The situation further changed when rest of Europe was witnessing the decline of feudalism, an authoritative feudal system emerged in the eastern part of Germany, see, Brenner (2005: 37–39), Byres (1996: 48–54).

[15]Feudalism can be understood as a system where, (a) labourer was unfree and exploited by extra economic means denoting different forms of servility (non -market means, like forced labour) and (b) production was for subsistence and system enjoyed ideological support by the church (one of the biggest controller of Land). Feudalism in Germany further varied based on the nature of servility and landed estates. Majorly, scholars have differentiated between Gutsherrschaft (estate lordship) that was prevalent in eastern Germany from Grundherrschaft (landlordship) that was prevalent in western and southern Germany. Whether or not there was feudalism in India has remained a matter of intense debate. Briefly, it can be pointed that at some stages feudal social relations did prevail but they differed from the manner in which feudalism as a system existed in Europe. For more refer to, Melton (1988: 315–318), Byres (1996: 62).

[16]Wilson and Wilson note that in 1949 the Federal Republic of Germany had almost 1.7 million farms, one-third of which were less than 2 ha in size. These were more compact in areas that followed impartible inheritance law and were scattered like strips around fields in area that followed partible inheritance. In Soviet Occupation Zone, as much as 28% of total farms were more than 100 ha in size where it was further concentrated in northern parts. See, Wilson and Wilson (1996: 17).

the land system in India developed out of diverse historical experiences under colonialism during which the British experimented with diverse set of local customs, and addressed conflicting claims of peasants and landlords by deploying 'historiographic modality'.[17] Following from this the British developed primarily three forms of land system in India namely, (a) Zamindari system in which a landed class was created with proprietary rights in land that was contingent on fixed payment of revenue, (b) Ryotwari System in which settlement was done directly with the individual cultivators that held proprietary rights in land and (c) Mahalwari system in which settlement was done with villages as the collective unit in which peasants contributed as per the size of their holdings (Mearns 1999, p. 7–9). Despite the distinctive nature and aims of these settlements intermediary interests in land developed. The outcome of all this was the development of a land system in which there were a series of hierarchy of interests in land that inhibited the prospects for involved production and burdened the peasantry with extra levies.

These different kinds of land systems in India and Germany (Federal Republic of Germany and German Democratic Republic) had similar political-economic ramifications. Considerations like developing a more efficient agrarian structure to ensure a constant and adequate supply of food, generating rural employment, addressing farmer's concerns (especially, for Federal Republic of Germany), historical inequality in land relations (especially, in Soviet Occupation Zone/German Democratic Republic) and ensuring accumulation from the countryside were on the agenda of war-torn Germany (Wilson and Wilson 1996, p. 38–39). Similarly, fulfilling the national promise of land reform,[18] economic reason of agrarian transformation through the development of a vibrant agrarian sector, and the need to pacify the radical movements (Lodhi et al. 2007, p. 5–8), etc., formed the objectives of reforms in India. Common to both was the aim of agrarian transformation that could serve these multiple goals. As far as the question of political choice is concerned, the tough task was to bridge the gap between the logic of improvement and the demand of land to the tiller by tenant, sharecroppers and landless labourers (particularly for India) and farmers' concerns (particularly of Germany).[19] It was in this context of challenges that the ushering of constitutional democracy in India and political formations in

[17]This footnote is reproduced from my unpublished M.Phil. dissertation titled 'The Politics of Land Reform: A Case Study of Bihar'. Historiographic modality was one of the many investigative modalities that the British deployed with relation to land and other things by the 1770s in India. It referred to those procedures through which 'the huge loads of information regarding the object of study were transformed into rational, definable concepts or categories for usage'. They based their enquiry on the prevalent idea of land relation in England. This meant that land was taxable, had owners in private property sense of the term and must be improved. For a brief and thoughtful understanding of the ways in which colonial forms of knowledge was produced and its impact on India, see, Cohn (1996: 5), Pandey (2018: 98).

[18]The promise of resolving the land question was a major base over which national movement in India had built consensus among a differentiated section of peasantry to form a larger alliance against the British.

[19]The differentiation is based on the social composition of land relations where landless agricultural labourers, sharecroppers were comparatively more in India in comparison to Germany.

Federal Republic of Germany and German Democratic Republic tried to resolve the land question.

Both India and Germany (Federal Republic of Germany and German Democratic Republic) adopted similar methods with an active role of the state in developing a more equitable and efficient agrarian structure with a marked difference of collectivization programme in German Democratic Republic. As far as German case is concerned, the process of resolution of the land question was carried out in a systematic manner in which land was expropriated from large landholders[20] and redistributed to landless beneficiaries in German Democratic Republic whereas small family farms were supported through economic policy measures in Federal Republic of Germany. The concern for improvement remained significant in both. Cooperatives were established, land was collectivized to achieve economies of scale in agriculture in East Germany whereas West Germany underwent active land consolidation programmes to make the agrarian structure more efficient.[21] Similarly, in India, the process of resolution was an incremental exercise beginning with the abolition of institutional structure of intermediaries with their characteristic attributes of unimproved agriculture and exploitative land tenurial relations that left no space for further improvement and social upliftment. This was followed by ceiling on landholdings, redistribution of acquired ceiling surplus land, securing of sharecroppers and others who were comparatively more vulnerable in the hierarchy of relations in land and consolidation of landholdings in the form of cooperatives for efficient land utilization (Appu 1975, p. A70–A75). Though these methods to resolve differed in their content and magnitude, the logic of improving the productivity of land and ensuring egalitarian land relations was a major concern. The situation changed with the reunification of Germany in the 1990s and liberalization of the Indian economy in the last decade of the twentieth century. The next section explores the way the land question has transformed and revived in both countries with qualitative similarities amidst quantitative differences.

11.4 The Emerging Land Question in India and Germany

The previous section briefly outlined the common concerns in the process of resolution of land question in India and Germany (Federal Republic of Germany and German Democratic Republic) from mid-twentieth century onwards. This section puts forward contemporary developments in the land question in India and Germany from the last decade of the twentieth century that witnessed the fall of Berlin Wall and reunification of Germany and liberalization of Indian economy. These events generated momentous shifts with regard to the land question in both countries.

[20]Eidson and Milligan have explained the process of expropriation between 1945 and 1949, in which agricultural farms with 100 ha or more and farms belonging to war criminals or Nationalist Socialist (small and large) were expropriated. See, Eidson and Milligan (2003: 47–92).

[21]Other policy measure like protection of farmer was also present. For the purpose of this paper, emphasis is on land.

11.4.1 In Search of the Land Question

As mentioned before, there is a common perception that the land question is not an important issue in the case of Germany as it got settled with the resolution of the compensation question that was raised after the reunification of Germany. Although land remains a vital question in the case of India, its significance is largely seen as confined to the domain of compensation in cases of acquisition by the state in the context of distributive conflicts arising out of such acquisition (D'Costa and Chakraborty 2017). In the agrarian sector, however, the concern with high productivity prevails over any other question related to land in India. Despite their importance, these views remain limited since they are unable to reflect upon the continuities and changes in the production relations in land of which the above-mentioned concerns are a part. Nevertheless, this issue has received serious attention in the case of Europe and Germany in the last few years to the extent that it made a mark in the European Parliament where land issue was discussed.[22] Similarly, new findings coming out of government based surveys, reports by erstwhile Planning Commission of India and private inquiries that received authentic response from the government have foregrounded this issue in India.

11.4.2 Emerging Land Concentration and Commercialization of Land

What kind of land question is emerging with regard to land in Germany and India and what implications does it have for constitutional democracies? Despite the changes brought about in land relations by the land reform and land consolidation programmes in Germany and halfhearted land reform processes in India, land remains concentrated. The major difference between the two is that agricultural land is becoming explicitly more concentrated in Germany whereas the trend of concentration of land seems to have diluted with regard to large landowners in India[23] but the nature of this dilution remains debatable.

---

[22] An event was organized on 7 December 2016 by the European Economic and Social Committee, the Greens/EFA group and European Coordination Via Campesina to discuss emerging land issues in Europe. Maria Noichl, member of European Parliament raised this issue and the European Parliament called for action to prevent this process of land concentration with 524 votes to 37 with 45 votes absent. Sylvia Kay has written a report on the extent of farmland concentration and farmland grabbing at the European level that was used as a source there. The report titled 'Land Concentration, Land Grabbing and People's Struggle in Europe' has important insights on the emerging changes in Germany. The finding of this report has received valid ratification as it was also cited as a study on land issues in Europe. It has used data provided by Eurostat and Common Agricultural Policy subsidy funding stature to reflect upon the emerging land question in many member states of Europe. See, European Parliament. 2016.

[23] Elite landowners controlled 43% of land at the time of India's independence in 1947. Gupta (2012: 460).

For instance in Germany, at present, the numbers of agricultural holdings of 100 ha and above comprise only 12.3% of total agricultural holdings but they control almost 57% of total agricultural land.[24] Though Germany (especially Federal Republic of Germany) has undergone a process of concentration of landholdings in the past, this process has intensified from the early 1990s despite the reunification process that brought forward the issue of splitting up of state-controlled large farms (Ibid.). The number of agricultural holding of more than 100 ha witnessed a 195% variation increase for the period 1990–2013, whereas the same period noted a steep decline of 79% in the number of agricultural holdings of less than 10 ha.[25] Further probing reveals that agricultural holdings having area between 2 and 5 ha and less than 2 ha witnessed a steep decline after the 1990s.[26] This has occurred along with an increase in utilized agricultural area of farms with landholding of 100 ha and above while the total utilized agricultural area of Germany has remained almost the same in the period.[27] Roman Herre points out that the land area covered by farms of less than 2 ha, shrunk from 123,670 ha in 1990 to a mere 20,110 ha in 2007. Farms of 50 ha and more expanded in area from 9.2 million ha in 1990 to 12.6 million ha in 2007. What is more significant is that in comparison to the steep fall witnessed by small farms between 2007 and 2012, the number of farms between 500 ha and 1000 ha grew by 200 or 3.4%.[28]

As far as India is concerned, around 95% of Indian farmers are marginal, small and semi-medium landholders owning or holding up to 2.47 (less than 1 ha), 4.94

---

[24] Agricultural holdings of more than 100 ha are 35,160 in present Germany whereas total holdings in Germany are 285,030. Herre (2013: 62).

[25] In 1990, the number of agricultural holdings for more than 100 ha was 11,920 that rose to 35,960 in 2013. The utilized agricultural area under it also rose from 6,278,240 in 1990 to 9,514,330 in 2013. The number of holdings of less than 10 ha in 1990 was 3,16,870 that declined to 66,310 in 2013 with a simultaneous decline in utilized agricultural area from 1,216,040 ha in 1990 to 370,440 ha in 2013. This information is based on the analysis of land relation data available at Bundesministerium für Ernährung und Landwirtschaft (BMEL) by Roman Herre.

[26] For instance, the number of agricultural holdings having area less than 2 ha, 2–4.99 ha, 5–5.99 ha were 1,08,170, 1,06,470, and 1,02,230 in 1990, respectively. The number of holdings in 2013 for less than 2 ha was 12,010, 9,720 for 2–4.99 ha and 4,458 for 5–9.99 ha. The holdings of 10–19.9 ha and 20–29.9 ha have faced similar decline. Only landholding size of 50–99.9 ha and 100 ha or more have seen a rapid increase in which the latter has witnessed an exponential increase. Ibid.

[27] The total utilized agricultural area of Germany in 1990 was 17,048,110 ha in 1990 and it came down to 16,699,580 ha in 2013. While the total number of holdings decreased from 6,49,620 in 1990 to 2,82,160 in 2013. The above-noted data reveals that the decline has been sharp in landholdings of small size as the utilized agricultural area of 100 ha and above rose from 6,278,240 in 1990 to 9,514,330 in 2013. Whereas the utilized agricultural area of landholdings size of less than 2 ha and less, 2–4.99 ha and 5–9.99 ha declined from 123670, 351980, 740390 ha in 1990 to 12090, 32580, 325770 ha in 2013 respectively. Similar trend is visible in case of utilized agricultural area of 10–19.9 ha and 20–29.9 ha. Herre noted that though there is a discrepancy in method as the Eurostat data was calculated on different basis in cases of landholdings and many landholdings of less than 5 ha were excluded. This can only change the number of landholdings but not the concentration of landholdings in larger farms. Ibid.

[28] Roman Herre and Sylvia Kay hold the opinion that changes in common agricultural policy and selective benefits provided to big landlords by the government are reasons behind this trend.

(less than 1.99 ha) and 9.88 (less than 3.99 ha) acres of land, respectively (Chaturvedi 2016). This situation of marginalized and fragmented landholdings has remained a recurring phenomenon in land system in India. Despite this and variations brought because of change in databases (urban plus rural and sometimes only rural) and categorical fixation (defining landless, land owned), some observation can be put forward regarding concentration of land in India. When taken together, the marginal and small landowners constituting 90% of the population owned only 43.43% of land in 2003 (Bandopadhyay 2008, p. 37–42). Whereas as per agricultural census of 2011–12 the marginal and small plus semi-medium landholders owned up to 68.2% of cultivated land in India. In contrast, the medium and large farmers comprising a miniscule minority of 9.60% owned around 56.21% of land in 2003 which declined to 31.8% of cultivated land as per agricultural census of 2011–12. It is problematic however to claim that decline marks a process of de-concentration of land under large landowners.[29] The question whether this decline of land under the control of large farmers is due to transfer of land from landed to the landless in the sense of both ownership and control remains unsettled especially in times when variation between landed and landless farmer is rampant. The variation can be understood from the fact that as per Agricultural Census of 2011–12 and 2011 Household Land Ownership Pattern (also known as Socio-Economic Caste Census), around '32% of India's farmland (agricultural land) is controlled by minority of 4.9% of farmers' (Chaturvedi 2016). To dig deeper to reflect upon land concentration, a 'large farmer controls as much as 45 times more land than the marginal farmer, whereas 101.4 million people or 56.4% of rural households own no agricultural land' (Ibid.). Moreover, owning 0.002 ha of land or homestead land leads to the inclusion of one in the category of landed despite the fact that the person might not be able to use such land for livelihood purpose and remains effectively landless.

Following from above, a related point pertains to the change in land's 'bio-material and social-institutional reality' in India and Germany through commercialization of land (Franco and Junior 2013, p. 20). To use insightful arguments of Saturnino Borrass Junior and others, the emerging land question is about changes in both (a) management plus control of land and (b) in the usage of land or the way production is organized. Presently, it is not just farmers or big landowners who are concentrating land, but also companies or business houses or non-agricultural investors who have developed an increased interest in land for both agricultural and non-agricultural activities. Due to this, land market has seen a rapid rise in prices of land and speculative activities and the viability of farming by small-medium farmers has receded since they cannot compete with large specialized farms under corporate control.[30]

[29]The NSSO survey 2013 shows a decline in area owned of this category in 2013. But in this survey it only looked at rural households. See, NSSO 2014. Other reports further reveal the nature of land concentration, see, Household Land Ownership Pattern (2011).

[30]9 out of 10 farms are specialized farms in Germany, either in animal husbandry or in crop farming. The development of a specialized, capital-intensive model has also meant land concentration, with a fast increase in the average farm size. The website was accessed in February 2018 for updated information. See, Federal Ministry of Food, Agriculture and Consumer Protection (2010).

For instance, land in Germany has become a safe investment site for banks, investment companies, pension funds that consider it as a secure place of investment and land has gone in the hands of big investors that are involved in biofuels production and organic farming.[31] Similarly, there has been a rise of contract and commercial farming in India (erstwhile planning commission report, 2006) that often dictates terms to small and medium farmers (Bandopadhyaya 2006, p. 10). Moreover, there has been a forced transfer of land from agricultural to non-agricultural uses like real estate development that has led to rise in conflicts and speculative activities in land. The major impact of this has been that small farmers or new farmers are unable to gain access to land and compete with these farms as they lack the capital which the big investors have.

Following from these is the policy shift with regard to land. The last decade of twentieth century witnessed retreat of the state from resolving the land question through redistributive land reform and agrarian reform and intrusion of market to deal with land issues globally.[32] To put it differently, resolving the land question now came to be considered as a goal to be carried by free-market force (if it existed)[33] that essentially meant smooth transfer of land to those who wanted to purchase from those who wanted to sell with the belief that through this transaction land will reach the efficient user.[34] This commodified the entire process of resolution of the land question, drifting away from the aim of altering the structures of power and developing equitable relations in land. The political task of bringing egalitarian land relations and agrarian structure was substituted by 'efficient' land management. This shift as enunciated by Junior has implications for both Germany and India as the emerging concentration of land is happening with the tacit support of the state through this kind of policy shift.

For instance, against the backdrop of reunification of Germany and utilization of formerly state-owned land, BVVG Company was charged by the government with the task of managing this land either through selling or by generating lease contracts in 1992 (BVVG 2018). It sold a good amount of land till 2007 when the policy was changed to renew only parts of leases and to accelerate land sales. Because of

---

There is huge rise in concentration of land by companies in Germany for biogas, agrofuels or flex crops production. See, Herre (2013: 62–69).

[31] Roman Herre, Sylvia Kay point out how new investors accrue benefit from rising prices of land. Roman Here points that companies like KTG Agrar control as much as 28000 ha land in Germany (majorly Eastern). Kaya Thomas points similarities with change in production of land with farms in West Germany. Information is based on personal conversation with Roman Herre, Sylvia Kay and Kaya Thomas.

[32] This argument and footnote is reproduced from my unpublished M.Phil. dissertation titled 'The Politics of Land Reform: A Case Study of Bihar'. From the 1980s onwards, land reforms—were gradually swept away from the agenda of many nation states, especially those where landlessness was a major problem due to debt crisis, discontent with the actual application of land reform, technological advancement in agriculture etcetera. See, Moyo and Yeros (2005: 1–8).

[33] This argument is reproduced from my unpublished M.Phil. dissertation titled 'The Politics of Land Reform: A Case Study of Bihar'. See, Nigam (2011: 49–50), Bagchi (2004).

[34] This is persuaded as the 'willing seller and willing buyer' argument as enunciated in policy documents of World Bank.

this emphasis on renewing fewer leases and enhancing the sale of land, land prices skyrocketed due to inflow of heavy capital investors because of which small farmers and new farmers were unable to renew their leases or gain access to land, respectively. While this concern with inequitable access to land because of commercialization may appear limited to eastern Germany, the allocation of subsidies under Common Agricultural Policy shatters this perception. The policy shift in common agricultural policy now offers a subsidy on per hectare basis which favoured the large landowners. Franco and Junior observe that a handful of 1.2% of beneficiaries received 28.4% of subsidies under common agricultural policy in Germany (Franco and Junior 2013, p. 62–69). This concentration of subsidies makes access to land more difficult for small landowners in Germany as they have to face shortage of capital on one hand and state's support to capital on the other.[35] Similarly, the post-liberalization period in India has witnessed a silent elision of redistributive land reforms from policy imperatives of the state.[36] Not only is the land declared surplus falling continuously but so is the land distributed to the landless. For example, as Sumit Chaturvedi points out from his inquiry that on an average 1,50,000 acres of land was declared surplus every year between 1973 and 2002 out of which an average of 1,40,000 acres was distributed every year (Chaturvedi 2016). The figures for 2003–2015 depict that average land declared surplus was 4000 acres each year and the figures for land taken under government possession and distributed to landless beneficiaries has declined from 29,000 acres in 2002 to 24,000 acres in 2015. Similarly, average land distributed to landless in 2002 was 0.95 acres per person which has fallen to 0.88 acres per person in 2015 (Ibid.). In addition to this, the dismal nature of agricultural subsidies makes marginal, small and semi-medium landholders further prone to market vagaries. On the other hand, the state is actively facilitating the process of transfer of land from agricultural to corporate investors as well as forwarding the path of market-led land transfer to develop a viable land market.

Taken together this commodification of land with characteristic attribute of financialization of agriculture is leading to exclusion of uncompetitive classic food producers or non-improving farmers in India and Germany from land. Moreover, this process is obstructing the entry of new farmers in Germany[37] with further marginalization of landless in India. To summarize, there are significant differences between

[35]The European Parliament took notice of this issue that land concentration has gone hand in hand with concentration of subsidies. See, European Parliament. 2017. Also, Roman Herre, Syliva Kay, Astrid and kaya Thomas emphasized this point in conversation on land issue in Germany.

[36]As far as reports of the government of India are concerned, till today, except abolition of intermediary tenures on paper and little democratization of landholdings, resolving the land question in its totality remains an unfinished agenda since independence except for marginal success in few states like Kerala and West Bengal.

[37]What is happening in Germany is synonymous with developments in Europe at large. Sylvia Kay notes that land concentration in Europe is significant: 3% of farms own 52% of farmland. Large-scale farming is spreading across Europe while small farms are disappearing: 4 million small farms, 33% of the total, have been lost in Europe between 2003 and 2013. Land inequality is structural, and distribution of farmland is dramatically more unequal than concentration of wealth. This trend is related to both exit of small farmers and entry denial for new farmers, with real implications for European food security, employment, welfare, and biodiversity, as well as for the well-being and

India and Germany with regard to their approach to the land question, but there are stark similarities that form the content of the emerging land question in the two countries. These can be summarized as (a) emerging and continuing land concentration, (b) commodification of land and supportive move to commercial farming and (c) active role of state in facilitating land concentration. This is leading to inequitable access to land for multitude of people, ratification of marketable relations in land that is often predominated by narrow economic logic and, advancement of all these processes or trends under the logic of improvement that these are rendering land more productive. The next section puts forward the questions of constitutional importance which this development is posing.

11.5 Questions for Constitutional Democracy: What Ought to be?

As evident from the previous section, the land question in India and Germany in the contemporary context can be located in the idea of improvement. This location presents a question pertaining to equitable access to land. Both the Indian Constitution and the Basic Law of Germany aspire to build an equitable social and democratic order. The Indian Constitution unequivocally states the ideal of substantive equality with regard to land through various parts present in the constitution. For instance, the Preamble emphasizes upon bringing economic and social democracy which gets further clarified with regard to land in Directive Principles of State Policy that insists on the state's duty of ensuring that means of production are not concentrated in a few hands (Article 39). Though the Basic Law of Germany is not as explicit as the Indian Constitution on this issue, the legal clause with regard to agricultural land transfer, land lease and judicial pronouncements[38] put forward the vision of equity. The law on agricultural land regulations and law on land lease in Germany states that such transfers should not be upheld if these do not improve the agrarian structure or lead to 'unhealthy accumulation of land'.[39] Moreover, equitable access to land is also considered as a foundation for a sustainable society. This vision received substantive ratification in Voluntary Guidelines on the Responsible Governance of Tenure of Land, Fisheries and Forests that argues for access to land for farmers (especially small and marginal) and its sustainable usage in Germany.[40] It is clear from the above that the current development in land relations with its characteristic attribute

viability of rural communities and European society as a whole. Saturnino Borrass Junior further note that almost 25 million people are involved in agriculture in Europe. See, Kay (2016:1–7).

[38]Way back in 1967, the Supreme Court in Germany had pronounced that land is different and cannot be dispensed like any other commodity. It further pronounced that an equitable legal and social order requires that public interest in land be taken into account. See, European Parliament. 2017.

[39]The clause on agricultural land transfer has been put under scrutiny by farmers in Germany with claim that it is often interpreted in marrow improving terms. See, Herre (2013: 68–69).

[40]Issue that is coming out in clear form in protests in favour of agroecology based usage of land.

of land concentration, continuing trend of exclusion and marginalization of marginal, small and semi-medium farmers goes against the equitable vision propounded in the Constitution and legal practices as well as the universal principles of human rights.

Another line of reasoning can be helpful in understanding the way this issue is posing significant questions for constitutional democracy in India and Germany. Often a consequential argument is put forward that because very few people are involved in agriculture or are in direct relation with land in Germany, despite these factual details and constitutional plus normative concerns, this question is not important. Similarly, argument about redundancy of land question in India is made on grounds that no big movements for developing equitable relations in land is being pursued presently and the matter is limited to nature of compensatory claims emerging in cases of acquisition by the state (with major exception of land rights movement by collective groups). Howsoever the conviction of these arguments, they are problematic or prone to at least two fallacies. Firstly, for these arguments land question's political and constitutional importance is dependent upon the quantification and magnitude which emerges solely on the ground of numbers, and not on the intrinsic value, essence or concerns of the question itself. Due to this, the comprehensive nature of the land question having basis in the structural changes remains untouched or out of reach. Secondly, following from the earlier point, I would argue that this view only takes into account the involvement of people with land at the level of existence and does not takes notice of the fact that dependence upon land is concrete in both absolute and relative sense. It can be stated at the level of theoretical argument that we are directly associated with land if we are eating food or consuming products that are produced by using land either as resource or as a place.[41] But more importantly, this brings us back to one of the foundational concerns of political science which constitutional democracy in India and Germany has to address: what kind of resource sharing (in this case of land) is morally and ethically desirable for their democratic future. Is it desirable to have a land system that considers land only as a commodity especially after being aware that land innately differs from other commodities? Is it desirable to continue this process of concentration of land especially after being aware that land is a historically shared good whose equitable sharing is indispensable for meaningful human survival?

11.6 Conclusion

This chapter attempted to enquire into the way the land question has taken shape in India and Germany with theoretical and empirical details. It is argued that resolving the land question to achieve similar goals was paramount during the initial years of independent India and post-war divided Germany for which similar methods were

[41] A view shared by Kaya Thomas and Sylvia Kay in personal conversation. They accepted that attachment to land and reliance over it is more in case of India in comparison to Germany, but this does not mean that this relation can only be of direct form.

used and deployed by the state. The situation changed after the 1990s which witnessed multiple changes like reunification of Germany, liberalization of Indian economy and adoption of commercialization of land as the global model or path to resolve the land question. The post-1990s' developments reveal that land question with similar groundings is developing in India and Germany having characteristic attribute of concentrated land with changes in its usage and conception. This development is posing constitutional and normative concerns that are relevant for both India and Germany.

Acknowledgments Sylvia Kay and Astrid Österreicher for sharing their views on land question and grassroot experiences on land issue in Europe and Germany. Special thanks to Paula Gioia for her responses during the entire course of writing of this paper despite her busy schedule on the farm and to Kaya Thomas for suggesting the names of people with whom I could have a conversation. I also thank Michael Becker. Anupama Roy and Matthias Gsänger for their comments and suggestions. This paper remains incomplete without mention of Shipra for her constant support and motivation.

References

Access to Land. (2018). *Background*. http://www.accesstoland.eu/Background-10. Accessed 25 Feb 2018.

Appu, P. S. (1975). Agrarian structure and rural development. *Economic and Political Weekly, 9*(39), A70–A75.

Bagchi, A. K. (2004). *The developmental state in history and in the twentieth century*. New Delhi: Regency publications.

Bandopadhyay, D. (2006). *Report of the working groups on land relations for the 11th five year plan*. Planning Commission, Government of India. http://planningcommission.nic.in/aboutus/committee/wrkgrp11/wg11_landrel.pdf. Accessed 11 Feb 2018.

Bandopadhyay, D. (2008). Does land still matter? *Economic and Political Weekly, 43*(10), 37–42.

Basole, A., & Basu, D. (2011). Relations of production and modes of surplus extraction in India: Part I—Agriculture. *Economic and Political Weekly, 46*(14), 41–58.

Bernstein, H. (2010). *Class dynamics of agrarian change*. Winnipeg: Fernwood Publishing.

Brenner, R. (2005). Agrarian class structure and economic development in pre-industrial Europe. In T. H. Ashton & C. H. E. Phipin (Eds.), *The Brenner debate: Agrarian class structure and economic development in pre-industrial Europe* (pp. 10–63). Cambridge: Cambridge University Press.

BVVG. (2018). https://www.bvvg.de/INTERNET/internet.nsf/HTML/START. Accessed 15 Feb 2018.

Byres, T. J. (1996). *Capitalism from above and capitalism from below: An essay in comparative political economy*. New York: Palgrave McMillan.

Byres, T. J. (2004). Introduction: Contextualizing and interrogating the GKI case for redistributive land reforms. *Journal of Agrarian Change, 4*(1, 2), 1–16.

Cesaire, A. (1955). *Discourse on colonialism*. New Delhi: Aakar Books.

Chaturvedi, S. (2016). Land reforms fail, 5% of India's farmers control 32% land. *The Wire*. https://thewire.in/agriculture/land-reforms-fail-5-of-indias-farmers-control-32-land. Accessed 13 Feb 2018.

Cohn, B. (1996). *Colonialism and its forms of knowledge: The British in India*. New Jersey: Princeton University Press.

D'Costa, A. P., & Chakraborty, A. (2017). *The land question in India: State, dispossession and capitalist transition*. New Delhi: Oxford University Press.

Eidson, J., & Milligan, G. (2003). Cooperative entrepreneurs? Collectivization and privatization of agriculture in two East German regions. In C. Hann (Ed.), *The postsocialist agrarian question: Property relations and the rural condition* (pp. 47–92). Münster: Transaction Publishers.

Ekta Parishad. (2009). *Landlessness and social justice: An assessment of disparities in land distribution and prospects for land reforms*. Patna: Ekta Parishad.

European Parliament. (2017). On the state of play of farmland concentration in the EU: How to facilitate the access to land for farmers (2016/2141(INI)). http://www.europarl.europa.eu/doceo/document/A-8-2017-0119_EN.html. Accessed 12 Feb 2018.

Federal ministry of food, Agriculture and Consumer Protection. (2010). *German agriculture, facts and figures*. https://www.bmel.de/SharedDocs/Downloads/EN/Publications/GermanAgriculture.pdf?__blob=publicationFile. Accessed 12 Feb 2018.

Franco, J., & Junior, S. B. (2013). *Land concentration, land grabbing and people's struggle in Europe*. Transnational Institute (TNI) for European Coordination Via Campesina and Hands off the Land network. https://www.tni.org/files/download/land_in_europe-jun2013.pdf. Accessed 12 Feb 2018.

Gaffney, M. (1994). Land as a distinctive factor of production. In N. Tideman (Ed.), *Land and taxation*. London: Shepheard-Walwyn Ltd.

Gupta, P. S. (2012). The peculiar circumstances of eminent domain. *Osgoode Hall Law Journal, 49*(3), 445–489.

Hall, D. (2013). *Land*. Cambridge: Polity Press.

Herre, R. (2013). Land concentration, land grabbing and options for change in Germany. In J. Franco & S. B. Junior (Eds.), *Land concentration, land grabbing and people's struggle in Europe* (pp. 62–69). Transnational Institute (TNI) for European Coordination Via Campesina and Hands off the Land network. https://www.tni.org/files/download/land_in_europe-jun2013.pdf. Accessed 12 Feb 2018.

Heubuch, M. (2016). *Land rush: The sellout of Europe's farmland*. The Greens/EFA, European Parliament. https://www.greens-efa.eu/files/doc/docs/19abd146a6f61773450e58f438b3d287.pdf. Accessed 10 Feb 2018.

Household Land Ownership Pattern. (2011). Socio economic caste census. http://secc.gov.in/statewiseLandOwnershipReport?reportType=Land%20Ownership. Accessed 15 Feb 2018.

Hubacek, K., & Bergh, J. V. D. (2002). *The role of land in economic theory*. Austria: International Institute for Applied Systems Analysis.

Kay, S. (2016). *Land for the few: The state of land concentration in Europe: Database for all EU member states*. Transnational Institute (TNI) for European Coordination Via Campesina and Hands off the Land network. https://www.tni.org/en/publication/land-for-the-few-infographics. Accessed 15 February 2018.

Lodhi, H. A., Jr., S. B. & Kay, C. (2007). *Land, poverty and livelihoods in an era of globalization: Perspectives from developing and transition countires*. Abidngon: Routledge.

Marx, K. (1996). Introduction to the grundrisse. In T. Carver (Ed.), *Marx: Later political writings*. Cambridge: Cambridge University Press.

Mearns, R. (1999). Access to land in rural India: Policy issues and options. Working Paper. World Bank. http://www.cpahq.org/cpahq/cpadocs/Access%20to%20Land%20in%20India.pdf. Accessed 12 Feb 2018.

Melton, E. (1988). Gutsherrschaft in East Elbian Germany and Livonia, 1500–1800: A critique of the model. *Central European History, 21*(4), 315–349.

Mills, C. W. (1959). *The sociological imagination*. New York: Oxford University Press.

Mishra, L. (2011). *Human bondage: Tracing its roots in India*. Delhi: Sage Publications Pvt Ltd.

Moyo, S., & Yeros, P. (2005). Introduction. In S. Moyo & P. Yeros (Eds.), *Reclaiming the land: The resurgence of rural movement in Asia, Africa and Latin America* (pp. 1–7). London: Zed Books.

Nigam, A. (2011). *Desire named development*. New Delhi: Penguin Books.

Nigam, A., & Menon, N. (2007). *Power and contestation: India since 1989*. London: Zed Books.

NSSO. (2014). Key Indicators of Situation of Agricultural Households in India. *NSSO 70th Round*. http://mospi.nic.in/sites/default/files/publication_reports/KI_70_33_19dec14.pdf. Accessed 15 Feb 2018.

Pandey, A. (2018). *The politics of land reform: A case study of Bihar (M.Phil. Dissertation)*. Delhi (Unpublished): Jawaharlal Nehru University.

Polyani, K. (1957). *The great transformation*. Boston: Beacon Press.

Sharma, R., & Jha, P. (2016). Land reform experiences some lessons from across South Asia: A research document prepared for the world forum for access to land. Research document. The Food and Agriculture Organization of the United Nations. http://www.fao.org/3/i8296en/I8296EN.pdf. Accessed 12 February 2018.

Ward, A., Wily, L. A., Cotula, L., & Taylor, M. (2012). *Land rights and the rush for land: Findings of the global commercial pressure on land research project*. (978-92-95093-75-1). https://www.landcoalition.org/sites/default/files/documents/resources/ILC%20GSR%20report_ENG.pdf. Accessed 10 Feb 2018.

Williams, R. (1973). *The country and the city*. London: Oxford University Press.

Wilson, G. A., & Wilson, O. J. (1996). *German agriculture in transition: Societies, policies and environment in a changing Europe*. New York: Palgrave Macmillan.

Wood, E. M. (2002). *The origin of capitalism: A longer view*. New York: Verso.

Aditya Pandey is Doctoral Research Candidate at Centre for Political Studies, Jawaharlal Nehru University. He is pursuing doctoral research on the centrality of land question in district of West Champaran in contemporary Bihar. His research explores the emerging land system in West Champaran (Bihar), the way in which structures of power through a configuration of social forces/classes accumulate around it, and the contestations or processes of democratization that emerge in the region. His other research interests are challenges of inclusive citizenship, constitutionalism and state practices, historical injustice and democratic rights, climate uncertainty, dispossession and sustainable urban/rural livelihood.

Index

© Springer Nature Singapore Pte Ltd. 2020
A. Roy and M. Becker (eds.), *Dimensions of Constitutional Democracy*,
https://doi.org/10.1007/978-981-15-3899-5

The manufacturer's authorised representative in the EU is Springer Nature Customer Service Centre GmbH, Europaplatz 3, 69115 Heidelberg, Germany. If you have any concerns regarding our products, please contact ProductSafety@springernature.com

Printed and bound by CPI Group (UK) Ltd, Croydon, CR0 4YY
30/09/2026
02225510-0005